D0340567

INTERNATIONAL SERIES IN PURE AND APPLIED PHYSICS

G. P. HARNWELL, Consulting Editor

DISLOCATIONS IN CRYSTALS

INTERNATIONAL SERIES IN PURE AND APPLIED PHYSICS

Leonard I. Schiff, *Consulting Editor*

The late F. K. Richtmyer was Consulting Editor of the series from its inception in 1929 to his death in 1939. Lee A. DuBridge was Consulting Editor from 1939 to 1946; and G. P. Harnwell from 1947 to 1954.

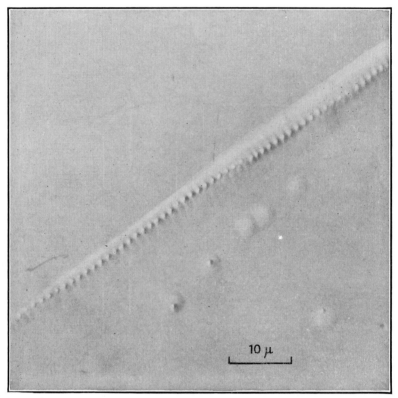

Etch pits at the dislocations that make up a grain boundary in germanium. The difference in orientation of the grains is about one minute of arc. After Vogel, Pfann, Corey, and Thomas (1953).

DISLOCATIONS IN CRYSTALS

W. T. READ, Jr.

Bell Telephone Laboratories
Murray Hill, New Jersey

New York   Toronto   London

McGRAW-HILL BOOK COMPANY, INC.

1953

DISLOCATIONS IN CRYSTALS

Library of Congress Catalog Card Number: 53-6049

To

MILDRED H. READ

PREFACE

The history of dislocation theory is divided into three overlapping stages. In the first stage ingenious simple ideas emerged and gave natural qualitative explanations for many of the mechanical properties of crystals—for example, the low mechanical strength. In the second stage, the explanations became more detailed and speculative and were extended to a wider range of observations; it became the fashion to invent a dislocation theory of almost every experimental result in plastic deformation. Finally, it became apparent that dislocations could explain not only any actual result but virtually any conceivable result, usually in several different ways. This led to the third stage which is a critical step-by-step development of basic theory from first principles and a search for clear-cut experimental checks of the theory; here the emphasis is on theories that apply directly in a limited area rather than comprehensive speculative theories that embrace, somewhat loosely, a wide range of phenomena. This book is an introduction to dislocations from the viewpoint of the third stage.

Some apology should perhaps be given for a textbook on a subject that is changing and growing as rapidly as the dislocation theory of crystals. My hope is that a clear introductory account of what has already been definitely established will help the subject grow more rapidly into a branch of solid-state physics capable of aiding practical metallurgy. There is a general impression that dislocation theory is an open field for the speculations of theoretical physicists who dabble in metallurgy; the different bits of theory appear as a hodgepodge of ingenious but arbitrary creations. I have tried to present the other side of the picture and develop the basic ideas as a coherent body of knowledge following directly from accepted physical principles and the definitions peculiar to dislocation theory.

The subject matter of the book can be divided roughly as follows:

Geometry and Crystallography. Only the simplest ideas of crystallography are required. A number of pictures illustrate what dislocations are and how they move. The pictures show both atoms and macroscopic crystals and illustrate the connection between what the atoms do and what one can observe. The figures are especially designed to clarify the three-dimensional concepts that are essential but cannot adequately be introduced in words.

Quantitative Theory. No mathematics beyond calculus is presupposed. A few basic ideas with concrete examples show how quantitative calculations can be made for particular crystals.

Applications. The dislocation theories of crystal growth and grain boundaries are discussed; these fields are outstanding because unique predictions can be made and compared with experimental measurements. In both fields speculation has been largely absent and basic theory has been applied successfully. A chapter is devoted to Frank's theory of crystal growth and its dramatic experimental verification. Four chapters deal with grain boundaries. For teaching dislocation theory, the theory of grain boundaries is an ideal application because (1) almost all dislocation theory can be used and no other specialized branches of physics are required; (2) the array of dislocations on a grain boundary is known, in contrast to most applications, where an array has to be postulated; and (3) good experiments are being done which test the theory.

It is a disappointment that I can offer only fragments of a theory of mechanical properties, strength, plastic deformation, and work hardening —these are the most important applications of dislocation theory from a practical viewpoint. However, it appears to me more profitable to recognize that at present there is no systematic general theory that is convincing or widely accepted. Instead of reviewing current speculations (or adding others), I have tried to give the student and prospective researcher a sound foundation that will help him to attack these problems successfully and eventually bring them from the area of speculation into the area of applied science.

Throughout the book, I have had in mind, especially, the reader who is using it as a text in a self-taught course. I have tried to play, as far as possible, the role of tutor as well as author. In particular I have encouraged the reader to anticipate steps in the argument and to work out proofs and answers to questions before reading on to the proofs and answers that follow. Exercises are included both in the text and at the ends of the chapters. Some of the text exercises are straightforward steps in the argument—steps conventionally covered by, "From the preceding results, it follows that. . . ." Some of the text exercises involve extending the arguments to new cases. Both the text and the exercises encourage a simple physical way of thinking based on pictures. Some of the exercises involve making drawings similar to those in the text. The problems at the ends of the chapters are similar to the text exercises but include also some mathematical thinking.

In a textbook of this type, it seemed undesirable to develop the subject from a historical viewpoint. Other authors and their works are mentioned where they are natural references for supplementing the text. I have made no particular effort to trace historical origins; the fact that many distinguished names are not often mentioned does not imply any lack of respect for their contributions.

I was encouraged to write this book by W. Shockley, J. H. Hollomon, and Morris Cohen. I wish to thank the many physicists and metallurgists who read the earlier mimeographed version and offered helpful comments. The comments of W. Shockley, F. C. Frank, J. D. Eshelby, and H. Brooks—to mention only a few—were especially valuable. In particular, I am indebted to two colleagues at the Bell Laboratories: Charles S. Smith analyzed the text in detail from the pedagogical viewpoint and suggested many improvements in presentation. J. F. Nye's thorough and stimulating discussion of the first two versions was responsible for much of the improvement in the final version.

I found A. H. Cottrell's forthcoming book on dislocations helpful and wish to thank him for sending me a manuscript.

The figures owe much to the painstaking work of Miss D. T. Angell, who did many of the original drawings. H. P. Gridley and Company did the final drawings and many of the original layouts.

I am especially grateful for the kind cooperation of the several typists, and in particular Mrs. L. E. Weinberger, who produced clear typescripts from my much revised handwritten notes.

W. T. Read, Jr.

CONTENTS

xiii

PART II APPLICATIONS

CHAPTER 10 APPLICATION TO CRYSTAL GROWTH

CHAPTER 11 SIMPLE GRAIN BOUNDARY

CHAPTER 12 GENERAL GRAIN BOUNDARIES

CHAPTER 13 MEASUREMENTS OF GRAIN BOUNDARY ENERGY

CHAPTER 1

WHY DISLOCATIONS?

Dislocations are responsible for the plastic deformation of metals and other crystalline solids. This book explains what dislocations are, what they do, and how they produce effects that one can observe and measure. The presentation is based on physical arguments and centers around the numerous drawings. What is definitely known about dislocations is distinguished from what is speculated; the latter is given little attention here (it is more than adequately covered in the literature).

This chapter outlines the plan of the book—after briefly discussing what dislocation theory is trying to do.

1.1 Imperfections in Crystals. Taylor, Orowan, and others introduced dislocations into physics in the 1930's; they were interested in understanding what the atoms do when a crystal deforms. The understanding of crystals in terms of atoms has two parts: (1) the theory of perfect crystals, (2) the theory of imperfections; dislocations come under 2.

In calling a crystal perfect, we mean that the atoms form a regular pattern (such as face-centered cubic or body-centered cubic). By an *imperfection* we mean a small region where the regular pattern breaks down and some atoms are not properly surrounded by neighbors. By small we mean that the region extends only a few atomic diameters in at least one dimension. A lattice vacancy is a simple example of an imperfection. We shall *not* use the term imperfection to include elastic strains, thermal vibrations, or other small distortions that leave the crystal structure clearly recognizable.

Most of the progress in crystal physics has been in 1 above. One can understand many properties of crystals by regarding them as perfect, that is, the imperfections contribute in proportion to their relative volume; therefore, in reasonably good crystals they can be neglected. Such properties are called *structure insensitive;* some examples are elastic constants, resistivity, density, and heat capacity. Other properties (such as mechanical strength) are highly sensitive to crystal perfection; even one imperfection of the proper type could reduce the strength by orders of magnitude. Internal friction and creep rate are other *structure-sensitive* properties.

This book deals with imperfections of structure; examples are vacancies,

1

interstitial and impurity atoms, stacking faults in close-packed crystals, twin boundaries, and in particular, dislocations. Structural imperfections should be distinguished from electronic imperfections (such as holes in the valence bonds of semiconductors).

This book develops dislocation theory as part of the study of imperfections. The concept of an imperfection is a shorthand for describing the positions of a large number of atoms—it is much easier to describe crystals by listing the imperfections than by giving the position of every atom. The theory of imperfections is useful for (1) describing structures, (2)

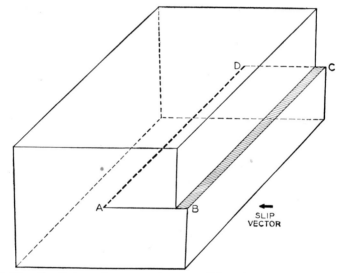

Fig. 1.1 The slip that produces an edge-type dislocation. Unit slip has occurred over the area $ABCD$. The boundary (within the crystal) of the slipped area is a dislocation. By definition, the edge dislocation AD is normal to the slip vector.

finding energies, and (3) describing processes such as deformation, annealing, and grain growth. This book shows that dislocation theory is a major part of the imperfections shorthand; throughout the book reasons will emerge for believing that the concept of a dislocation describes—at least to an approximation—what actually goes on when, for example, a metal deforms.

The remainder of this section gives a simple example to illustrate what a dislocation is. Section 1.2 discusses the nature of dislocation theory; Sec. 1.3 outlines the plan of the book. Section 1.4 enumerates some of the practical problems that dislocation theory is trying to solve. At present, dislocation theory is the most promising theoretical approach to these extremely difficult and important problems.

Now the simple example of a dislocation. Begin with the idea of slip: In the ideal case, a crystal deforms by planes of atoms sliding over one another—like cards in a deck. There is one unit of slip on a slip plane if every atom on one side of that plane has moved into a position originally occupied by its nearest neighbor in the direction of slip. Thus unit slip leaves the atoms in register across the slip plane and does not disturb the

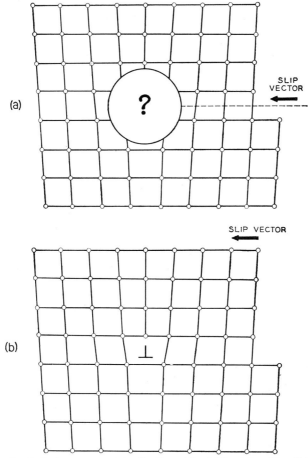

FIG. 1.2 A plane of atoms normal to the line AD of Fig. 1.1. The dislocation is a region of severe atomic misfit, where atoms are not properly surrounded by their neighbors. (*a*) The elastic strain around the dislocation; the arrangement of atoms at the center of the dislocation is not known exactly. (*b*) An approximate arrangement. The symbol ⊥ denotes the dislocation. Note that the dislocation is the edge on an incomplete atomic plane; hence, the name edge dislocation.

crystal perfection. In most real crystals, however, slip is not uniform over a slip plane. Figure 1.1 shows a crystal where unit slip has occurred over only a *part* of a slip plane; the rest of the plane remains unslipped. The line AD is the boundary within the crystal of the slipped area $ABCD$. Figure 1.2 shows the atoms viewed along AD. The imperfect region along AD is one type of dislocation—called an edge dislocation. It is denoted by the symbol $\perp$. Observe that one atom in the figure is not properly surrounded by neighbors. Observe also that, if the dislocation were to move across the slip plane (from one side of the crystal to the other), the crystal would deform (see Fig. 4.2)—hence the connection between dislocations and plastic deformation.

1.2 The Nature of Dislocation Theory. At present there is no unique dislocation theory of crystals. Rather, dislocation theory is a conceptual scheme for describing possible atomic mechanisms. Which mechanisms operate in actual crystals can be determined only by decisive experiments. The second part of the book shows how dislocation theory has stimulated several decisive experiments.

In this field (as in other fields of physics) the hand-in-hand advance of theory and experiment requires that we do two things: The first (and by far the easier) is to develop dislocation theory systematically from explicitly stated definitions and assumptions. Following this procedure, we find the possible dislocation types, derive the properties of individual dislocations, study the interactions between pairs of dislocations (or dislocations and other imperfections), and find the properties of simple symmetrical arrays of dislocations. However, when we have to deal with more than simple combinations of dislocations, the field of possibilities becomes practically unlimited; further progress must then wait on the second (and by far the more difficult) task of doing decisive experiments. Such experiments are difficult because dislocation theory is an atomistic theory and the experiments that can readily be performed are too macroscopic in scale to be directly related to the behavior of atoms. Little is gained in trying to explain any and all experimental results by dislocation theory; the number of possible explanations is limited only by the ingenuity, energy, and personal preference of the theorist. However, the second part of the book will show that some very decisive experiments have been performed during the past few years. Historically, these appear to approximate the dislocation equivalent of the oil-drop experiment in electron physics.

1.3 Plan of the Book. The purpose of Part I is to (1) develop and clarify the fundamental ideas of dislocation theory, (2) derive the basic geometrical and analytical properties of dislocations, and (3) discuss some of the ways in which dislocations can play an important role in the plastic deformation of crystals. Part II applies dislocation theory to the study of crystal growth and grain boundaries.

The development of basic theory follows an implicitly logical course; however, the emphasis is not on logical rigor, but on a pictorial representation designed to encourage a physical feeling for dislocations. Actually, one could deduce the geometry of dislocations from a set of definitions in the manner of Euclid. Chapters 2 to 7, although largely descriptive, try to convey some feeling for the underlying logical unity of the theory. Chapters 8 and 9 are more mathematical; they deal with quantitative properties that have been calculated exactly (in particular the elastic stress fields around dislocations).

Most of the basic ideas of Part I have to be illustrated by concrete examples which, although physically possible, are somewhat simpler than actual crystals. Therefore, we do not apply every result immediately to the explanation of some experimental observation; instead we concentrate on establishing a basis for the applications in Part II.

Part II applies dislocation theory to two problems of physical metallurgy: (1) the growth of a crystal from the vapor or dilute solution, and (2) the structure, energy, and motion of a small-angle-of-misfit grain boundary. Although these problems are not the most urgent from a practical viewpoint, they are especially important from a research standpoint; at present they represent the principal examples where dislocation theory has given definite predictions that have subsequently been checked by experiment. Such predictions should be distinguished from explanations that can be altered to fit the data.

The basic ideas of dislocation theory immediately suggest qualitative explanations for many properties of crystals; however, it is difficult to obtain unique and detailed predictions for specific cases. This difficulty is not due to any vagueness or indeterminacy in the theory itself; a dislocation is a well-defined concept with definite properties. If we specify the distribution of dislocations in an otherwise perfect crystal, we have specified the position of every atom in the crystal; we could then predict the behavior of the crystal under any set of conditions (for example, the application of a tensile stress). However, we do not know the distribution of dislocations in actual crystals; we, therefore, have to assume a distribution or "dislocation model"; by proper choice of a model, we can explain almost any experimental result. We are like a mathematician who knows his differential equation but not the boundary conditions; he finds that, by proper choice of boundary conditions, he can obtain almost any solution. In this analogy, dislocation theory is the differential equation; the distributions of dislocations in actual crystals are the unknown boundary conditions.

Part II discusses two ways in which the problem of finding a model has been handled successfully. One way is to deal with phenomena that involve only a single dislocation (or very few dislocations). The properties of single dislocations are well understood; if only one or a few dislocations are involved, the theory applies directly and unique predictions are made without the necessity (and consequent uncertainty) of postulating a dislocation model. F. C. Frank used this approach successfully in his theory of crystal growth. Because of the atomistic nature of the theory, its experimental verification required techniques of high resolution.

The other approach deals with the usual situation where hundreds of thousands of dislocations contribute to the experimental result; however, an experiment is chosen where some symmetry, periodicity, or other geometrical necessity specifies the dislocation model. Read and Shockley used this approach in their theory of small-angle-of-misfit grain boundaries; here the geometry of the boundary uniquely specifies—or at least rigidly limits—the choice of a model. At worst the choice is limited to only a few models. Read and Shockley show how to calculate the energy of each model. The model having the lowest energy should represent a well-annealed specimen. Chapter 13 shows how the calculated boundary energies agree with experiment.

In problems of plastic deformation, it is more difficult to get a clear-cut correlation between theory and experiment. Most explanations of experimental results have been either qualitative or speculative. However, throughout Part I, the elements of a theory of plastic deformation will turn up in the fundamental ideas of dislocation theory. Most of the basic properties of dislocations will immediately suggest a qualitative explanation for some observed mechanical property (the most outstanding example is the mechanical weakness of good single crystals). We shall not stop to pursue these explanations in detail; instead we proceed logically from the simplest ideas to the more complex without introducing *ad hoc* assumptions to explain some particular result.

Part II discusses two cases where the crystal-growth and grain-boundary studies have opened up promising approaches for the combined experimental-theoretical attack on plastic deformation.

This book makes no effort to review, even briefly, speculative theories that cannot as yet be experimentally tested.

1.4 Dislocations and Plastic Deformation. Before beginning the systematic development of dislocation theory, it may be helpful to review briefly some of the problems in plastic deformation where dislocation theory has been applied. This section makes no effort to explain or clarify these applications; instead, it merely enumerates examples to give some advance idea of why dislocations are important in plastic deformation.

Weakness of Single Crystals in Shear. A dislocation (like a lattice vacancy) is a configuration that can move through the lattice. The motion of a dislocation (like the motion of a vacancy) is a convenient shorthand for describing the motions of a large number of atoms; each atom moves only one interatomic distance or less as the configuration moves through many atomic spacings. The motion of a dislocation through the crystal produces a macroscopic deformation in which the crystal yields to applied stresses. The stress required to move a dislocation is at least several orders of magnitude smaller than the stress required to shear one entire plane of atoms simultaneously over another in a perfect crystal; this explains the otherwise mysteriously low yield stress in single crystals.

Slip Bands. A certain simple form of dislocation can produce a large amount of slip on one slip plane by a simple motion; it can also generate a large number of additional dislocations by a process of expansion and subdivision. This mechanism—known as the Frank-Read mechanism— is the most plausible explanation for (1) the concentration of slip in slip bands and (2) the origin of the dislocations that accumulate during deformation.

Work Hardening. Dislocations are surrounded by elastic stress fields. The stress fields of different dislocations interact strongly and lock the dislocations into a metastable configuration. The externally applied stress required to produce plastic deformation must be sufficient to make dislocations move through the opposing stress fields of other dislocations. Thus the dislocations accumulated during cold work harden the crystal.

Reducing the density of dislocations allows the few dislocations left to move more easily and, therefore, weakens the crystal. However, if all the dislocations were eliminated, the crystal would be very strong. If a crystal were made small enough—smaller than the mean distance between dislocations—it should contain no dislocations; it would therefore have the strength calculated for a perfect crystal. (In a perfect crystal the critical stress for plastic deformation corresponds to an elastic strain of 1 to 3 per cent. The strength of actual good single crystals is about 10^3 times lower than this.) Galt and Herring (1952) verified that tin crystals about a micron in diameter have the calculated strength of perfect crystals.

Effect of Impurities. Impurity atoms diffuse toward dislocations. Oversized atoms are attracted to the region of tension around a dislocation; undersized substitutional atoms are attracted to the region of compression. Note that the distortion around the dislocation in Fig. 1.2 would be partially relieved if an undersized atom replaced the atom just above the symbol ⊥. Cottrell and Bilby (1949) calculated the rate of diffusion of impurities in the stress field around a dislocation; from this they correctly predicted the time law of strain aging.

Cottrell has explained the yield point observed in iron and other crystals as a breaking away of dislocations from the surrounding impurity atoms; once the dislocation has broken away, it can keep moving under a lower stress—hence the drop in the stress-strain curve.

Effect on Elastic Constants and Internal Friction. A small applied stress (lower than the stress required to cause slip) causes a small reversible displacement of the dislocations; this adds a small reversible strain to the elastic strain. Therefore the strain (for a given stress) is increased; hence the apparent elastic moduli are decreased.

A small alternating stress causes the dislocations to move back and forth; the moving dislocations dissipate energy and thereby contribute to internal friction. Thus changes in the elastic constants and internal friction (during cold work or annealing) can be explained by changes in the density of dislocations.

Annealing. The arbitrary motion of a dislocation (as distinct from a pure slipping motion) involves mass transport by diffusion. Suppose a configuration of dislocations is stable if only pure slipping motion can occur; in general it will be unstable if the dislocations are permitted to move arbitrarily. Thus annealing at a high temperature (where appreciable diffusion occurs) allows the dislocations to move into a configuration of lower energy. If dislocations that have an interaction energy of attraction are allowed to move freely, they will come together and annihilate one another or combine to form a single dislocation; in either case, energy is released and the number of dislocations decreases. The effect of annealing is thus explained by the elimination of dislocations.

Polygonization. A bent crystal contains a preponderance of dislocations of one type; these are more or less uniformly distributed on parallel slip planes. In the process of polygonization, dislocations on different slip planes line up one above the other and form a small-angle grain boundary. (Chapter 11 shows that a row of like dislocations is a small-angle-of-misfit grain boundary.) The energy per dislocation is reduced when the dislocations are so arranged.

The above examples are not intended to be exhaustive but merely to give an idea of why dislocations are important in the practical problems of plastic deformation and strength of materials.

1.5 Bibliography. We shall not review, even briefly, the extensive literature on dislocations. However, here are a few suggestions for supplementing this book:

The most important reference is Cottrell's "Dislocations and Plastic Flow in Crystals" (1953); this is a lucid introduction to dislocations and their role in plastic deformation. Cottrell gives a thorough review of the outstanding facts of plastic deformation; he also covers the quantitative development of dislocation theory in a simple and thorough way and applies it to a number of practical problems. The student who wants to go still further into the quantitative development of dislocation theory can profitably study Nabarro's (1952) thorough treatise, The Mathematical Theory of Stationary Dislocations in *Advances in Physics*.

Advances in Physics should be watched for other timely reviews of dislocations and related subjects; several have already appeared: Frank's "Dislocations and Crystal Growth" forms the basis of Chap. 10 of this book and covers the subject more fully, especially in regard to the kinetics of crystal growth. Brown's "Surface Effects in Plastic Deformation" summarizes a number of pertinent experiments and their relation to current theory.

Orowan (1953) has a valuable paper on the dislocation theory of plastic deformation in the AIME monograph, "Dislocations in Metals."

The following reports of conferences have already become standard references:

"Report of a Conference on the Strength of Solids," The University of Bristol, England, 1947. Published by the Physical Society (London), 1948 (commonly called the Bristol Report).

"The Plastic Deformation of Crystalline Solids," Carnegie Institute of Technology, May, 1950, O.N.R. (commonly called the Pittsburgh Report).

"Imperfections in Nearly Perfect Crystals" (Shockley, Seitz, Hollomon, Maurer, editors), Wiley, New York, 1952 (report of the October, 1950, N.R.C. Conference at Pocono, Pa.—called the imperfections book).

There is no better way to develop a feeling for dislocations than to see Bragg and Nye's (1947) moving pictures of dislocations in the bubble model (distributed by Kodak Ltd., Wealdstone, Harrow, Middlesex, England, as 16-mm "cinegraph" No. 2015, "Bubble Model of a Metal").

In concluding this introductory chapter, it may be well to review quickly the background assumed on the part of the reader: The descriptive Chaps. 2 to 7 assume an elementary knowledge of crystallography. The text and figures refer explicitly to only four crystal structures: the (hypothetical) simple cubic, the face-centered cubic (Al, Cu, . . .), the body-centered cubic (αFe, Na, . . .), and the hexagonal structure (Zn, Cd, . . .). Miller indices are used in, and only in, the cubic system. Pages 1 to 9 of Barrett's "Structure of Metals" (1952a) is adequate background for crystallography.

A knowledge of the definitions of stress and strain and the stress-strain relations is necessary; a passing acquaintance with the conditions of static equilibrium for stress would be useful in the quantitative Chaps. 8 and 9. For this purpose, references to Timoshenko's "Theory of Elasticity" are given wherever necessary.

Some knowledge of the principal facts of plastic deformation will help in appreciating the significance of dislocation theory—although it is not necessary for understanding the book. The mathematics required goes only through the elements of calculus (except in a few of the problems). The physics includes only such fundamentals as are covered in a general undergraduate course.

PART I
THEORY

CHAPTER 2

SOME SIMPLE EXAMPLES

This chapter shows pictures of the basic types of dislocations. Each example is introduced by (1) a picture of how the dislocation could be produced—starting with a perfect crystal—and (2) a picture of how the atoms are arranged. The last section discusses interatomic forces and their effect on the arrangement of atoms near a dislocation.

2.1 Dislocations and Nonuniform Slip. Section 1.1 gave a simple example of a dislocation, namely the line separating slipped and unslipped areas on a slip plane. This is a possible way of visualizing all types of dislocations. There are other ways of visualizing dislocations and other processes that could form dislocations; however, slip provides a single pictorial representation in familiar terms.

Several observers have watched slip lines through a microscope during plastic deformation. Recently, Chen and Pond (1952) took moving pictures of growing slip lines during deformation at a controlled rate. When they viewed the slip lines on a surface at right angles to the slip vector, they saw that a typical line begins as a short fine line; it then broadens in the center and increases in length with time. Even after the middle part of the line has become well developed (indicating slip of many thousands of atomic spacings), the line still does not extend all the way across the specimen; instead it fades out gradually at the ends. The amount of slip is therefore not uniform; it varies from none at the ends of the line to many thousands of atomic spacings at the center. This chapter introduces dislocations by examples of nonuniform slip.

First, consider the simple case where one unit of slip has occurred over part of a slip plane; the rest of the plane remains unslipped. In the slipped area, the atomic planes adjoining the slip plane have been displaced relative to one another by one interatomic spacing in the direction of slip. In other words, the slip vector is a translation vector of the crystal (a vector that connects atoms, or lattice points, having identical surroundings). We can distinguish the following three regions on the slip plane: In one region, no slip has occurred; on another, slip has taken place and the atoms are again in register across the slip plane; in the third region (which separates the other two), there is a transition from the slipped to the unslipped state. Here the atoms are not in register, and

13

nearest neighbor relations are not satisfied; therefore, the region has a larger average energy per atom. To minimize the total energy, the transition region will be only a few atoms wide. The exact width is not known at present; Sec. 2.7 discusses its dependence on atomic structure. On a macroscopic scale, the boundary between the slipped and unslipped areas is a line; on an atomic scale, it is a region where the atoms are not properly surrounded by neighbors (that is, an imperfection). Since the imperfection is contained within a few atomic diameters of a line, it is called a line imperfection. This chapter is based on the following pictorial definition: *a* **dislocation** *is a line imperfection forming the boundary within the crystal of a slipped area.* Chapter 3 gives a more general treatment and defines dislocations independently of their origin. A consequence of the general definition is that any dislocation can be eliminated from a crystal by slip; conversely, it could have been formed by slip. One can therefore visualize dislocations in terms of slip without loss in generality.

The discussion begins with the hypothetical simple cubic structure, where atomic arrangements in three dimensions are relatively easy to visualize. Once the basic ideas have become familiar, it will be easier to visualize dislocations in real crystals—especially in the face- and body-centered cubic metals. The results obtained for the simple cubic are extended to more general structures in Sec. 2.6.

Sections 2.2 and 2.3 discuss two simple examples: the edge dislocation and the screw dislocation. These names are slightly misleading—they represent not discrete types but special orientations. Strictly speaking one should say "dislocation in the edge orientation" rather than "edge dislocation"; this will become clear as the discussion proceeds. Section 2.4 shows how a curved dislocation can change from edge to screw along its length. Sections 2.2 and 2.3 deal with only straight dislocations which are either all edge or all screw.

2.2 Edge Dislocation. Taylor and Orowan originally interpreted plastic deformation by what is now called an edge dislocation (also, a Taylor-Orowan dislocation). The example in Chap. 1 (Figs. 1.1 and 1.2) is an edge dislocation; here *the slip vector is at right angles to the dislocation.* Slip has occurred over the area $ABCD$; the slip vector is a $<100>$ translation vector of the lattice. The line AD is the boundary (within the crystal) of the slipped area; along AD the atoms are not properly surrounded by neighbors in the simple cubic pattern (note that one atom per atomic plane does not even have the right number of nearest neighbors). The line imperfection AD is called a dislocation line, or just a *dislocation*.

The exact arrangement of atoms along AD is not known; to find it would require a difficult calculation using quantum mechanics. The arrangement in Fig. 1.2 is a good enough approximation to show some of the properties of an edge dislocation. Observe that $n + 1$ atomic planes above the slip plane try to join onto n planes below; therefore, one vertical plane of atoms has to terminate on the slip plane; the dislocation is the edge of this extra plane—hence the name edge dislocation.

Besides the atomic disorder along AD, there is an elastic stress field, which falls off inversely with distance from AD. The stress field of a dislocation plays an important role in work hardening; for example, at a distance of 1 micron, the stress has dropped to about 10^7 dynes/cm^2— which is the yield stress for typical good single crystals. The mathe-

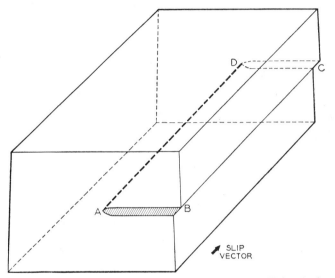

FIG. 2.1 The slip that produces a screw-type dislocation. Unit slip has occurred over $ABCD$. By definition, the screw dislocation AD is parallel to the slip vector.

matical theory of elasticity gives the stress distribution exactly except near the dislocation.

An alternative way of forming an edge dislocation is to remove half a plane of atoms below the slip plane (or insert an extra half plane above); this, of course, requires mass transport; it might occur in real crystals by diffusion of vacancies or interstitial atoms. Sometimes it is helpful to imagine an edge dislocation as the boundary (within the crystal) of an extra plane of atoms. However, it is only for an edge dislocation that a densely packed plane is inserted between two portions of crystal (which are simply wedged apart without tangential displacement); in the general case the slip picture is better.

2.3 Screw Dislocation. Burgers (1939) generalized the idea of a dislocation and introduced the screw (also called Burgers) dislocation. A screw dislocation by definition *is parallel to the slip vector*. Figure 2.1

shows how to create a screw dislocation by slip; the dislocation AD is the
boundary within the crystal of the slipped area $ABCD$.   Figure 2.2 shows
a screw dislocation parallel to a cube edge in a simple cubic crystal; the
unit cells are shown as distorted cubes.   Figure 2.3 shows the atomic
planes above and below the slip plane; the open circles represent atoms
just above the slip plane, and the solid circles, atoms just below.   Again
the exact arrangement of atoms near the dislocation is not known.

Figure 2.2 shows why this dislocation is called screw: *the crystal is not
made up of parallel atomic planes one above the other; rather it is a single
atomic plane in the form of a helicoid, or spiral ramp.*

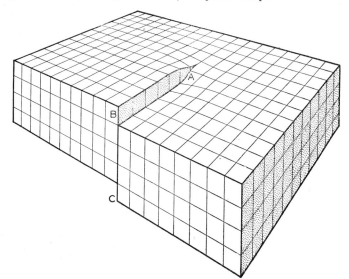

Fɪɢ. 2.2 Another view of a screw dislocation.   The dislocation AD (of which only the
end A is visible) is parallel to the line BC, which is parallel to the slip vector.   The
atoms are represented by distorted cubes (see Fig. 10.4, which represents the same
situation by undistorted cubes).   Note that the crystal is a *single* atomic plane in the
form of a helicoid, or spiral ramp.

The distortion around a screw dislocation is mostly pure shear; therefore the unit cells can also be represented by undistorted cubes displaced
relative to one another in the direction of the slip vector.   The arrangement of atoms around the point A is represented in this way in Fig. 10.4
(see Chap. 10).   Figure 10.4 is especially useful when thinking about
crystal growth.

The same screw dislocation can be produced by slip on *any* plane containing AD—or on any slip surface ending on AD.   The reason is as
follows: A screw dislocation has no unique slip plane; the slip plane must
contain both the dislocation and the slip vector; when these are parallel,
the slip plane is not uniquely defined.   Chapter 3 will discuss this point

in more detail.   The method of representing the distortion in Fig. 2.2 (by distorted cubes) makes the dislocation *appear* to have a unique slip plane; near the center of the dislocation, the distortion is so severe that some arbitrariness is involved in drawing the cubes.   As an exercise, use Fig. 10.4 to show graphically that the same arrangement of atoms results from slip on any surface ending on a line parallel to the slip vector.

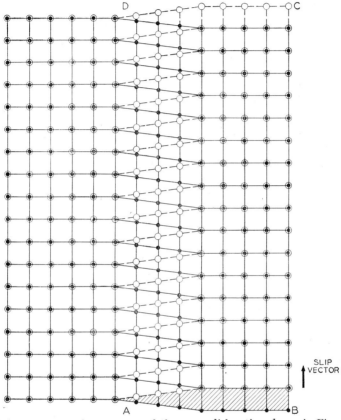

FIG. 2.3 Arrangement of atoms around the screw dislocation shown in Figs. 2.1 and 2.2.   The plane of the figure is parallel to the slip plane.   *ABCD* is the slipped area and *AD*, the dislocation.   The open circles represent atoms in the atomic plane just above the slip plane and the solid circles, atoms in the plane just below the slip plane.

2.4 Curved Dislocation Line on Plane Slip Surface.   The two examples above were straight dislocation lines.   Now let the slipped area lie in a single plane but otherwise have an arbitrary shape; its boundary (the dislocation) is then an arbitrary plane curve.   Figure 2.4 is an example of the more general case; here the slipped area *ABC* is bounded (within the crystal) by the curved dislocation *AC*.   The atomic disorder varies along the curve.   Figure 2.5 shows the arrangement of atoms; as before, the

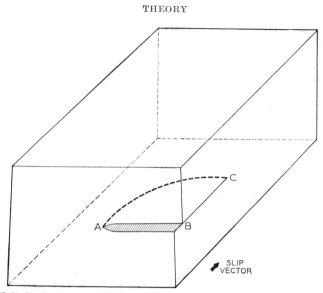

Fig. 2.4 Unit slip in the area *ABC* produces a curved dislocation *AC* lying in a single plane (the slip plane).

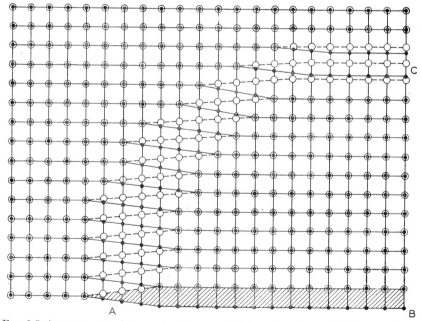

Fig. 2.5 Arrangement of atoms for the curved dislocation shown in Fig. 2.4. Open circles represent the atomic plane just above the slip plane; closed circles represent the atoms just below.

plane of the drawing is the slip plane; the open circles represent atoms directly above the slip plane, and the closed circles, atoms directly below. At A the dislocation is parallel to the slip vector and is therefore in the screw orientation; the atomic arrangement is the same as in Fig. 2.3. Near C the dislocation is in the edge orientation and the arrangement of atoms is the same as in Fig. 1.2; however it is now viewed along the normal to the slip plane (instead of along the dislocation). Notice that near C in Fig. 2.5 three rows of open circles must join onto two rows of solid circles; the middle row of open circles is therefore the edge of the extra atomic plane. Follow this extra plane into the crystal and observe that, when the dislocation curves (and ceases to be pure edge), the extra plane ceases to be "extra"; instead it joins onto an atomic plane below the slip plane.

Figure 2.5 shows that *edge* and *screw* refer not to properties of the whole dislocation, but to the local orientations.

2.5 Arbitrary Slip Surface. The curved dislocation in Fig. 2.4 lies in a single plane; that plane contains the slip vector and is therefore the slip plane. However, the most general slipped area (for a given slip vector) is not a plane but a surface, which must be parallel at all points to the slip vector. For example, in α iron, the traces of the slip surfaces on the external surface are very wavy when viewed along the slip vector. In other crystals, slip prefers to occur on definite crystallographic planes, usually of low indices and high atomic density (for example, the basal plane in hexagonal crystals). In face-centered cubic metals, the most general slip surfaces appear to be made up of segments of {111} planes, which intersect along lines parallel to their common slip vector. On an atomic scale, we can always resolve any dislocation into straight segments; however, in the most general case, these segments may be only a few atoms long.

An example of a segmented slip surface is shown in Fig. 2.6; here the slipped area has two parts, $ABCD$ and $DEFA$; these are parallel to cube faces and intersect along the line AD (which of course must be parallel to the slip vector). The dislocation line is shaped like an L; both sections DC and DE are perpendicular to the slip vector and are therefore pure edge. Looking down ED from above or into DC from the right, we see the same arrangement of atoms shown in Fig. 1.2. Figure 2.7 shows the atoms just above (open circles) and just below (solid circles) the slip plane $ABCD$. The section of dislocation DC (in the plane of the figure) and the section DE (normal to the figure) are both edges of the same extra plane.

Now imagine that DC is rotated counterclockwise through 45°, as shown in Fig. 2.8; now DC is between the edge and screw orientations (visualize the corresponding slipped area with the aid of Fig. 2.6). Figure

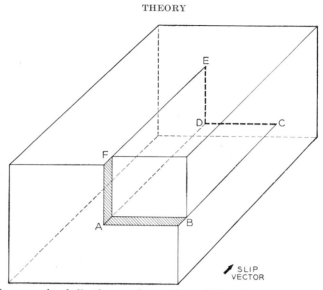

FIG. 2.6 An example of slip that produces a bent dislocation which does *not* lie in a single plane parallel to the slip vector. Unit slip has occurred over the bent slip surface *ABCDEF*. The boundary *CDE* (within the crystal) of the slipped area is an edge-type dislocation.

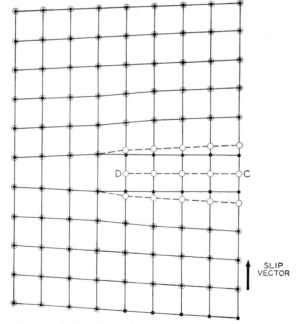

FIG. 2.7 Arrangement of atoms in a plane parallel to *ABCD* of Fig. 2.6. The open and solid circles represent atomic planes, respectively, above and below the slip plane *ABCD*. The section of dislocation *CD* lies in the plane of the drawing; the section *DE* is normal to the drawing.

2.9 shows the atoms after DC has rotated through 90°; now DC is parallel to AD; it is therefore in the pure screw orientation. The section ED stays the same in all these figures.

The dislocation CDE in Fig. 2.9 is similar to AC in Fig. 2.5 except that the bend is abrupt instead of smooth; in both figures, the dislocation lies in a single plane parallel to the slip vector.

This completes the crystallographic picture of four elements which make up any dislocation: (1) an edge segment, (2) a screw segment, (3) a

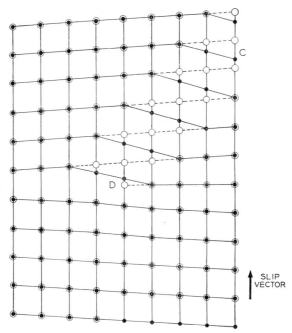

FIG. 2.8 Same as Fig. 2.7 except that DC is rotated 45° counterclockwise about the fixed point D. In the area swept out by DC, unit slip has occurred and open circles have moved up one interatomic spacing relative to solid circles.

bend lying in a plane parallel to the slip vector, and (4) a bend lying in a plane normal to the slip vector.

2.6 More General Structures. At this point it is convenient to introduce what we shall call **t vectors**. A **t** vector is defined by the following two conditions:

1. It must connect atoms that have identical surroundings (identical here means identical except for elastic strains).
2. It cannot be made up of a combination of shorter vectors that satisfy condition 1.

In other words a **t** vector is a lattice translation vector of minimum length. It could always be an edge of a primitive unit cell. The accompanying table gives the directions and magnitudes of the **t** vectors in the common cubic structures. The cube edge is taken as unit length. The table also

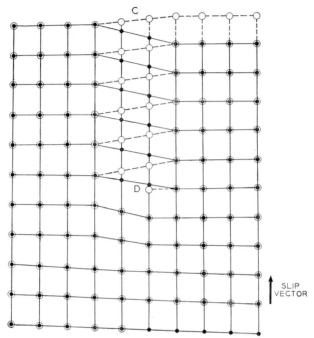

Fig. 2.9 Same as Figs. 2.7 and 2.8 except that *CD* has rotated 90° and is in the pure screw orientation.

gives the number of different **t** vectors in each case (not counting as different vectors that differ only in sign).

Structure	Direction	Magnitude	Number
Simple cubic	$<100>$	1	3
Body-centered cubic	$<111>$	$\frac{1}{2}\sqrt{3}$	4
Face-centered cubic	$<110>$	$\dfrac{1}{\sqrt{2}}$	6
Close Packed hexagonal	$\langle 11\bar{2}0 \rangle$	*1a*	*3*
	$\langle 000\bar{1}\rangle$		

In each of these structures, all the **t** vectors have the same length. This is not so in general. For example, take the hexagonal structure (by hexagonal structure we mean almost close-packed structures such as zinc, cadmium, etc.); here there are three **t** vectors of equal length in the basal plane; the fourth **t** vector is normal to the basal plane and equal in length to twice the spacing between basal planes.

By changing the angles between the t vectors in simple cubic, we can produce either the body- or face-centered cubic structure. Changing both the lengths and directions of t vectors gives still more general structures. The simple cubic can thus be transformed to any structure having only one atom per lattice point. The transformation does not give the hexagonal structure, which has two atoms per lattice point. Chapter 7 deals separately with the hexagonal case.

Most of the figures so far represent atomic planes that contain two orthogonal t vectors. These figures apply not just to the simple cubic but to any atomic plane where the atoms form a square array with each atom surrounded by four nearest neighbors in the plane of the figure.

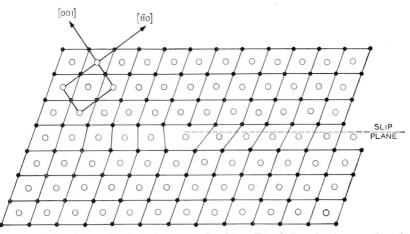

Fig. 2.10 Edge dislocation in body-centered cubic. The dislocation is normal to the plane of the figure, (110). Solid and open circles represent parallel neighboring planes in different elevation.

For example Fig. 1.2 applies to the (100) atomic planes in face-centered cubic; however, a parallel plane of atoms in different elevation should be added to complete the picture in face-centered cubic, see Prob. 2.[1]

When the slip plane contains two t vectors, it is again helpful to draw the atomic planes above and below the slip plane. Figures 2.3, 2.5, and 2.7 to 2.9 can be transformed to represent other structures by changing the squares to parallelograms and displacing the two planes so that they have the proper relation in the unslipped state. Changing the angle between close-packed rows from 90° to 70°32′ gives a picture of the (110) slip planes in body-centered cubic; 60° gives the close-packed planes in either face-centered cubic or hexagonal crystals.

[1] Unless otherwise indicated, the problems mentioned in the text refer to those at the end of the chapter in which the reference occurs.

A similar transformation applies to Fig. 1.2, but in general, one or more parallel planes of atoms in different elevation must be added for completeness. For example, Fig. 2.10 shows an edge dislocation parallel to a <110> direction in body-centered cubic.

2.7 Effect of Atomic Structure on the Form of a Dislocation. Around a dislocation, the distortion is so severe that elastic continuum theory does not apply; it is necessary to take account of the periodic nature of the crystal. An exact (quantum mechanical) treatment has not yet been carried out. At present such an analysis appears to be impractical. This section discusses several approximate approaches, which are based on the idea of interatomic forces—an idea which, in itself, is an approximation from a quantum mechanical viewpoint. We shall show how the forces between atoms determine the form of a dislocation—and in particular the width. By **width** we mean the *width of the area on the slip plane where the atoms are out of register by more than a certain amount, which is conventionally taken as one-half the maximum shear strain.*

The Peierls-Nabarro Theory. Begin with the edge dislocation in Fig. 1.2. Above the slip plane, the atoms are squeezed together (in the direction of slip); below the slip plane, the atoms are pulled apart. Shear stresses acting across the slip plane hold the upper and lower halves of the crystal in equilibrium. Peierls (1940) and Nabarro (1947) treat the parts of the crystal above and below the slip plane as elastic continua; they take account of the periodic structure of the crystal by recognizing that the shear stress τ acting across the slip plane is a periodic function of the relative displacement δ of the adjoining atomic planes. For example, when $\delta = b =$ (magnitude of the slip vector), the atoms are again in register across the slip plane; hence the period is b. Peierls and Nabarro take a simple periodic function—the sine function—and set

$$\tau = \frac{G}{2\pi} \sin \frac{2\pi\delta}{b}$$

where G is the shear modulus. The constant $G/2\pi$ was chosen so that the relation would reduce to the linear stress-strain law $\tau = G(\delta/b)$ at small strains.

Peierls and Nabarro used their approximation to calculate the form of an edge dislocation. They found that the width is about $1.5b$. Eshelby (1949a) used the same method and got essentially the same result for a screw dislocation. Except within about one interatomic spacing of a dislocation, the Peierls-Nabarro solution is almost the same as the elasticity solution (Chap. 8), in which the center of the dislocation is a singularity.

The advantage of the Peierls-Nabarro approximation is that it takes account of the periodic nature of the crystal and yet is simple enough to apply to imperfect crystals. The chief criticisms of it concern the simple sine law, which appears to be a poor approximation for real crystals (as will be discussed later in this section). The use of the sine law causes the width of a dislocation to be *underestimated*.

The Central-force Approximation. Here the interatomic force is assumed to act along the line of centers and to depend only on distance between atoms. The force is represented by the sum of the following two terms:

1. A short-range repulsion that is very sensitive to the distance between atoms. It increases almost abruptly as the atoms move closer together than the normal interatomic spacing, and it drops to nothing as the atoms move farther apart than the normal separation.
2. A long-range attraction that is relatively insensitive to distance but drops off at large distances.

The normal interatomic distance is determined by a balance between 1 and 2. Now consider how the *net* force varies with distance: If the atoms move only very small distances from the equilibrium position, then the net force varies linearly with displacement (elastic range). As the atoms move closer together than the elastic range, the net repulsive force increases more and more rapidly with decreasing separation. The opposite is true if the atoms move farther apart; beyond the elastic range, the net attractive force increases less and less rapidly with increasing separation; finally it reaches a maximum and begins to decrease (now we say that the bond is broken, or the crystal has cracked on an atomic scale). In other words, the curve of interatomic force vs. separation of atoms is concave downward (taking a net attraction as positive). We now define the **hardness** of the atoms as the *curvature* of the force-separation curve. Hardness, in this sense, describes a nonlinear property of the structure and has no relation to the elastic properties; the latter are determined by the *slope* of the force-separation curve.

As an exercise show that the maximum net attractive force occurs at a larger separation for softer atoms (for the same elastic constants).

We next discuss the behavior of the structure in large shear. First, however, it is necessary to consider the structure of a crystal whose atoms are held together by central forces. We can think of such a crystal as a collection of spheres under pressure—the pressure comes from the long-range attractive forces. As an exercise, prove that only a close-packed structure (such as face-centered cubic or hexagonal close-packed) is stable under central forces; in any other structure (such as simple or body-centered cubic) there must be directional bonds (we consider the effect of directional bonds later in this section). In a close-packed structure with central forces, the resistance to large shear comes from the fact that shear disturbs the close packing: one atomic plane cannot be sheared directly over another; it must move *up and over*.   Thus, in large shear, the crystal expands at right angles to the shear (or slip) plane and work is done against the long-range attractive forces, which try to hold the crystal in close packing.   This expansion normal to the shear plane is a nonelastic effect (it is still an *expansion*—and not a compression—if the direction of shear is reversed).   The maximum expansion in large shear depends on the plane and direction of shear.   In all cases, the shear stress is a periodic function of shear strain (as in the Peierls-Nabarro approximation). However the relationship departs from a sine function—especially for hard atoms.   As an exercise, show that the shear stress reaches its maximum at a lower shear strain for harder atoms—this point is discussed further in the problems, and the complete shear stress vs. strain curve is calculated for several slip systems.   Approximate formulas are used to represent the forces between atoms.   The same formulas could be used to calculate the form of a dislocation; the calculation, however, would be fairly laborious and has not yet been done.   We next consider an experimental method of studying interatomic forces and their effect on the form of a dislocation.

The Bubble Model.   Bragg, Nye, and Lomer constructed a soap-bubble model of a metal to study the form of a dislocation and the role of dislocations in deformation.   The bubble model is a monolayer raft of bubbles of uniform size floating on liquid.   The bubbles form a close-packed layer.   The attractive force between bubbles comes from the surface tension; the repulsive force acts only between bubbles in contact and comes from the excess pressure inside the bubbles (excess pressure is inversely proportional to bubble radius).   The size of the bubbles determines their hardness: large bubbles are soft, small bubbles, hard.   Bubbles about 1.1 mm in diameter represent fairly well the forces between (hard) copper ions as calculated by K. Fuchs.   Figure 2.11 shows a dislocation in a raft of bubbles 1.9 mm in diameter (relatively soft).   Figure 2.12 shows the same type of dislocation for (relatively hard) bubbles 0.76 mm in diameter. Observe, in each figure, how the structure is expanded normal to the slip plane where the shear across the slip plane is large.   As an exercise, explain why dislocations are wider for harder bubbles—for the answer see Lomer (1949).

Bragg and Nye (1947) used the bubble model to study many phenomena observed in real crystals—for example, elastic deformation, slip, recrystallization, and annealing after severe deformation.   They found that slip occurs by the motion of dislocations, which originate at irregularities in the external surface.   Their moving pictures (see Sec. 1.5 for reference) show graphically how moving dislocations account for plastic deformation, recovery, etc., in metals.

Some caution should be used in applying the two-dimensional bubble model to real crystals. Even if the forces between bubbles were *exactly* the same as the forces between atoms, the model would not represent

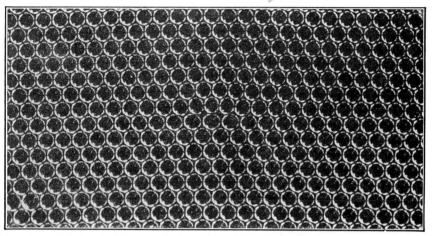

FIG. 2.11 A dislocation in the bubble model. The relatively soft bubbles—1.9 mm in diameter—give a narrow dislocation (after Bragg and Nye, 1947).

exactly a close-packed atomic plane intersecting a dislocation in a three-dimensional crystal. The reason is this: in any real crystal, atoms in one close-packed plane experience a net force (in that plane) due to atoms in the adjoining planes. Therefore the distortion of one close-packed plane

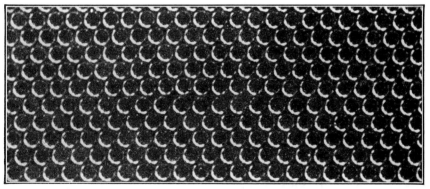

FIG. 2.12 A dislocation in the bubble model. The relatively hard bubbles—0.76 mm in diameter—give a wide dislocation (after Bragg and Nye, 1947).

would change if it were removed from the crystal. The distortion of a plane normal to an edge dislocation would *not* change on removal from the crystal if the crystal were made up by stacking such planes one directly above the other—as simple cubic is made up by stacking (100) planes one above the other; thus Fig. 1.2 would apply both to a monolayer or to one atomic plane in a three-dimensional crystal. There is, however, no crystal made up by stacking close-packed (hexagonal-type) planes one directly above the other (see Sec. 7.2 for a discussion of close-packed stacking).

Directional Bonds. Directional bonds are important in any non-close-packed structure—the latter would be unstable under purely central forces. For example, take the simple cubic and consider the edge dislocation (Fig. 1.2): Directional bonds provide the main resistance to shear on the slip plane—central forces actually favor such shear. Strong directional bonds across the slip plane always make for narrow dislocations—it is energetically unfavorable to have many atoms out of register across the slip plane.

Form of a Screw Dislocation. So far the discussion has concerned the edge dislocation. The screw presents a somewhat different problem. To illustrate the problem, take again the simple cubic. Figures 2.2 and 10.4 represent the distortion as symmetrical about the screw dislocation. The strain is pure shear on planes containing the dislocation. The atoms all lie on a helical surface. (As an exercise, prove from symmetry that this arrangement of atoms is an equilibrium one.) A symmetrical screw dislocation is necessarily narrow. However, it is not known whether a symmetrical screw dislocation is stable—it might be able to lower its energy by spreading out in one slip plane; on that plane a large shear-type misfit would extend over a relatively wide area, with only elastic distortion elsewhere. As an exercise draw such an unsymmetrical screw dislocation; use cubes to represent atoms as in Fig. 2.2 or 10.4.

PROBLEMS

1. The edge dislocation in Fig. 1.2 is symmetrical about a plane of atoms on the compression side of the slip plane. Draw a dislocation having the same direction and slip vector but symmetrical about a plane of atoms on the tension side.

2. Add a second plane of atoms (in different elevation) to make Fig. 1.2 represent the (100) plane in face-centered cubic (again with the dislocation normal to the figure).

3. The (hypothetical) simple cubic structure is held together by both central forces and directional bonds. Show how the arrangement of atoms for the edge dislocation (Fig. 1.2) varies with the hardness of the atoms (as defined in Sec. 2.7) and the stiffness of the directional bonds (in large distortion). Draw the dislocation for the following cases:

a. Soft atoms and strong (stiff) directional bonds.

b. Hard atoms and weak directional bonds.

4. Show that the crystal in Fig. 2.2 will be one continuous atomic plane provided only that the dislocation is *not* pure edge. Illustrate by drawing the case where the dislocation is at 45° to the slip vector.

Show that a stack of close-packed planes always form one continuous plane if they intersect a dislocation whose slip vector has a component normal to those planes.

5. Sketch the shear stress-strain curve for a perfect crystal made up of perfectly rigid spheres held together by long-range attractive forces. Calculate the curve exactly, using a hydrostatic pressure P to represent the long-range attraction. How is the curve modified if the atoms are slightly soft?

6. A close-packed structure is expanded radially around a symmetrical pure screw dislocation. Why? (HINT: This is a nonelastic effect; use the ideas of Sec. 2.7.)

7. Consider an (edge) dislocation in the two-dimensional bubble model with hard bubbles. The dislocation in Fig. 2.12 is wide. Show that, if a high enough compressive stress were applied normal to the slip plane, the dislocation would become narrower. Draw the narrow dislocation. Show that the same result holds for any edge dislocation in a close-packed structure of relatively hard atoms.

8. Consider a face-centered cubic structure made up of hard spheres. Find the maximum expansion normal to the shear plane for large shear on the following shear systems: [110] ($1\bar{1}0$), [110] (001), [$11\bar{2}$] (111).[1] Compare with the corresponding expansion in the two-dimensional bubble model; show that the latter expansion is the same as for shear on a plane normal to the basal plane in a hexagonal close-packed structure.

9. Calculate the stress-strain curve for shear of a perfect face-centered cubic structure on the [$11\bar{2}$] (111) system. Let z be the normal separation of neighboring (111) planes, and let x be the relative tangential displacement. Take the unstrained spacing of (111) planes as the unit of length (thus, in the unstrained state, $z = 1, x = 0$). Consider two atoms i and j in neighboring (111) planes; let r_{ij} be the distance between i and j. Nabarro (1947) has suggested the expression

$$W_{ij} = Bz^2 + Ae^{-\beta r_{ij}^2}$$

for the potential energy of i and j. Find the total potential energy (per atom) of the crystal as a function of x and z. Only nearest neighbor interactions need be included in summing W_{ij} over pairs of atoms. Show that (with no stress normal to the slip plane) the shear stress τ is related to x by

$$\frac{\tau}{G} = \frac{6\sqrt{2}}{2p-3}\left[\frac{2(1-x)e^{px} - (2+x)}{1 + 2e^{px}}\right]$$

where G is the elastic modulus for [$11\bar{2}$] (111) shear and $p = 6\sqrt{8}\,\beta$. Plot the curve for $p = 10$ (estimated from Fuchs's calculations for copper). Plot the maximum of the τ vs. x curve as a function of the parameter β.

---

[1] In the [$11\bar{2}$] (111) system, large shear produces a stacking fault. Continued shear would take place by a zigzag sequence of alternate [$11\bar{2}$] and [$\bar{1}2\bar{1}$] movements. Chapter 7 will discuss this more fully.

CHAPTER 3

IMPERFECTIONS IN CRYSTALS

Given an imperfection of unknown origin, how should it be described? Chapter 2 derived the properties of dislocations from their (assumed) origin in slip. This chapter starts with the *imperfection* and describes it independently of its origin. Various classes of imperfections are distinguished, and their properties are derived from a simple method of description. The discussion brings out the radical difference between dislocations and other imperfections, such as vacancies and impurities.

3.1 Introduction. Chapter 2 defined a dislocation by a vector (the slip vector) and a line (the dislocation line, or boundary of the slipped area). The line and vector together determine the slip surface—or, when the line is straight, the slip plane. This chapter gives a general definition that associates a vector with a given line imperfection without presupposing a slip process. The definition is used to (1) classify dislocations and distinguish them from other imperfections, (2) describe networks of intersecting dislocations, (3) prove a conservation theorem that describes the fundamental topological property of dislocations.

Section 3.1 gives two examples to illustrate the conservation theorem. Then the discussion turns to imperfections in general; Sec. 3.2 deals with the properties of point and line imperfections. Sections 3.3 to 3.5 define dislocations by a neat construction due to J. M. Burgers (1939) and known as the Burgers circuit. Section 3.6 proves the general conservation theorem. Section 3.7 discusses the various ways of forming a given dislocation. The chapter concludes with a brief discussion of low-energy plane imperfections, such as stacking faults, and their relation to partial dislocations; the latter are defined and distinguished from the dislocations in Chap. 2.

Before going into the more general analysis, we give some simple examples—still using the slip picture—to introduce and illustrate the idea that something is conserved along a dislocation. The following theorem is a good example to begin with: *a dislocation cannot end inside the crystal*—or, for a polycrystal, *inside a crystal grain*. The proof follows directly from the picture of incomplete slip. The boundary of a slipped area must be a closed curve; part of this curve may be the external surface; therefore the dislocation must either close on itself or end on the boundary of the crystal or crystal grain.

Next take a slightly more general case: suppose several dislocations lie in a single plane which is their common slip plane; the dislocations are then boundaries of areas that have slipped by different amounts or in different directions, or both. If the three dislocations meet at a point, there must be a relation between their slip vectors, where now the slip vector of a dislocation is defined as follows: look along each dislocation toward the intersection point; subtract the slip in the area on the right from the slip in the area on the left. Defined in this way, the slip vectors of the three dislocations add up to zero (this is almost obvious physically; prove it rigorously as an exercise). Frank extended the result to dislocations that do not have a common slip plane (Sec. 3.6).

The above examples illustrate what may be called the conservation of the slip vector. As a basis for the general theory of dislocations, Sec. 3.2 introduces a broader view of imperfections. Chapter 2 introduced each dislocation as the result of incomplete slip. This chapter reverses the procedure: given an imperfection, what are its properties and how could it have originated?

3.2 Point and Line Imperfections. Read and Shockley (1952a)—following a suggestion of J. C. Slater—call imperfect material **bad**. Bad material is understood to be structurally imperfect (imperfect in the sense defined in Chap. 1); in a bad region, the atoms are not properly surrounded by neighbors. **Good** material is material that is perfect except for elastic strains, thermal vibrations, or other perturbations that leave the crystal structure clearly recognizable. Hereafter we shall use the terms "good" and "bad" freely, bad being synonymous with imperfect (as defined in Chap. 1).

In a single crystal only a small fraction of the material is bad; for example, even in heavily cold-worked crystals, only about one atom in 10^4 is in a bad region. Any given bad region has to be small in at least one dimension; otherwise it would be, not an imperfection, but a second phase. This chapter distinguishes the following three classes of imperfections: (1) point imperfections are small (a few atoms in extent) in all three dimensions, (2) line imperfections are small in two dimensions, (3) plane—or more generally surface—imperfections are small in only one dimension. Plane imperfections are discussed in Sec. 3.9. We now consider, in order, point and line imperfections.

Point Imperfections. These are conveniently described in the following way: Surround the imperfection by a closed surface; then remove the material from within the surface and replace it with good material; let the good material deform elastically to join continuously onto the surrounding good material. This (imaginary) process eliminates the imperfection and leaves in its place only (elastically strained) good material. The best way to describe the imperfection is to compare it with the good material that replaced it. For example, suppose the bad material contains one less atom than its good replacement; then the imperfection is a vacancy; if it contained a different kind of atom (or atoms), the imperfection would be an impurity (or small precipitate).

Line Imperfections. If the imperfection is small in two dimensions, then the surface that separates good from bad material is a long tube of atomic cross section. The most important line imperfections are dislocations. Dislocations differ from point imperfections in more than shape; they also differ radically from other line imperfections. The distinguishing feature of a dislocation is that it *cannot* be eliminated simply by substituting good material for bad. A common misunderstanding is to think of a dislocation as similar to an extra row of atoms or a row of vacancies or impurity atoms.

3.3 Burgers Circuit and Vector. We shall define and describe dislocations by a simple construction due to J. M. Burgers (1939). Burgers showed that a dislocation is uniquely characterized by what is now called a Burgers vector. This section defines the Burgers vector; the following section gives some concrete examples of the definition.

A Burgers vector is the closure failure of a particular type of loop called a Burgers circuit. A Burgers circuit is made up of atom-to-atom steps along t vectors in good material; the t vectors are considered to vary elastically with the local elastic deformation; when we say that two t vectors are the same, we mean that they would be the same if the elastic strain were relaxed. A Burgers circuit is defined by the following two requirements:

1. The circuit must lie entirely in good material—although it may encircle bad material.
2. The same sequence of atom-to-atom steps in a perfect crystal must form a closed path. For example, consider the following path in a face-centered cubic crystal: n atom-to-atom steps in the $[1\bar{1}0]$ direction, n along $[\bar{1}01]$, and n along $[01\bar{1}]$; such a path would form a closed circuit if the crystal were perfect.

In a real crystal, the Burgers circuit does not necessarily close. The closure failure of the Burgers circuit is called the *Burgers vector* and denoted by **b**. The fact that the Burgers circuit may not close even though it lies in good material is due to the elastic strain; the cumulative effect of the elastic strain around the circuit can result in a closure failure. As an exercise prove that the closure failure must be a lattice translation vector, that is, a t vector or the sum of several t vectors (a simple proof is given by Read and Shockley, 1952a).

Next we consider some concrete examples that illustrate Burgers circuits and vectors.

3.4 Examples of Burgers Circuits and Vectors. First consider a fine needlelike precipitate. A Burgers circuit around the needle will close. Observe that matrix atoms could replace precipitate atoms and thereby eliminate the imperfection.

Next take a dislocation—for example the one in Fig. 1.2. Construct a Burgers circuit beginning at the atom in the upper left-hand corner; go seven atomic spacings down, seven to the right, seven up, and seven to the left. Such a circuit would close in a perfect crystal. In Fig. 1.2 it fails to close by the slip vector **b**. In this example, replacing the disordered atoms by good material cannot eliminate the imperfection.

As a third example, make a Burgers circuit on the top surface of the crystal in Fig. 2.2. If the circuit encircles the point A, then it fails to close by the step height—which, again, is the slip vector. Section 3.7 will show that (1) the slip and Burgers vectors are always equal, (2) slip is only one of many ways of forming any given dislocation.

3.5 General Definition of a Dislocation. *If a Burgers circuit around a line imperfection fails to close, the imperfection is a dislocation; the closure failure is the Burgers vector of the dislocation.* The sign of the Burgers vector depends on the direction of traversing the Burgers circuit—which, in turn, depends on which way the dislocation is considered to run. (The dislocation AD in Fig. 2.1 can be considered to run from A to D or from D to A.) Once we have choosen (arbitrarily) the positive direction of advance along the dislocation, the following two conventions specify the Burgers vector:

(1) *Go around the Burgers circuit in the direction of rotation of a right-handed screw advancing along the dislocation.* (2) *The Burgers vector goes from the end of the Burgers circuit to the start.* For example, in Fig. 1.2 let the z axis come out of the figure; take xz as the slip plane and let the dislocation run in the $+z$ direction; then the Burgers circuit goes counterclockwise and the Burgers vector is in the negative x direction. (The incomplete plane of atoms is on the $+y$ side of the slip plane; hence it is called a positive edge dislocation.)

3.6 Conservation of the Burgers Vector. This section proves the conservation theorem for (1) a single dislocation and (2) several intersecting dislocations. Both proofs rest on a theorem about what we call *equivalent Burgers circuits*. Two Burgers circuits are defined as equivalent if one can be gradually moved or deformed to coincide with the other without cutting through any imperfect material. Now the theorem: *equivalent Burgers circuits have the same Burgers vector.* As an exercise, illustrate the theorem by drawing several equivalent Burgers circuits in Figs. 1.2 and 2.2. Then prove the theorem rigorously.

Now consider a Burgers circuit around a single dislocation; slide the circuit (through good material) along the dislocation; at all positions the circuit is equivalent to the original circuit; thus *the Burgers vector is conserved along a dislocation.*

As an exercise show rigorously that the closure failure of a Burgers circuit around several dislocations is equal to the sum of their Burgers vectors; then show that, if a dislocation branches, the sum of the Burgers vectors of the branches is equal to the Burgers vector of the original dislocation. From here it is an easy step (below) to the conservation theorem for intersecting dislocations.

The point where several dislocations meet is called a **node.** In a network of dislocations, any individual dislocation must close on itself, go into a node, or terminate on the external surface of the crystal (or on a grain boundary). Chapter 6 discusses the role of nodes in deformation. Frank (1951) first applied the conservation theorem to nodes; he states it as follows: *The sum of the Burgers vectors of the dislocations meeting at a node must vanish if each dislocation is considered to go into the node.* Frank's theorem is the dislocation equivalent of Kirchhoff's law for electric currents (the currents are replaced by Burgers vectors). As an exercise the reader may wish to construct a proof of Frank's theorem before going on to the proof in the following paragraph.

Think of one dislocation as going into a node and branching into the other dislocations. We have already seen that the sum of the Burgers vectors of the branches is equal to the Burgers vector of the original dislocation. Thus the sum of the Burgers vectors of the dislocations going *into* a node is equal to the sum of the Burgers vectors of the dislocations coming *out* of the node. Hence, if all the dislocations are considered to go *into* the node, the sum of their Burgers vectors vanishes (reversing the direction of the dislocation reverses the direction of traversing the Burgers circuit and therefore changes the sign of the Burgers vector).

3.7 Physical Meaning of the Burgers Vector. In this section, we relate the Burgers vector to the possible ways of forming (or eliminating) the dislocation.

Every *closed* circuit around a dislocation is a Burgers circuit plus the Burgers vector **b**. Thus any method of eliminating the dislocation must somehow introduce an atom-to-atom step equal to $-\mathbf{b}$ into every closed circuit around the dislocation (so that every closed circuit becomes a Burgers circuit). The elimination of a dislocation, therefore, involves not only the material in the bad region but also the surrounding good crystal—rearranging or substituting atoms in the bad region will have no effect on the closure failure of a surrounding Burgers circuit that runs at a large distance from the dislocation.

The simplest way to eliminate a dislocation is as follows: First make a cut connecting the dislocation with the external surface of the crystal. Such a cut intersects every closed circuit around the dislocation. Next displace the two sides of the cut by $-\mathbf{b}$ relative to one another (this may require taking out or adding atoms to the sides of the cut). Now a step equal to $-\mathbf{b}$ has been introduced into every closed circuit around the dislocation; hence (as shown in the above paragraph) the dislocation has been eliminated. If we begin with a perfect crystal, make the cut, and give the two sides an offset $+\mathbf{b}$, then we have created the dislocation; that is, we have changed every (originally) closed circuit around the dislocation into a Burgers circuit with closure failure $\mathbf{b}$.

The choice of a cut connecting the dislocation with the external surface is arbitrary. Thus the dislocation is uniquely defined by a line (the dislocation line) and a vector (the Burgers vector).

Many different physical processes can produce the same dislocation. A simple example is the screw dislocation, which has no unique slip plane; therefore all slip systems having the same slip vector could produce the same screw dislocation. Another example is the edge dislocation; incomplete slip could produce it; so could removing half an atomic plane or inserting an incomplete plane. Figure 3.1 shows several different ways of making the same edge dislocation; the cut is different in each case—the displacement $\mathbf{b}$ is the same.

For an arbitrary cut, $\mathbf{b}$ has components both normal and tangential to the cut. A layer of material equal in thickness to the normal component has to be removed from (or added to) the sides of the cut. To make a dislocation by pure slip, we take the cut parallel to $\mathbf{b}$; then no mass transfer is needed. Since the cut can always be taken parallel to $\mathbf{b}$, pure slip can form any dislocation; therefore we can represent every dislocation by slip without loss in generality. Hereafter, *slip vector* and *Burgers vector* will be used interchangeably—without implying, however, that every dislocation originates in slip.

When the slip (or Burgers) vector has been found for a given dislocation, it is a simple matter to construct the slip surface. By definition, the **slip surface** is the surface generated by lines that (1) go through the dislocation line and (2) are parallel to the slip vector. The *slip plane* is the plane which is tangent to the slip surface; for a curved dislocation, the slip plane varies along the length of the dislocation.

One might ask, "Why not picture every dislocation in terms of slip? It is always a possible picture." The answer is that slip provides an adequate picture for a stationary dislocation or a dislocation moving on its slip plane; slip, however, *cannot* represent motion normal to the slip plane. A dislocation in motion is, in fact, sweeping out a cut whose sides have been displaced by $\mathbf{b}$. If the area swept out is not parallel to $\mathbf{b}$, then the motion requires mass transport (by diffusion of vacancies or interstitial atoms). However, we are now getting into the subject of Chap. 4.

3.8 Frank's Rigorous Treatment of the Burgers Circuit and Vector.
Frank (1951) has given a more rigorous treatment of the Burgers circuit
and vector. Frank uses two crystals. One is the real (imperfect)
crystal; the other is an ideally perfect crystal of the same crystal structure;
the latter is called the reference crystal. The real crystal would be
identical with the reference crystal if all the imperfections were eliminated

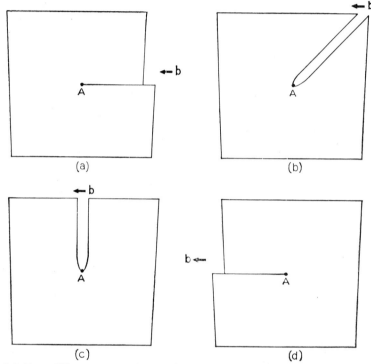

Fɪɢ. 3.1 Four different ways of making the same dislocation. The cut is different
in each case; the Burgers vector (relative displacement of the two sides of the cut) is
the same. In *a* and *d* only pure slip is required; in *b* and *c* atoms must be added to
fill the gap.

and the strain was relaxed. Thus there is a one-to-one correspondence
between atoms in the real and reference crystals. Frank defines a Burgers circuit as a *closed* circuit C in the good material of the real crystal.
He then constructs the corresponding circuit C' in the reference crystal.
Frank's Burgers vector is the closure failure of C'.

Frank's procedure has the advantage of referring the Burgers vector to
the unstrained reference crystal, where all **t** vectors of a given class are
exactly the same; in our procedure the **t** vectors vary from atom to atom
with the local deformation and rotation of the good material. As an

exercise the reader may find it profitable to go through some of the preceding proofs and arguments using Frank's approach.

3.9 Internal Surface Imperfections and Partial Dislocations. One class of imperfections remains, namely, those of atomic extent in only one dimension; here the imperfect region is an extended surface within the crystal. Internal surface imperfections fall into two classes as follows:

1. The energy of atomic misfit per atom is close to the maximum for the solid state; bonds are broken or badly distorted and nearest neighbor relations severely violated. An example is a noncoherent twin boundary or a large-angle-of-misfit grain boundary; here the misfit energy per atom is close to the latent heat of melting.
2. The misfit energy per atom is small compared with the maximum value; nearest neighbor requirements are violated only slightly or not at all. An example is a coherent twin boundary in a face-centered cubic crystal; here nearest neighbor requirements are completely satisfied; the energy of misfit comes from violations of next-nearest neighbor requirements. Other examples are the stacking faults in face-centered cubic and hexagonal crystals.

In this book we shall be concerned primarily with internal surface imperfections of type 2 and in particular with stacking faults. *Low-energy internal surface imperfections in single crystals are called faults.* Barrett (1952) has discussed the evidence for stacking faults; he finds that faults have a pronounced effect on plastic deformation. At present no one knows whether there are any other important faults besides stacking faults. Chapter 7 will discuss faults in some detail.

Another important type of imperfection is a high-energy line imperfection forming the boundary (within the crystal) of a fault. Suppose, for example, that a stacking fault does not extend all the way through the crystal, it must terminate on a line imperfection. Figures 7.2 and 7.4 show faults ending inside face-centered cubic crystals. Notice that the edge of the fault is a high-energy imperfection, where nearest neighbor relations are violated. (On the fault, only next-nearest neighbors are unhappy.) The boundary (within the crystal) of a fault is called a *partial dislocation.* There are various partial dislocations; two of the most important are those shown in Figs. 7.2 and 7.4. Chapter 7 deals with partial dislocations and faults in detail; this section merely shows how they fit into the general picture of imperfections.

Chapter 7 extends Frank's treatment of the Burgers circuit and vector to partial dislocations. The Burgers vector of a partial dislocation is not a **t** vector. Chapter 7 shows how slip can produce certain types of partial dislocations; others seem to require some form of mass transport, such as the condensation of vacancies on one plane. Partial dislocations will be easier to appreciate after further discussion of total dislocations, in Chaps. 4 to 6.

Partial dislocations are also called imperfect, incomplete, or half dislocations. Total dislocations are sometimes referred to as complete or perfect dislocations. Unless otherwise specified, we shall assume that *dislocation* means *total dislocation*.

A partial dislocation can also be the dividing line between two plane sections of fault. Another type of partial dislocation is the so-called *twinning dislocation* in a twinned crystal; an example is shown in Fig. 7.5. The twin interface is not exactly coherent (parallel to the twinning plane) but is made up of sections of coherent twin interface connected by steps. One step is shown in the figure; at the step, the twin boundary jumps from one (111) plane to the next; the step is defined as a twinning dislocation. Chapter 7 discusses twinning dislocations and their role in twinning.

3.10 Large Dislocations. These have Burgers vectors which are sums of **t** vectors. Probably not many large dislocations are stable enough to exist—they could break up into smaller dislocations, which would then move apart. A possible exception is a dislocation having a $<100>$ Burgers vector in body-centered cubic: Sec. 9.7 will discuss large dislocations in relation to the combination and splitting of dislocations.

PROBLEMS

1. What pair of dislocations is equivalent to a row of lattice vacancies? What, to a row of interstitial atoms?

2. What is the minimum number of dislocations (having Burgers vectors equal to **t** vectors) that can meet at a node in (*a*) simple cubic, (*b*) face-centered cubic, (*c*) body-centered cubic, (*d*) hexagonal close-packed?

3. Consider a plastically deformed crystal containing dislocations. Suppose the macroscopic stress (average stress over a volume of material that contains many dislocations) vanishes at all points. Find the distribution of dislocations for the following cases of plastic deformation:

a. Pure bending in simple cubic where the (010) planes are bent about the [001] axis. Show that the dislocations are parallel to [001] and have [100] Burgers vectors. Show that the density of dislocations is κ/b per unit area (normal to the dislocations), where κ is the curvature.

b. Pure bending in simple cubic with (110) planes bent around the [001] axis.

c. Pure bending in face-centered cubic with (110) planes bent about [001]. Same for (010) planes.

d. Pure bending in face-centered cubic where the planes parallel to [001] and inclined at an angle ϕ to (110) are bent about the [001] axis. Express the density of each type of dislocation as a function of κ and ϕ.

e. Pure torsion about the [001] axis in simple or face-centered cubic. Let θ be the angle of (plastic) twist per unit length.

4. When the macroscopic stress (as defined in the last problem) vanishes at all points, then the deformation of the crystal is defined by the macroscopic rotation ω

(rotation of an element of material that contains many dislocations). Let $\mathbf{N}_i$ be the flux of dislocations having Burgers vector $\mathbf{b}_i$; that is, the magnitude and direction of $\mathbf{N}_i$ are equal to the density and direction, respectively, of the corresponding dislocations; $i = 1, 2, 3, \ldots, n$ where n is the number of different types of dislocations. Use the Burgers circuits and vectors to show that the $\mathbf{N}_i$ must satisfy the dyadic relation

$$\sum_i \mathbf{b}_i \mathbf{N}_i = \boldsymbol{\nabla}\omega - \mathbf{I}(\boldsymbol{\nabla} \cdot \boldsymbol{\omega})$$

where $\mathbf{I}$ = the (dyadic) idemfactor. HINT: Use Stokes's theorem relating line and surface integrals. An alternative proof is given by Nye (1953), who first discovered the result.

5. The screw dislocation in Fig. 2.2 is a right-handed screw. Consider an L-shaped dislocation: One arm runs along the $+z$ axis and is in the edge orientation; the extra plane of atoms is on the $+y$ side. The other arm of the L runs along the $+x$ axis and is pure screw; is it a right- or left-handed screw? For a general rule see Bilby (1950).

CHAPTER 4

DISLOCATIONS IN MOTION

4.1 Introduction. Moving dislocations are responsible for plastic deformation. This chapter shows how dislocations move, why they move easily, and what their motion does to the crystal.

A section of dislocation can move either in its slip plane or normal to it. Motion on the slip plane (or, more generally, the slip surface) simply enlarges the slipped area; since only slip is involved, the motion is called slipping or gliding, or just glide. Motion normal to the slip plane is called climb. We shall find that climb requires mass transport by diffusion of vacancies or interstitial atoms. Since glide and climb have different mechanisms, we discuss them separately. Sections 4.2 to 4.5 deal with glide and discuss (1) the macroscopic strain, (2) the motions of the atoms, and (3) the resistance to glide. The resistance to glide is several orders of magnitude smaller than the resistance to shear of a perfect crystal. Dislocations were originally introduced to explain the low critical stress for slip. It now appears that, at least in soft metal crystals, the stress required to move dislocations is lower than the observed stress at which slip begins; the latter stress is probably that required to move dislocations through internal obstacles such as other dislocations or other types of imperfections, for example, impurities. (Chapters 6 and 9 will discuss some of the factors that impede the motion of dislocations and thereby contribute to strength and work hardening.)

Section 4.6 discusses the deformation, atomic motions, and driving force for climb. Section 4.7 discusses motion in general and proves a useful theorem. When a dislocation moves and the crystal deforms plastically, the work done by the applied stress goes into several forms of energy, which are distinguished and discussed in Sec. 4.8. Chapter 5 will show how the work done by the applied stress defines a force on the dislocation.

4.2 Macroscopic Strain in Glide. A dislocation is a configuration that can move through the crystal; as the dislocation moves, the crystal deforms plastically. This section discusses the glide of the pure edge dislocation in Fig. 1.2 and considers (1) how the atoms move and (2) how the crystal deforms. Finally, the results are extended to the glide of an arbitrary dislocation.

First consider the atomic displacements when the dislocation in Fig. 1.2 glides. Figure 4.1 shows the same dislocation (solid circles); the open circles represent the atoms after the dislocation has moved one interatomic spacing to the left. The configuration of atoms is the same in the two positions and is symmetrical with respect to a vertical plane through the dislocation. The figure shows that the motion of the dislocation through one repeat distance involves only a minor rearrangement of the atoms in the bad material. Section 4.3 will discuss the atomic displacements in more detail and consider the variation of atomic misfit energy as the dislocation moves.

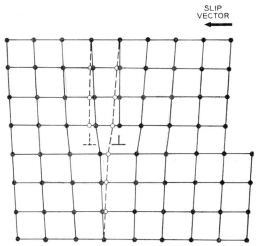

FIG. 4.1 An edge dislocation moves one interatomic spacing to the left on its slip plane. The solid circles represent the positions of the atoms before motion, the open circles, the positions after.

Now let us see how the crystal deforms as the dislocation in Fig. 4.1 glides. First suppose the dislocation moves all the way across the crystal, starting at the extreme right. Figure 4.2 shows four successive positions of the dislocation beginning with a perfect unslipped crystal and ending with a perfect slipped crystal. In the final state (d), the upper half of the crystal is offset by one interatomic spacing b relative to the lower half. When the dislocation is in the crystal, the crystal is strained and the offset of one half relative to the other is not uniform; we then define *offset* as the *average offset* of the upper surface relative to the lower. Figure 4.2 shows how the offset increases as the dislocation moves. The solid circles in Fig. 4.1 show the dislocation halfway across the slip plane; the offset is $b/2$. Figure 4.2 shows also the one-fifth and four-fifths positions. In all cases, the offset is approximately proportional to the distance that the dislocation has moved starting from the extreme right;

this result appears physically reasonable—the slipped area wants an offset b, the unslipped area, no offset; the result is a weighted average. It will be easy to treat the macroscopic deformation more rigorously and thoroughly after the discussion of work and force in Chap. 5.

Next consider the macroscopic shear strain, which is (offset)/(height of the crystal). For example, in Fig. 4.1, the dislocation moves one inter-atomic spacing, or one-eighth of the way across the slip plane. The offset

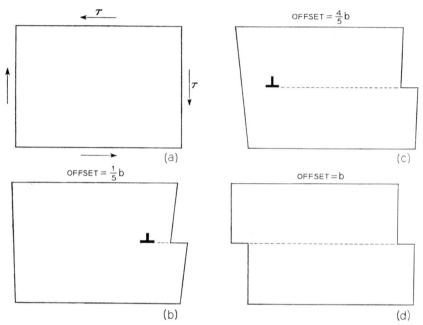

FIG. 4.2 When a dislocation moves on its slip plane, the crystal deforms; an applied stress can do work in the deformation. (a) The applied stress that does work when the dislocation in Fig. 4.1 moves by slip. In b a dislocation, coming in from the right-hand surface, has moved one-fifth of the way across the slip plane; the (average) offset of the upper surface is $b/5$. (c) The same except that the dislocation has moved four-fifths of the way across and the offset is $4b/5$. When the dislocation has moved all the way across, d, the offset is b. Note that the stress shown in a does work τb per unit area when the dislocation moves across the slip plane.

associated with the motion is therefore $b/8$. (This is too small an incre-ment to show up in the figure.) Since the crystal is seven atomic planes high, the increment of strain is $\frac{1}{56}$. As an exercise show that, when the dislocation moves so as to sweep out an area A on its slip plane, the macro-scopic shear strain is bA/V where V is the volume of the crystal. Figure 4.2a shows the stress that provides the driving force trying to make the dislocation move. Observe that this stress—a shear stress on the slip plane and in the slip direction—does work in the macroscopic deformation. Chapter 5 will show how the applied stress defines a force on the dislocation.

The same general discussion applies to glide of a screw dislocation. As an exercise, show how the atoms move when the dislocation in Fig. 2.3 glides. Since a screw dislocation has no unique slip plane, it can glide in any direction. Show how the macroscopic strain varies with the direction of glide; draw the deformation for two mutually perpendicular directions of glide.

Finally consider the glide of a dislocation of arbitrary or variable orientation. As an exercise, show how the atoms move and how the crystal deforms when the dislocation in Figs. 2.4 and 2.5 glides. Show that, when a dislocation with given slip vector glides completely over a given slip plane, the associated macroscopic strain is the same whether the dislocation is edge or screw. This result is a consequence of the following general theorem, which will be easy to prove after the discussion of force in Chap. 5: *The macroscopic strain associated with the glide of a dislocation (or section of dislocation) is a shear strain corresponding to the slip plane and slip direction of the dislocation. The magnitude of the strain is proportional to the area of slip plane swept out by the moving dislocation.* Thus the macroscopic strain is independent of the orientation of the dislocation in its slip plane. This point is often a source of confusion. It may be helpful to remember that, when a dislocation sweeps out an area on its slip plane, the slip in the slipped area is uniquely determined by the slip vector.

4.3 Resistance to Glide—Edge Dislocation. In this section we consider the resistance to glide of an edge dislocation—in particular the dislocation in Fig. 4.1. Section 4.4 will extend the analysis to the general case of glide of an arbitrary dislocation.

Figure 4.1 showed that the atoms move very short distances when the dislocation moves one interatomic spacing. The magnitude of the atomic displacements depends on the width of the dislocation. (Section 2.7 defined the width of a dislocation as the width of the area on the slip plane where the atoms are out of register by more than half the maximum amount.) As an exercise show that the atomic displacements (for a given motion of the dislocation) are inversely proportional to the width of the dislocation. The dislocation in Fig. 4.1 is narrow, probably narrower than dislocations in real crystals of metals.

Consider the variation in the atomic misfit as the dislocation in Fig. 4.1 moves on its slip plane. The atomic misfit varies periodically with the displacement of the dislocation, the period of the variation being b; in other words the configuration of atoms shown in Fig. 4.1 repeats itself every time the dislocation moves an integral number of atomic spacings. Now consider the energy E of atomic misfit, which must also vary with period b.   The configuration of atoms is symmetrical at the two positions of the dislocation shown in Fig. 4.1; E is a minimum at these positions. There is another symmetrical position—and another minimum in E—at a position halfway between the two shown in Fig. 4.1 (see Prob. 1, Chap. 2). Between the minima in E, there are maxima, which provide the resistance to motion.   To get over the maxima the dislocation needs help from applied stress, thermal energy, or both.   The following paragraph shows that the resistance to motion decreases with the width of the dislocation. (As an exercise, the reader may wish to prove this himself before going on.)

We have already seen that the atomic displacements (for a given displacement of the dislocation) are less for a wider dislocation.   Thus the change in the configuration of atoms is also less, and so is the change in misfit energy E.   Consequently, the energy hump $E_{max} - E_{min}$ is less for a wider dislocation.   The resistance to motion is, in fact, an extremely sensitive function of dislocation width.   Nabarro (1947) has shown that the stress required to move a dislocation (at the absolute zero of temperature) varies by many orders of magnitude when the width changes by a factor of 2.   As we discussed in Sec. 2.7, the widths of dislocations in real crystals are not known and probably vary considerably with atomic structure.

The resistance to glide has not yet been calculated exactly for any real crystal—largely because the resistance is a sensitive function of the unknown details of the atomic arrangement near the center of the dislocation.   It is easy to show, however, that the resistance to motion is orders of magnitude smaller than the resistance to shear of a perfect crystal.   In fact, calculating the resistance is difficult simply because the resistance *is* so small; all the effects that we can easily calculate add up to zero resistance.   The following brief consideration of interatomic forces shows why the dislocation in Fig. 4.1 moves easily:

Consider the three atoms nearest the center of the dislocation.   Let A denote the atom just above the symbol $\perp$ (that is, the atom forming the edge of the incomplete atomic plane).   Let L be the atom below and to the left of A; R is the atom below and to the right.   The atom A is not in a stable position; both L and R want A as a normal nearest neighbor.   If we now apply the stress shown in Fig. 4.2a, then A is pushed to the left. Consequently L's claim on A is favored and R's weakened.   Therefore A moves still farther to the left.   Thus the dislocation appears to move under vanishingly small stress.   A fairly elaborate calculation is necessary to estimate even approximately the resistance to motion—see Nabarro (1947) and Foreman, Jaswon, and Wood (1951).

Cottrell (1953) summarizes the mobility of a dislocation as follows: Consider the shear on the slip plane.   On the unslipped side of the dislocation, the atoms want to return to the unslipped state; on the slipped side, the atoms want to go on to the completely slipped state. The atom at the center—atom A above—is in a dead-center position. When the dislocation is at a symmetrical position, there is no change of energy with an infinitesimal displacement of the dislocation—by symmetry, the work done *against* the interatomic forces on one side of the center of the dislocation equals the work done *by* the interatomic forces on the other side. Thus at a symmetrical position the dislocation moves under zero applied stress. However, before the dislocation can move to the next *symmetrical* position, it has to go through *unsymmetrical* positions, where the interatomic forces do not balance out and the change in energy with dislocation position does not vanish; hence an applied stress is needed to move the dislocation.

The same arguments about resistance to glide apply also to a pure screw dislocation. Section 2.7 mentioned that we do not know how symmetrical screw dislocations are in real crystals; an unsymmetrical screw will move the most easily on the slip plane in which it is the widest. As an exercise, construct a drawing similar to Fig. 2.2 showing a highly unsymmetrical screw dislocation; show why its resistance to motion would be highly anisotropic.

Section 4.5 will discuss the effect of temperature on the motion of a dislocation that lies on the average parallel to a close-packed direction. First however we consider the resistance to glide in the general case of a dislocation that has an arbitrary orientation.

4.4 Resistance to Glide—General Case. The dislocations discussed in the preceding section are simple examples but also, in a way, misleading examples. Both the edge dislocation in Fig. 4.1 and the pure screw dislocation are parallel to densely packed directions. This section will show that the resistance to motion is greatest when the dislocation lies in a densely packed direction; for an arbitrary irrational direction (where the direction cosines are not in the ratios of integers), the resistance to glide vanishes. (The reader may wish to prove this as an exercise before going on to the following proof.)

Define the orientation of the dislocation by the plane that is normal to the slip plane and parallel to the dislocation (or section of dislocation); let h, k, and l be the Miller indices of that plane. The dislocation then lies along the intersection of the slip plane and the $(h\ k\ l)$ plane. As the dislocation glides, its successive positions are parallel to neighboring $(h\ k\ l)$ planes. Define δ as the normal distance between neighboring atomic planes that (1) are parallel to $(h\ k\ l)$ and (2) have the same density and arrangement of atoms. In a cubic crystal

$$\delta^2 = \frac{a^2}{h^2 + k^2 + l^2}$$

where a is the cell constant, or length of the cube edge.

Consider how the atomic misfit varies as the dislocation glides. Again the configuration of atoms (and the misfit energy E) varies periodically with the distance moved by the dislocation. *The period of the variation is δ.* Thus, for a dislocation parallel to a close-packed direction in simple cubic, $(h\,k\,l) = (100)$ and $\delta = a = b$. The following paragraph shows that the resistance to motion decreases as δ decreases and vanishes as $\delta \rightarrow 0$.

The distance that the dislocation has to move to go over the energy hump is less than δ and decreases as δ decreases. The atomic displacements and the associated change in energy are smaller for a smaller displacement of the dislocation. Therefore the energy hump that the dislocation has to go over decreases as δ decreases. When $\delta = 0$, all positions of the dislocation have the same energy; so the resistance to motion vanishes. Thus a dislocation lying in an arbitrary irrational direction has zero resistance to motion; it moves at random because of thermal vibrations and drifts under a vanishingly small stress.

Seitz (1950) has summarized the motion of an arbitrary dislocation as follows: If a dislocation has an arbitrary orientation, the nature of the atomic misfit and the misfit energy per atom vary from point to point along the dislocation. Now suppose the dislocation moves normal to itself; as the dislocation moves, the atomic configuration simply moves along the dislocation. There is a redistribution of energy along the length of the dislocation, but no net change in energy.

4.5 Kinks in Dislocations.[1] In this section, we consider a dislocation that is almost but not quite parallel to a densely packed direction. Figure 4.3 represents the slip plane of the dislocation; the dashed lines are parallel to a densely packed direction, such as the direction of the slip vector in Fig. 2.3 or the normal in Fig. 4.1. Consider a dislocation almost parallel to the densely packed direction. The dashed lines represent positions of minimum energy of the dislocation; for example, each dashed line could represent one of the positions shown in Fig. 4.1. The energy of atomic misfit per unit length of dislocation varies periodically along the normal to the dashed lines; the period is the spacing δ between dashed lines. The energy maxima lie between the dashed lines.

Let ψ_a be the (small) angle between the dashed lines and the average direction of the dislocation. The minimum energy form of the dislocation will be a curved line; the form of the curve is determined by a balance between the following two opposing factors:

1. The dislocation wants to lie as much as possible in the energy minima. This factor alone would give the shape shown by curve A in Fig. 4.3.

---

[1] The author is indebted to W. Shockley (private communication) for the basic ideas in this section.

2. The dislocation tries to reduce energy by being as short as possible—which favors the straight line shape B.

The actual form of the dislocation is something like curve C. (Problem 4 involves calculating C as a function of ψ_a.) The curved part of C is called a *kink in the dislocation* (it has no connection with the so-called kink bands observed in certain crystals).

As an exercise, describe how the length of a kink depends on the energy hump or amplitude of energy variation normal to the close-packed direction. How does the added energy associated with the kink depend on the

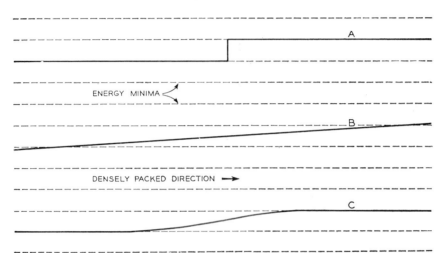

FIG. 4.3 Shapes of a dislocation running almost parallel to a densely packed direction. The energy per unit length of the dislocation is a minimum along the dashed lines and varies periodically at right angles to these lines. The shape of the dislocation (curve C) is somewhere between the extremes A and B.

energy hump? The answer is as follows: If the energy hump is a large fraction of the average energy, then factor 1 above dominates and the kink is short and has a relatively high energy. As the energy hump decreases, the kinks become longer and the dislocation approaches the straight line shape B and kink energy decreases.

Consider how the form of the dislocation changes with ψ_a. As ψ_a approaches zero, the kinks become infinitely far apart. When ψ_a is so small that the spacing between kinks is large compared with the kink length, then the kinks are independent of ψ_a; as ψ_a increases, the straight sections between kinks become shorter. When the kinks are close enough to begin to overlap, then the dislocation is almost straight. The value of ψ_a above which the dislocation is straight depends on the (at present) unknown magnitude of the energy hump. In Prob. 5 we use the

Peierls-Nabarro approximation (Sec. 2.7) to calculate the shape of the dislocation as a function of ψ_a. In this approximation, the energy hump is about 10^{-4} electron volt per atom and the dislocation is found to be straight for ψ_a above about $1°$.

Now consider the motion of a kinked dislocation: the kinks can move along the length of the dislocation; such motion causes the dislocation to move normal to itself; for example in Fig. 4.3 the dislocation moves up when the kinks move to the left. The sections of dislocation between kinks have a high resistance to motion; the kinks however have a very low resistance to moving along the dislocation. Thus a kinked dislocation can move much more easily than one parallel to a close-packed direction.

Now consider a dislocation that runs at least on the average parallel to a close-packed direction; $\psi_a = 0$. Except at the absolute zero of temperature, there will be some probability of finding kinks in the dislocation; since $\psi_a = 0$, there will be equal numbers of opposite kinks. The mobility of the dislocation will be limited mainly by the number of kinks; hence the motion of the dislocation will be characterized by an activation energy equal to the energy E_k of a kink. The calculation of E_k (using the Peierls-Nabarro approximation) forms Prob. 6.

To conclude the discussion of dislocation mobility we may say that the mobility of a dislocation appears to be a very sensitive function of both atomic structure and orientation of the dislocation. In some cases, and especially when the dislocation is parallel to a close-packed direction, temperature probably has an important effect. The mobility has not yet been calculated for any real crystals and remains a big question mark in the theory. At present it is believed that, in soft metals (such as the face-centered cubic and hexagonal close-packed), the measured critical stress for slip is *not* the stress necessary to move a dislocation but rather the stress required to overcome internal stresses such as the stress fields of other dislocations; in other crystals, and especially in those having the diamond structure, the motion of a dislocation may involve breaking bonds and the resistance of a dislocation to motion may provide the principal resistance to observable plastic deformation. In Chap. 14, we shall see how the motion of a known array of identical dislocations can be studied; such studies may provide the answer to the question of how stress, temperature, and dislocation orientation affect the motion of dislocations in real crystals.

4.6 Motion Normal to the Slip Plane (Climb). Any dislocation can be constructed from edge and screw segments and any motion resolved into components in the slip plane (glide) and normal to the slip plane (climb). We have already discussed the glide of edge and screw dislocations; the motion of a screw is always glide. Thus there remains only the climb of an edge, which we discuss in this section. Climb requires mass transport, as the following argument will show:

Suppose the edge dislocation in Figs. 1.2 and 4.1 moves up one atomic spacing so that it lies on the next higher slip plane. The extra row of atoms then ends on the higher slip plane; hence there is one less atom in the row. The motion therefore requires some method of removing the atom (which we have called atom A) just above the symbol $\perp$. One such atom must be removed for every atomic plane in which the dislocation climbs up one atomic spacing. If the dislocation moved down, then atoms would have to be added to the edge of the extra plane. It is conventional to define the positive direction of climb as the direction for which atoms must be *taken away* from the extra plane, so that the extra plane shrinks. In negative climb the extra plane grows.

Consider now the atomic mechanism of climb. The atom A on the edge of the extra plane could be removed in two ways: (1) A lattice vacancy could diffuse to the dislocation and combine with A, A jumping into the vacant site. (2) Atom A could break loose, become an interstitial atom, and diffuse away. In negative climb, atoms are added to the extra plane; this also could occur in two ways: (1) Interstitial atoms could diffuse to the dislocation. (2) Atoms from the surrounding crystal could join the extra plane (leaving vacancies to diffuse away). Thus an edge dislocation is both a source and a sink for both vacancies and interstitial atoms.

Now look at climb from a three-dimensional viewpoint. Figure 4.4 shows a crystal containing a circular loop of edge dislocation. This crystal is equal to a perfect crystal plus an incomplete plane of atoms; the edge dislocation is the boundary of the incomplete atomic plane. To illustrate glide and climb, draw the slip surface; this is generated by lines that (1) pass through the dislocation and (2) are parallel to the Burgers vector. In Fig. 4.4, the slip surface is a cylinder (shown by dotted lines). If the dislocation moves off the slip surface, the incomplete atomic plane grows (or shrinks); therefore atoms must be transported to (or from) its edge. Read and Shockley (1952a) have described the same picture as follows:

The crystal in Fig. 4.4 is made up of unit cells; consider a vertical column of cells (that is, a column parallel to the Burgers vector); this column has either $N + 1$ or N cells depending on whether or not the dislocation encircles it. Climb changes the number of columns which have an extra cell; therefore it requires mass transport.

Vacancies and interstitial atoms are most likely to be absorbed or emitted at what are called **jogs**; Fig. 6.7 shows two jogs (Sec. 6.7 describes their formation). The circles in Fig. 6.7 are atoms that form an incomplete atomic plane parallel to the plane of the figure. The boundary

of the incomplete atomic plane is a closed loop of edge dislocation
$ABQQ'CDP'P$; the Burgers vector is normal to the figure (ignore the vector
$\mathbf{b}_i$ shown in the drawing—it refers to something else). The segments of
dislocation PP' and QQ' are *jogs*. On an atomic scale, an edge dislocation
of arbitrary shape contains jogs.

Notice that the atoms at P and Q' are the least tightly bound to the
extra plane; they could therefore break away more easily than the others.
Notice also that an atom that joined the extra plane at a jog would be
more likely to stick there than anywhere else on the dislocation. The
reason is as follows: Because of the reentrant corner at the jog, an atom
arriving there can form two bonds with nearest neighbors (in the plane

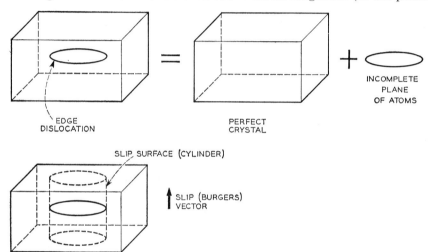

FIG. 4.4 A closed loop of edge dislocation in an otherwise perfect crystal. The dislocation surrounds an incomplete plane of atoms. The slip surface of the dislocation
is a cylinder with axis parallel to the Burgers vector.

of the drawing); at any other point on the dislocation, an additional atom
forms only one such bond. Thus jogs are favorable spots for both the
emission and absorption of both vacancies and interstitial atoms. As an
exercise, illustrate all four processes.

In thermal equilibrium, atoms join and leave a jog with equal frequency. Consider what happens if, for example, we increase the concentration of vacancies in the surrounding crystal above the equilibrium
value; the rate of arrival of vacancies at the jog increases; therefore the
extra plane shrinks. Thus an excess of vacancies is a driving force for
climb; for a fuller discussion, see Bardeen and Herring (1952); see also
Prob. 3.

Now observe what climb does to macroscopic strain. When atoms are
removed from the extra plane, the crystal collapses locally (compressive

strain); when atoms are added, the growing atomic plane expands the crystal locally (tensile strain). Tensile and compressive stresses therefore do work in climb; an applied compressive stress tries to squeeze out the extra plane; a tensile stress encourages it to grow (just as a shear stress encourages a slipped area to expand).

4.7 A Theorem on Slipping vs. Diffusive Motion. Figure 4.4 illustrates a theorem about a closed loop of dislocation. The dislocation can

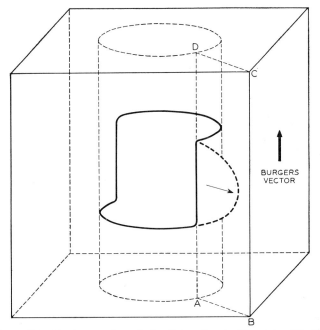

FIG. 4.5 A possible slipping motion of the dislocation in Fig. 4.4. The dislocation can glide into any position on the cylindrical slip surface; also, the screw (vertical) segments can glide on any slip plane—for example, the plane $ABCD$, as shown by the dashed line.

glide into any position on the slip surface; Fig. 4.5 shows one possible position (two screw sections connect semicircular edge sections). A screw has no unique slip plane; therefore, a dislocation can increase its freedom of glide by moving into the screw orientation—which it can always do by glide. For example, the screw sections in Fig. 4.5 can glide off the original cylindrical slip surface and glide on the plane $ABCD$ as shown by the dashed line. Wavy slip lines (observed in α iron and other crystals) are probably caused by screws shifting from one slip plane to another.

Now the theorem: *If a closed loop of dislocation moves so as to change its projected area on a plane normal to the Burgers vector, then mass transport is required.* As an exercise, prove this rigorously.

4.8 Moving Energy and Energy Dissipation. Let W be the work done on the external surface in the deformation produced by a dislocation in motion. W goes into the following three forms of energy:

1. E_d, the energy dissipated and converted into heat
2. E_m, the energy of motion, which moves with the dislocation and depends on dislocation velocity: $E_m = 0$ for zero velocity
3. E_s, the potential energy of distortion, which includes both elastic energy and energy of atomic misfit

The law of conservation of energy for moving dislocations is

$$\delta W = \delta E_d + \delta E_m + \delta E_s$$

Chapters 5 and 9 will discuss W and E_s, which depend only on the position of the dislocation and not on its velocity. We conclude this chapter with a brief discussion of E_m and E_d, which depend on the velocity v of the dislocation and vanish for a stationary dislocation.

Energy Dissipated, E_d. A dislocation in motion can dissipate energy by interacting with thermal vibrations of the crystal (scattering phonons or generating heat or sound waves). In steady-state motion all the work done by the driving forces is so dissipated. The dependence of rate of energy dissipation on velocity is at present unknown and is probably not a simple function except at low velocities, where energy dissipated per unit distance moved is probably proportional to v. The energy dissipated at the moving dislocation spreads out over the crystal and either raises the temperature or is withdrawn as heat. Cottrell (1953—Sec. 6.4) discusses the various mechanisms of energy dissipation for a fast moving dislocation; he also brings out the difficulties of treating the problem exactly.

Energy of Motion, E_m. E_m arises from the motion and moves through the crystal with the dislocation. We can distinguish the following two contributions to E_m:

1. A dislocation is a configuration of atomic positions; therefore associated with a moving dislocation is a configuration of atomic velocities. Each atom moves only a short distance as the dislocation moves through the crystal. The atomic velocity is greatest at the center of the dislocation and decreases with distance from the dislocation. As an exercise, show that the ratio of maximum atomic velocity to dislocation velocity increases as the width of the dislocation decreases. The distribution of kinetic energy that moves with the dislocation is called the kinetic energy of the dislocation; it is similar to the kinetic energy of a sound wave; however, the ratio of atomic velocity to configuration velocity is much greater for a dislocation than it is for an ordinary sound wave.

2. As the dislocation velocity increases, the form of the dislocation changes; in particular, the width decreases, so that the misfit is spread over a narrower area on the slip plane. As the dislocation becomes narrower, the distortional energy increases. We arbitrarily define this increase as belonging to E_m rather than E_s. By definition E_s is the distortional energy for a stationary dislocation at the same position in the crystal. The additional distortional energy due to the motion comes under E_m.

The decrease in width of the dislocation is similar to the relativistic contraction of a particle; in both cases, the width (in the direction of motion) approaches zero and the energy approaches infinity as the velocity approaches a limit, which for a dislocation is sound velocity. For a thorough mathematical discussion of the relativistic effect in dislocation dynamics, see Frank (1949) and Eshelby (1949a); a simple derivation, for the special case of a screw dislocation, forms Prob. 6 of Chap. 8.

PROBLEMS

1. Consider two parallel edge dislocations on orthogonal slip planes in a crystal that contains no other imperfections. Construct a sequence of atomic displacements by which the two dislocations move closer together without any glide. What stress would provide a driving force for such motion?

2. Show how, by pure glide, the dislocation in Fig. 4.5 could divide into two separate closed loops of pure edge dislocation.

3. What is the direction of climb (positive or negative) for an edge dislocation when the surrounding crystal has (a) an excess of vacancies (over the equilibrium value), (b) a deficiency of vacancies, (c) an excess of interstitial atoms, (d) a deficiency of interstitial atoms?

4. In Fig. 4.3 take the x axis along the close-packed direction. Let the angle ψ between the dislocation and the x axis be small enough that (1) ψ^2 can be neglected compared with unity and (2) the energy E per unit length of the dislocation depends only on the y coordinate (and not on ψ).

a. Show that the differential equation of the dislocation line (curve C in Fig. 4.3) is

$$E \frac{d^2y}{dx^2} = \frac{dE}{dy}$$

Show that ψ is given by

$$\psi^2 - \psi_m{}^2 = \ln \frac{E^2}{E_m{}^2}$$

where E_m and ψ_m are the maxima of E and ψ, respectively.

b. Taking E_0 and ψ_0 as the minima of E and ψ, respectively, use the relation

$$\psi_m - \psi_0 = \frac{\ln (E_m/E_0)}{\frac{1}{2}(\psi_m + \psi_0)}$$

to prove the results stated in Sec. 4.5 about how the form of the dislocation changes with ψ_a.

c. From the Peierls-Nabarro theory, $E_m - E_0 \approx 10^{-4}E_0$. Use this to find (1) the value that ψ_m approaches as ψ_a approaches zero, and (2) the value of ψ_a at which

$\psi_m \doteq \psi_a$ so that the dislocation is approximately straight. Estimate the length of a kink when ψ_a is low enough that the kinks are separated by distances large compared with their length.

5. In the preceding problem let E vary sinusoidally with y (Nabarro, 1947). Show that x is given as a function of y by

$$x = \frac{F(k,y)}{\psi_m}$$

where $F(k,y)$ is the elliptic integral of the first kind (Pierce, "A Short Table of Integrals," p. 122) and $k = \epsilon/\psi_m$ where $\epsilon^2 E_m$ is the amplitude of variation of E with y. (Neglect ϵ^2 compared with unity.) Show that

$$\frac{\psi_a}{\psi_m} = \frac{\pi}{2K}$$

where K is the complete elliptic integral of the first kind.

6. Show that, if $E(y)$ varies sinusoidally with y, the energy E_k of a kink is

$$E_k = \frac{b}{\pi} \sqrt{2E_m(E_m - E_0)}$$

CHAPTER 5

FORCES ON DISLOCATIONS

The last chapter showed how dislocations move; this one shows *why* they move when stress is applied to the crystal. The effect of the applied stress is represented by a force on the dislocation.[1]

5.1 Stress, Work, and Force. As Chap. 4 showed, a moving dislocation can cause the crystal to yield to an applied stress. The total work done by the applied stress varies with the position of the dislocation. Whenever energy (or work) varies with the position of a configuration, we can define a force on the configuration. However the force on a *configuration* has to be defined carefully—it should not be confused with the force on a mass. The two may have similar properties; this however has to be proved—not assumed. Section 5.2 introduces the concept of force in the simple case of glide illustrated in Fig. 4.2. Sections 5.3 and 5.4 treat glide in the general case. Since glide and climb use different mechanisms, it is convenient to separate the components of force in and normal to the slip plane. Section 5.5 discusses the force normal to the slip plane, and Sec. 5.6, the general formulas for force. The chapter concludes by applying the idea of force to static equilibrium and steady-state motion.

Before defining the force on a dislocation, we distinguish the following two types of stress distributions:

Internal Stress. We define as internal stress any state of stress in which the external surface is stress free. Examples are the stress field around a dislocation, impurity atom, or other type of imperfection. A component of internal stress may act *at* the surface but not *on* the surface; for example, let $x = $ constant be a stress-free surface; then σ_x, τ_{xy}, and τ_{xz} must vanish at the surface but not σ_y, σ_z, and τ_{zy}.

External, or Applied, Stress. This is any distribution of stress that is produced by forces or constraints applied to the external surface. The applied stress, by definition, vanishes when the external surfaces are stress free. Common examples are tension, bending, and torsion; the latter two are nonuniform stress distributions. *The applied stress field is*

---

[1] The author is indebted to J. D. Eshelby (private discussion) for suggesting the general approach to force presented in this chapter.

considered to include both the stress acting on the external surface and the associated stress distribution inside the crystal.

This chapter considers the case where the dislocation itself is the only imperfection in the crystal and the stress field of the dislocation is the only internal stress. We suppose that an arbitrary distribution of stress is applied to the crystal. When the dislocation moves, the crystal deforms and the applied stress does work W on the external surface. W represents energy transferred to the crystal from an external source, such as a weight or tensile machine. The force on the dislocation is defined by the variation of W with position of the dislocation. We shall find that the force at each point on the dislocation is determined by the value of the applied stress *at that point*.

The discussion in this chapter is specialized in that the only distribution of internal stress is the stress field of the dislocation itself and the total force is the force due to the applied stress. Chapter 9 considers the general case where there are other imperfections (which contribute to the internal stress) and shows how dislocations (or dislocations and other imperfections) exert forces on one another. The total force on a dislocation is the sum of (1) the force due to the applied stress (discussed in this chapter) and (2) the force due to the stress fields of other dislocations or other types of imperfections (defined and discussed in Chap. 9). Chapter 9 will show that the *total* force on a dislocation is defined by the change in $W - E_s$ with position of the dislocation. The work done by the total force is $\delta W - \delta E_s$, which (by the conservation of energy) is equal to $\delta E_d + \delta E_m$. In other words the total force on the dislocation does work which goes into energy of motion or energy dissipated—as in the motion of a mass. The work $-\delta E_s$ is done by the forces exerted on the dislocation by other imperfections.

Another way of looking at the energy relations is as follows: When the crystal deforms, it acquires energy δW (in the form of mechanical work) from the external source. All of δW that does not go into stored energy E_s goes into the work done by the force on the dislocation.

In this chapter we shall be concerned entirely with applied loads that remain constant as the dislocation moves—which is usually the case in conventional methods of stressing, such as simple tension. Similar arguments apply for other methods of stressing; in all cases the same formulas give the force on a dislocation. (The case where the external surface of the crystal is held fixed as the dislocation moves forms Prob. 6.)

5.2 Simple Example of Glide. This section introduces the concept of force through the example of glide illustrated in Figs. 4.1 and 4.2. Figure 4.2a shows the applied stress τ that does work when the dislocation moves and the crystal deforms. When the dislocation moves all the way across the slip plane, the work done is τb per unit area (the upper surface is offset by b; the force on it is τ per unit area). We define the force (per unit length of dislocation) as the work done when unit length of dislocation moves unit distance. Hereafter, *force* will mean *force per unit length*. The force, by definition, is the work done per unit area swept out by the dislocation. Thus, in the above simple example, the force (or at least the average force) on the moving dislocation is τb. The following section will show rigorously that the applied stress exerts a constant force τb on the moving dislocation; in other words, if A is the area swept out by the moving dislocation and W the work done, then $F = dW/dA = \tau b$. However, before going on to the more general analysis, we use the simple case (Fig. 4.2) to illustrate some energy relations that are important in the general derivation.

First consider a hypothetical case where uniform slip is taking place at a constant rate on the slip plane in Fig. 4.2. The half of the crystal above the slip plane is moving as a whole relative to the fixed lower half. Assume that the resistance to motion comes from friction on the slip plane, where one atomic plane is sliding over the other (there is no dislocation in this hypothetical case). Observe that there is no net force on the upper half of the crystal (since it is moving at constant velocity); the force on the upper surface is τ (take the area as unity for convenience); the force on the lower surface of the upper half crystal is $-\tau$. Thus the applied stress field does no work; it *does*, of course, do work on the *external surface* of the crystal; but an equal amount of work is done *against* the applied stress on the slip plane. The work done on the external surface is mechanical energy transferred to the crystal from an external source; the work done on the slip plane represents energy dissipated in friction. (The situation is exactly analogous to a horse pulling a sleigh: no work is done on the sleigh; the work done by the horse is equal to the energy dissipated by friction.)

In all cases, when slip occurs and the crystal deforms, the applied stress does work *both* on the external surface *and* on the slip plane, and the two amounts of work are equal and of opposite sign. (Section 5.3 will prove this rigorously for the general case.) For example, suppose the slip in Fig. 4.2 occurs because the dislocation is moving, with uniform velocity, across the slip plane. Consider an element of area dA swept out by the moving dislocation. In the area dA, the two sides of the slip plane are offset by b; the stress acting across the slip plane and in the slip direction is τ; therefore the work done *against* the applied stress is $\tau b\,dA$ (verify that work is done *against* τ on the slip plane if the dislocation moves so that τ *does* work on the external surface). By hypothesis, the dislocation is moving with uniform velocity; therefore all the work done on the slip plane is dissipated as heat or acoustical waves. Thus (work done by the applied stress on the external surface) = (work done by the force τb on the dislocation) = (energy dissipated on the slip plane). If the dislocation were accelerating (instead of moving with constant velocity), some of the work $\tau b dA$ would go into energy of motion E_m (Sec. 4.8) instead of energy dissipated E_d.

5.3 General Case of Glide. The example in Sec. 5.2 is a simple case in that (1) a straight dislocation moved uniformly and swept out the whole area of the slip plane, (2) the crystal had a simple shape, (3) the applied stress was a uniform distribution of pure shear. As an exercise, carry through the same argument for a pure screw dislocation with the same stress, slip plane, and slip vector; show that the force on it is the same.

In this section we consider the general case: an arbitrarily curved dislocation glides in a crystal of arbitrary shape with an arbitrary distribution of applied stress. Let τ be the component of applied stress that acts in the direction of the slip vector and on the slip plane of the dislocation. In general τ varies—not only because the applied stress is nonuniform but also because the slip plane of a curved dislocation varies along the dislocation.

Focus attention on a short segment of dislocation (short enough to be considered straight, so that we can speak of its slip *plane*). Let the segment move a short distance, sweeping out a small element of area dA. Associated with this incremental displacement of the dislocation is an increment of macroscopic strain, in which the applied stress does work dW on the external surface. Now comes the principal result of this section (the proof comes later): The value of τ in the area dA (*inside* the crystal) determines the work dW done on the *external* surface. In the limit $dA \rightarrow 0$, $dW = b\tau dA$. By definition dW/dA is the force on the segment of dislocation. Thus the dislocation experiences a force $F = b\tau$. In general F varies along the dislocation since τ varies. It is important to emphasize that the work done by an arbitrary distribution of stress on the external surface is uniquely given by the stress at a point inside the crystal; this follows from the fact that the externally applied surface stress uniquely determines the stress distribution inside the crystal.

We have defined τ as the component of applied stress on the slip plane and in the slip direction. The slip direction is conserved along the dislocation, but the slip plane may vary (being always the plane containing the slip vector and the tangent to the dislocation line). For example in Fig. 2.6 the segment of dislocation CD lies on the slip plane $ABCD$, which is normal to the slip plane of DE. If $\tau = \tau_{xz}$ for one segment, $\tau = \tau_{yz}$ for the other (where z is the slip direction). Thus the force on a curved or bent dislocation can vary along its length even when the applied stress field is constant throughout the crystal.

We now turn to the proof of $F = b\tau$ for the general case: The proof rests on the theorem that the applied stress field does no work when the dislocation moves—a result that we have already illustrated for a simple case in Sec. 5.2. The proof in the general case requires that we consider the energy of a crystal containing a dislocation and subject to applied stress. The total stress is the sum of (1) the stress field of the dislocation and (2) the applied stress; that is, the two stress distributions add. (Actually they do not quite add in the bad region at the center of the dislocation, where the distortion due to the dislocation is nonlinear; however, we can ignore this effect without error provided the applied stress does not vary appreciably over the width of the bad region, which is only a few atoms.) The energy of distortion in the crystal is the sum of the following three terms:

1. $E_\perp$ is the energy of the dislocation alone.
2. E_a is the energy of the applied stress field alone.
3. $E_{\perp a} = E_{a\perp}$ is the interaction energy, or energy required to superpose one stress field on the other. $E_{\perp a}$ is the work that the stress field of the dislocation does in the deformation associated with the applied stress; $E_{a\perp}$ is the work that the applied stress does in the deformation associated with the dislocation. (Prove $E_{\perp a} = E_{a\perp}$ from the conservation energy.)

Consider how these three terms vary with position of the dislocation. If the applied stress remains constant as the dislocation moves, E_a remains constant. Unless the dislocation is near the external surface, $E_\perp$ does not change. (Chapter 9 will show that the effect of the surface can be represented by an image dislocation, which exerts a force on the real dislocation.) In this chapter we are primarily interested in the interaction energy. We have seen that the deformation of the crystal (due to the presence of the dislocation) varies with the position of the dislocation. Thus, when the dislocation moves and the crystal deforms, the work done by the applied stress is (by definition) the change in $E_{a\perp}$. The following paragraph will prove, by a simple physical argument, that $E_{\perp a}$ is identically zero; hence no work is done by the applied stress field as the dislocation moves. Therefore, when the dislocation moves, the work dW done on the external surface must be equal and opposite to the work done on the slip plane. In the area dA the two sides of the slip plane are offset by b; hence work $b\tau\, dA$ is done against the applied stress; so $dW = b\tau\, dA$ and $F = b\tau$ (as in the simple example in Sec. 5.2).

To complete the argument, it remains only to prove that $E_{\perp a} = 0$. The proof is as follows: Let the crystal already contain the dislocation. Superpose the applied stress. Since the dislocation does not move, no work is done on the slip plane; therefore any work done must be done on the external surface. However, the stress field of a dislocation—or, in fact, any internal stress field—can do no work on the external surface since an internal stress field gives no stress acting on the external surface (see definition of internal stress in Sec. 5.1). It is easy to generalize this result and show that there is no interaction between *any* internal stress field and *any* applied stress field. In general, however, two external stress fields—or two internal stress fields—*will* have an energy of interaction.

Let us now summarize the argument of this section: No work is done by the stress field of the dislocation in superposing the applied stress on the dislocation. Therefore, by conservation of energy, no work is done by the applied stress in superposing the dislocation on the applied stress field. Thus, when the dislocation is superposed on an applied stress field, equal and opposite amounts of work are done by the applied stress on (1) the external surface and (2) the slip plane of the dislocation.

In elasticity theory the argument would go as follows: $E_{a\perp}$ is the work done on the boundary of the elastic region when the dislocation is superposed on the applied stress. The boundary of the elastic region includes not only the external surface but also the two sides of the slip plane (since slip is not an elastic strain). Thus the vanishing of the interaction energy gives

$$W - \int_A b\tau \, dA = 0 \tag{5.1}$$

where A is the slipped area. Differentiating gives $dW = b\tau \, dA$ as before.

We are now in a position to prove rigorously the statements about macroscopic strain in Chap. 4: Assume that a uniform but otherwise arbitrary stress is applied. When the dislocation moves, the component of stress τ does work in the macroscopic deformation. The other (arbitrary) stress components do no work; therefore the corresponding macroscopic strain components must vanish. Thus when a dislocation moves, the macroscopic deformation produced is a shear strain corresponding to the slip plane and direction of the dislocation. As an exercise prove that the macroscopic (or average) strain is bA/V where A is the area swept out on the slip plane and V, the volume of the crystal.

In conclusion consider how energy is absorbed at the dislocation. First suppose we move the dislocation from one position to another as follows: (1) make a cut connecting the two positions, (2) apply forces to the sides of the cut to maintain equilibrium, and (3) slowly displace the two sides by b. Work is done on both the external surface and the cut. In the (equilibrium) process, the work done on the external surface is removed from the crystal by the forces applied to the cut. In an actual motion (where equilibrium is not maintained), the work done on the area

dA goes into E_d or E_m. However, the work done on the external surface is independent of the method of absorbing energy at the dislocation; it is therefore the same for both equilibrium and nonequilibrium processes.

5.4 Direction of the Force in Glide. Section 5.3 defined only the *magnitude* of the force; what is the *direction?* First consider the direction of glide; take a point on the dislocation; what is its direction of motion? This is a purely geometrical problem; it is simply a matter of describing the arbitrary motion of a line in a plane. This means giving the velocity at every point. It is only necessary, however, to give the component of velocity normal to the line. The tangential component is arbitrary— moving the points along the tangent to the line has no effect on the motion of the line—thus there are a number of equivalent descriptions, all differing in the tangential velocities. Which description we use is a matter of convenience. In dislocation dynamics, it is better to use only normal velocities—for example, both E_m and the rate of energy dissipation are functions of only normal velocity. In other cases some other description is much simpler; an example is any curved dislocation that moves without change in form. What we want is, therefore, a definition of force that gives the right amount of work for *any* description of motion. (As an exercise show that **F** should be taken at right angles to the dislocation; the proof is in the following paragraph.)

Suppose **ds** is taken as the displacement of a point on the dislocation; let the force at that point be **F**. The following requirements nail down the direction of **F**: (1) The work should be the dot, or scalar, product **F · ds**. (2) The work should not depend on the (arbitrary) tangential component of **ds**. Conclusion: **F** *is normal to the dislocation.*

Perhaps a simple analogy will bring out the physical meaning of the above argument: Take a gas under pressure in a container. The pressure produces a force on the surface of the container. The *direction* of the force is normal to the surface. The magnitude is the pressure (which can be defined as the work done per unit increase in the volume of the gas). Now think of a slipped area as a two-dimensional gas trying to expand under a pressure τb (= work done per unit increase in slipped area). The pressure of the slipped area trying to expand produces a force τb normal to the dislocation that bounds the slipped area.

To summarize this section: The magnitude of the force is equal to the magnitude of the slip vector times the component τ of applied stress in the slip plane and slip direction. The magnitude does *not* depend on the orientation of the dislocation in the slip plane. The direction of the force (in the slip plane) is at right angles to the dislocation and is independent of the applied stress. A common error is to give the force the direction of the resultant applied shear force on the slip plane.

5.5 Force Normal to the Slip Plane. This is found from the work done in climb just as the force in the slip plane was found from the work done in glide.

Any dislocation can be made up of edge and screw segments; the screws can glide in any direction. (As an exercise take a screw dislocation parallel to the z axis and express the force $\mathbf{F}$ on it in terms of the stress components τ_{zy} and τ_{xz}.) It therefore remains to find the force normal to the slip plane of an edge dislocation.

Section 4.6 discussed the climb of an edge dislocation and showed that the edge of the extra plane has to acquire (or loose) atoms as the growth (or shrinking) of the extra plane expands (or collapses) the crystal. Therefore the tensile stress σ normal to the extra plane does work. When unit area of extra plane is removed, the adjoining planes move together through the distance b; the tensile stress σ does work $-\sigma b$. Thus the force, by definition, is $-\sigma b$. The minus sign comes from the convention that positive climb is a shrinking of the extra plane (upward motion of the dislocation in Figs. 1.2, 4.1, and 4.2). As an exercise show how work is done, and derive the force for climb of the edge dislocations in Figs. 4.4 and 4.5.

5.6 General Formulas for Force. It is now a short step to the general formulas for force on an arbitrary dislocation in an arbitrary stress field having components $\sigma_x, \sigma_y, \sigma_z, \tau_{xy}, \tau_{yz}, \tau_{zx}$. Figure 5.1 shows the three stress components that contribute to the force. In the xyz coordinate system, x is along the Burgers vector and z, along the normal to the slip plane. Let AC be unit length of dislocation making an arbitrary angle α with the x axis. Define the sign of the Burgers vector by taking AC in the direction A to C; then the Burgers circuit goes in the clockwise direction looking from A toward C (see the conventions in Sec. 3.5). In graphical terms, the Burgers vector is the displacement of the material above the slip plane relative to that below when the dislocation glides to the right (toward B).

The stress τ_{xz} produces a force in the slip plane

$$F_s = b\tau_{xz} \tag{5.2}$$

F_s acts at right angles to the dislocation and tries to make the dislocation glide toward B.

To find the force F_n normal to the slip plane, replace AC by AB and BC. AB is a screw segment of length $\cos \alpha$ and BC, an edge segment of length $\sin \alpha$. F_n is the work done when ABC moves unit distance upward (sweeping out the area $ABCDEF$). First take the work done on $ABEF$. AB moves over $ABEF$ by pure glide. τ_{xy} is the shear stress in the slip direction and on the plane $ABEF$; it does work $+b\tau_{xy}$ per unit area swept out by AB. (As an exercise verify the positive sign.) The area of

$ABEF$ is $\cos \alpha$; therefore the work done on $ABEF$ is $b\tau_{xy} \cos \alpha$. Now take the area $BCDE$: BC is the edge of an incomplete atomic plane parallel to $BCDE$. (Verify that the extra plane is *above* the slip plane.) As BC climbs upward, atoms are removed from the extra plane in the area $BCDE$. The crystal collapses, and σ_x does work $-b\sigma_x$ per unit area of

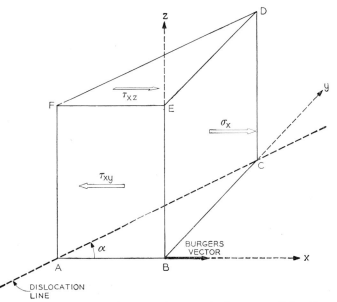

FIG. 5.1 The stress components that contribute to the force on a dislocation. AC is unit length of dislocation making an arbitrary angle α with the Burgers vector. The components of force on the dislocation are $F_s = b\tau_{xz}$ in the slip (xz) plane and normal to the dislocation and $F_z = F_n = b(\tau_{xy} \cos \alpha - \sigma_x \sin \alpha)$ normal to the slip plane.

extra plane. The area of $BCDE$ is $\sin \alpha$; therefore the work done is $-b\sigma_x \sin \alpha$. Thus the work per unit displacement of ABC is

$$F_n = b(\tau_{xy} \cos \alpha - \sigma_x \sin \alpha) \qquad (5.3)$$

F_n acts normal to the slip plane and tries to make the dislocation climb.

It may be asked whether the above argument is justified in replacing the straight section of dislocation AC by the bent dislocation ABC; the two are not equivalent; for example, ABC is longer and has more energy than AC. The justification is as follows: Suppose AC is transformed to ABC; work is done on the dislocation to provide the added energy. The upward displacement (which can be made arbitrarily small) carries ABC into FED. Now let FED straighten out and become FD; we now get back the same energy that was required to change AC to ABC. Thus replacing the straight dislocation by the bent one has no net effect on the energy argument that gave F_n.

We now present an alternative derivation that gives F_n without replacing AC by ABC. Let AC move upward into the position DF, sweeping out unit area $ACDF$. This is the same as making a cut on $ACDF$ and giving the two sides of the cut a relative displacement equal to the Burgers vector. Take one side of the cut as a reference and consider the force on the other side and the work that it does. The relative displacement is b in the x direction. As an exercise show that the force in the x direction is $\tau_{xy} \cos \alpha - \sigma_x \sin \alpha$. Thus the work done ($= F_n$) is the same as in Eq. (5.3).

Sometimes it is more convenient to refer stress and force to axes lined up with respect to the dislocation and slip plane—instead of with respect to the Burgers vector and slip plane. As an exercise, take the z axis along the dislocation, the y axis normal to the slip plane, and show that

$$F_x = -b(\tau_{yz} \cos \alpha + \tau_{xy} \sin \alpha)$$
$$F_y = b(\tau_{xz} \cos \alpha + \sigma_x \sin \alpha)$$

(5.4)

where α is again the angle between the dislocation and its Burgers vector. (HINT: Consider the dislocation as the superposition of an edge with Burgers vector $b \sin \alpha$ and a screw with Burgers vector $b \cos \alpha$; the two must, of course, move together, but their effects can be treated separately.) Here F_x is in the slip (xz) plane and tries to make the dislocation glide in the $+x$ direction; F_y promotes climb.

In vector form, the force $\mathbf{F}$ on the dislocation is

$$\mathbf{F} = \mathbf{v} \times (\mathbf{P} \cdot \mathbf{b})$$

(5.5)

where $\mathbf{P}$ is the stress dyadic and $\mathbf{v}$, unit vector tangent to the dislocation (see, for example, Peach and Koehler, 1950).

In vector form, the definition of $\mathbf{F}$ in terms of W is

$$\mathbf{F} = \nabla W$$

(5.6)

where $\nabla = $ gradient of.

The following two sections apply the concept of force to static equilibrium and steady-state motion; these applications form a bridge to Chap. 6.

5.7 Static Equilibrium. The force defined in the previous sections is the force due to the applied stress field; it vanishes when the external surface is stress free. Chapter 9 will show how the internal stress (such as the stress fields of other dislocations) also produces a force on the dislocation; that force is equal to $-\nabla E_s$. The total force is therefore $\nabla(W - E_s)$, which (by the conservation of energy, Sec. 4.8) is equal to $\nabla(E_d + E_m)$. Thus (as discussed earlier for glide) all the work W that does not go into stored energy of distortion E_s goes into the work done by the force on the dislocation. The work done by the force on the dislocation either goes into energy of motion E_m or is dissipated.

This section deals with static equilibrium, where there is no energy of motion and no energy dissipated; the net force $\nabla(W - E_s)$ vanishes. Without going into the more quantitative problems of Chap. 9, we shall discuss briefly the three sources of internal stress that cause changes in E_s and thereby contribute to the force $-\nabla E_s$:

1. Neighboring dislocations and other types of imperfections are surrounded by stress fields.
2. An arbitrary curved dislocation lies in its own stress field; one part of the dislocation exerts forces on another part (as in the case of force between different parts of a curved charged wire).
3. A dislocation near the external surface also lies in its own stress field—which, as one would expect, urges the dislocation toward the surface (the crystal wants to reduce its energy by getting rid of the dislocation).

Chapter 9 treats 1 for straight dislocations and 3 for straight dislocations and plane surfaces. This section deals only with a single dislocation far from the external surface; thus 1 and 3 can be neglected. 2 has been analyzed exactly only in a few simple cases (such as a closed circular or rectangular loop). In general the calculation of 2 is too laborious to be practical. In what follows, we present an approximate treatment of 2 that is useful for many practical calculations.

Let T be the stored energy per unit length of dislocation. In general T varies along the dislocation; T depends, for example, on both the local orientation and the form of the whole dislocation. In the approximation we neglect this variation and take $T = $ constant; so the dislocation is treated like a one-dimensional soap film which has a constant line tension equal to T (note that line tension = energy per unit length). When the dislocation is curved, the line tension produces a sidewise restoring force on the dislocation. The restoring force tries to reduce energy by straightening out the dislocation. The magnitude of the restoring force is T times the curvature, or T/R where $R = $ radius of curvature. The direction of the restoring force is normal to the dislocation and toward the center of curvature (as for a soap film or string under tension).

Chapter 4 gave several examples where T implicitly played a role. For example in Fig. 4.3 the line tension tries to straighten out the kink so that the equilibrium shape is like C instead of A. In Fig. 4.4 the closed loop tries to shrink under its line tension; therefore in equilibrium it glides into the shape of minimum length; if the temperature were raised to permit climb, the loop would shrink to nothing.

We conclude the discussion of static equilibrium with the following example, which is simple and yet has wide application in plasticity: Take a straight dislocation of length L lying on a plane slip surface.   Let L run between two nodes N_1 and N_2 where it meets other dislocations in other slip planes.   Take the temperature low enough that only glide occurs. The nodes are held fixed by the other dislocations (Sec. 6.5).   Now apply a uniform stress τ which produces a force $F = b\tau$ on the dislocation.   How does the shape of the (initially straight) dislocation change as τ increases? The following paragraph gives the answer.

The equilibrium condition is $F = T/R$; thus the dislocation is part of a circle of radius $R = T/F$.   The dislocation must also connect the fixed points N_4 and N_2.   Draw the dislocation for several values of F; show that, as the applied stress increases, R decreases and reaches a minimum $R = L/2$, for which the dislocation is a semicircle.   Observe that, for a force larger than $F = 2T/L$, static equilibrium is not possible (the applied force is larger than the maximum possible restoring force); now the dislocation becomes unstable and expands indefinitely (Chap. 6 will discuss the motion in detail).   Chapter 8 will show that $T \approx Gb^2$ where G is the (average) shear modulus of the crystal.   Thus the dislocation becomes unstable when the applied stress $\tau \approx Gb/L$.

5.8 Steady-state Motion.   In steady-state motion, E_m is constant; all the work done by the net force is dissipated.   The rate of energy dissipation is an unknown function of normal velocity v; however, it probably increases monotonically with v.   In this section we show that, even without knowing the exact form of the function, we can reach several useful results.

First consider pure glide on a plane with uniform applied stress.   If the restoring force increases monotonically with curvature $1/R$, and energy dissipated increases monotonically with v, then the normal velocity toward the center of curvature increases monotonically with curvature (or normal velocity away from the center of curvature decreases as $1/R$ increases). Use this result to sketch (roughly) a curved dislocation that could glide without change in form.

At low velocities energy dissipated per unit distance moved is proportional to v; therefore

$$F - \frac{T}{R} = \frac{v}{\mu} \qquad (5.7)$$

where μ is a constant which we shall call the mobility of a dislocation under small stress.   For higher velocities the right-hand side of (5.7) is an unknown nonlinear function of v.

By definition of steady-state motion, the shape of the dislocation remains constant; the motion is therefore either a pure translation or a rotation of one part of the dislocation around a fixed point—for example, a point where the dislocation leaves one slip plane and goes onto another.

The steady-state rotation is discussed in Chap. 6 in relation to the Frank-Read theory of slip.

In describing, for example, the steady-state translation of a curved dislocation, we say every point has the same velocity $\mathbf{V}$. However, the normal component v of $\mathbf{V}$ varies along the dislocation; this is an example where the description in terms of v is not the simplest.

PROBLEMS

1. Show that there is no *net* force on a closed loop of dislocation (not necessarily lying in one slip plane) when the applied stress field is constant throughout the crystal.

2. Surround a dislocation with a tubular surface separating the good material from the bad. Consider the stress acting across this surface; prove that the *net force* exerted *by* the good material *on* the bad material vanishes. Distinguish the force on the configuration from the force on the bad material.

3. Consider an oversized or undersized impurity atom that strains the surrounding crystal isotropically. Here we have an imperfection that is *both* a configuration and a material mass. What force does a local stress field exert on the *configuration?* (For the answer see sec. 9.10.)

What type of force acts on the *mass* (that is, the impurity atom itself), and what form of energy is involved? Is the force on the *mass* affected by the local elastic stress field?

4. Consider a stacking fault that extends completely through a crystal. What is the pressure on the fault in an applied stress field (the pressure is defined as the work done per unit area of fault per unit distance moved)? HINT: The pressure would vanish if the applied stress were constant throughout the crystal.

5. A hexagonal crystal in the form of a rod is stressed in pure bending; the axis of bending lies in the basal planes, which are at 45° to the axis of the rod. Find the force on a dislocation that lies in the basal plane and show that like edge dislocations tend to accumulate inside the crystal.

6. A dislocation moves in an applied stress field; the external surface of the crystal is held fixed. Use the general definition of force $\mathbf{F} = \boldsymbol{\nabla}(W - E_s) = \boldsymbol{\nabla}(E_d + E_m)$ to derive the formulas of this chapter for force in terms of applied stress. (Since the external surface is held fixed as the dislocation moves, $\boldsymbol{\nabla}W = 0$.)

7. Consider a closed dislocation loop lying on a prismatic slip surface of rectangular cross section. Take the z axis parallel to the Burgers vector and let X and Y be the lengths of the two sides of the rectangular cross section. If only glide is permitted, find the equilibrium shape of the loop for the following two stress distributions: (a) $\tau_{xz} = 0$, $\tau_{yz} = \tau = $ constant; (b) $\tau_{xz} = \tau_{yz} = \tau = $ constant. In each case find the critical value of τ at which static equilibrium becomes impossible. (Use the constant-line-tension approximation.)

8. Consider a closed loop of dislocation on a cylindrical slip surface of radius R (as in Fig. 4.4). Find the shape of the dislocation under an arbitrary applied stress which is constant throughout the crystal. Use the constant-line-tension approximation.

a. Sketch the shape roughly.

b. The loop becomes unstable and expands indefinitely when which component of applied stress reaches what critical value? (Obtain the answer by a simple physical argument.)

c. Solve for the exact equilibrium shape of the loop.

The answer, in cylindrical coordinates R θ z, is

$$z = R \ln (\beta \sin \theta + \sqrt{1 - \beta^2 \cos^2 \theta})$$
$$\beta = \frac{\tau b R}{T}$$

where θ has the range 0 to π; the formula represents half the closed curve; the other half is a mirror image. The $\theta = 0$ plane is so chosen that the stress in the z direction is a maximum τ on the $\theta = \pi/2$ plane.

9. Consider the steady-state pure translation of a dislocation in a uniform stress field; all points have a constant velocity V in a given direction. Assume a restoring force that increases monotonically with curvature and a damping force that increases monotonically with normal velocity.

a. Show that for any given stress and V the solution has four branches—two straight lines and two curved lines that approach the straight lines asymptotically. Show that one curved line could represent a physical situation; the other curved line in its entirety is physically unreasonable.

b. Using Eq. (5.7), show that the straight-line asymptotes in *a* make an angle

$$\phi_0 = \sin^{-1}\left(\frac{\tau b \mu}{V}\right)$$

with the direction of pure translation. Here $F = \tau b$ is the constant force on the dislocation.

c. Solve Eq. (5.7) for the form of the dislocation lines. Take the x axis in the direction of translation; show that x and y are given by the parametric equations

$$x = -\frac{1}{2} \ln (\sin \phi_0 - \sin \phi)^2$$
$$y = -\phi - \frac{1}{2} \tan \phi_0 \ln \left[\frac{1 - \cos (\phi_0 - \phi)}{1 + \cos (\phi_0 + \phi)}\right]$$

Plot the four branches for $\phi_0 = 45°$, $90°$.

CHAPTER 6

MULTIPLICATION AND INTERSECTION OF DISLOCATIONS

This chapter fits together the results of the previous ones; what emerges is a simple picture of

1. Why a large amount of slip occurs on a single slip plane, as observed in slip lines
2. The origin of the dislocations that accumulate during plastic deformation
3. How dislocations get tangled up and interfere with one another's motion so that the crystal is hardened
4. How moving dislocations can produce vacancies and interstitial atoms

The argument proceeds by applying the already developed ideas of dislocation motion; no *ad hoc* assumptions are introduced.

6.1 Slip on Intersecting Planes.   The central idea of this chapter is the motion of one or more dislocations on intersecting slip planes.   Sections 6.2 to 6.6 discuss the motion of a single dislocation on a bent slip surface consisting of two plane sections; Secs. 6.7 to 6.10 discuss the intersection of *two* dislocations moving on intersecting slip planes.   The former leads to a mechanism of dislocation multiplication, the latter to a mechanism of work hardening.

Chapter 2 discussed the geometry of several simple dislocations including both dislocations that lie in a single slip plane and dislocations, such as the one in Fig. 2.6, that lie on a bent slip surface.   When a dislocation lies in one slip plane or on a smoothly curved slip surface, then it moves as discussed explicitly in Chap. 4.   However, when the slip surface is sharply bent (as in Fig. 2.6), a simple but strikingly important type of motion is possible that has not yet been discussed explicitly although it is a straightforward consequence of the ideas discussed in Chaps. 4 and 5.   The sharp bend in the dislocation (where it shifts from one slip plane to the other) permits the dislocation to produce a very large amount of slip on a single slip plane.   This slip mechanism, called the Frank-Read mechanism, is at present the most plausible explanation for the fact that, in typical crystals, slip is not homogeneous but is concentrated on a relatively few active slip planes which slip by many atomic spacings.   A number of drawings show

how the atoms move and how the crystal deforms as the mechanism acts. The resolved shear stress law determines the driving force for the mechanism. Sections 6.2 to 6.5 discuss the mechanism in detail and show how it can produce new closed loops of dislocation. Section 6.6 applies the same principle to climb. In climb the mechanism produces plastic deformation by mass transport; such deformation is observed, for example, in the Kirkendall effect.

Section 6.7 considers two dislocations—one on each of two intersecting slip planes. Whenever a dislocation moves across a slip plane, it will have to cut through other dislocations on other slip planes. Section 6.7 shows why, in general, intersecting dislocations have trouble getting past one another—they become stuck and thereby harden the crystal. Section 6.8 shows how a dislocation that has cut through another dislocation is restricted in its further motion—in fact, as it moves, it leaves behind a trail of vacancies or interstitial atoms. Section 6.9 discusses the role of dislocation intersections in work hardening. Section 6.10 shows how dislocation intersection can produce the bent dislocation of the Frank-Read mechanism.

6.2 The Frank-Read Mechanism—A Simple Example. Figures 2.4 and 2.5 show a dislocation bounding a plane slipped area. If the dislocation glides over the slip plane, the result is an offset b, or one unit of slip. Until 1950 the general picture of slip was that one dislocation produces one unit of slip by sweeping out all its slip plane, thus moving out of the crystal. The second unit of slip would then require a second dislocation, and so on. The origin of all these dislocations remained a mystery. Orowan (1953), Cottrell (1953), and Brown (1952) review the historical efforts to explain the origins of dislocations. It was a simple matter to show that a combination of thermal energy and applied stress was *not* sufficient—even if the stress were taken at a severe stress concentration, such as the tip of a crack. (In typical metals, the necessary crack would have to be about a millimeter deep—which is often larger than the specimen diameter.) Frank suggested that moving dislocations could reach sufficiently high velocities that some of their kinetic energy could go into forming new dislocations (see Frank's paper in the Bristol Report referred to in Sec. 1.5). This "dynamic multiplication mechanism" still remains an ingenious possibility, although less importance is attached to it now that the simpler Frank-Read mechanism is available.

The Frank-Read mechanism, despite its almost obvious simplicity, remained so long unnoticed because before 1950 most thinking in dislocation theory was two dimensional. Extensive speculations were made with two-dimensional thinking, while simple and important three-dimensional ideas were overlooked. The three-dimensional concepts are not merely an extension of two-dimensional ones; instead they introduce striking new possibilities, of which the Frank-Read mechanism is an out-standing example. Consequently, in the preceding chapters, we have taken a three-dimensional viewpoint from the beginning. This procedure follows from the main point of Chap. 1—that a thorough study of basic ideas should precede applications of the theory.

To introduce the Frank-Read mechanism, let us return to Fig. 2.6 and consider a simple motion of the dislocation *CDE*. Figures 2.7 to 2.9 show successive positions of the atoms in what is perhaps the simplest conceivable motion of *CDE*—the arm *DE* remains fixed and *CD* moves,

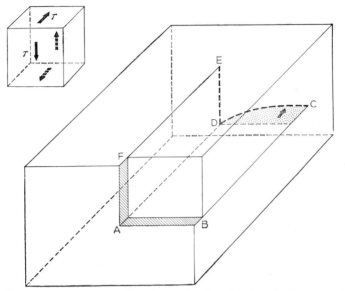

FIG. 6.1 Same as Fig. 2.6 except that the section *DC* of dislocation has moved on its slip plane sweeping out the shaded area. The stress shown at the upper left produces no force on *DE*. *CD* experiences a force $b\tau$ normal to itself and in its slip plane. Thus the stress tends to make *CD* rotate about *DE*.

rotating about *DE*. We now discuss, with the aid of figures, (1) how a simple stress makes *CD* rotate about *DE*, (2) the associated macroscopic deformation (which, in fact, could shear the crystal in two), and (3) how the atoms move.

Driving Force. Figure 6.1 (upper left) shows a simple stress that would make *CD* rotate around *DE*, namely, a pure shear stress τ in the direction of the slip vector and on the slip plane (*ABCD*) of *CD*. Observe that slip on *ABCD* causes the crystal to yield to τ; on the other hand, no work is done by τ if slip occurs on the slip plane *DEFA*. Thus *the applied stress exerts a force τb on CD and no force on DE*. Assume that, under no force, *DE* remains fixed (Sec. 6.5 discusses ways of anchoring *DE*). The stress τ tries to expand the slipped area *ABCD* and make it cover the whole slip plane. Thus all along CD there is a force on CD urging it to rotate about the fixed point D. Remember that the force on CD is always at right angles to CD; thus if CD rotates about D (like the hand of a clock) the applied stress continues to provide a driving force for the rotation; in other words, the torque causing CD to rotate about ED remains constant as CD moves.

Macroscopic Deformation.   Figure 6.1 is the same as Fig. 2.6 except that CD has moved.   Figures 6.2 and 6.3 show still further stages in the motion.   As CD moves it sweeps out the shaded area in Figs. 6.1 to 6.3; unit slip has occurred in the shaded area since CD started to move.   (The

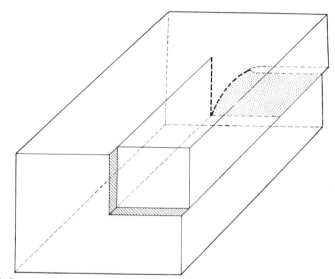

Fig. 6.2 Same as Fig. 6.1 except that the slipped (shaded) area has increased farthei as CD in Fig. 6.1 rotates about the fixed point D.

visible offset on the rear surface of the crystal in Figs. 6.2 and 6.3 is the beginning of a visible *slip line*.)   In one complete revolution, CD produces unit offset over the whole slip plane.   Figure 6.4 shows CD starting on its second revolution; here the area that has slipped by *two* units since CD started to move is shaded.   Remember that when CD started to move (Fig. 2.6) there was already unit offset b on $ABCD$.

The macroscopic deformation shows up clearly in Fig. 6.4.   The upper half of the crystal is offset by b for every revolution of CD.   As the upper half of the crystal moves along (relative to the bottom half), it carries DE with it.   By making enough revolutions, this simple mechanism could shear the crystal in two, or at least until D reaches the external surface.   Such large offsets, of half a crystal diameter or more, occur on a single slip plane in certain hexagonal close-packed crystals at high temperatures.

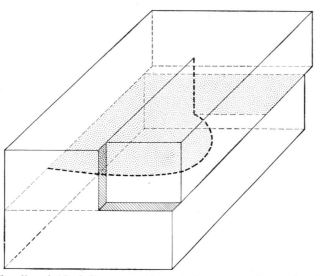

FIG. 6.3 The slipped (shaded) area continues to increase as the moving dislocation rotates about the fixed point and sweeps over the slip plane.

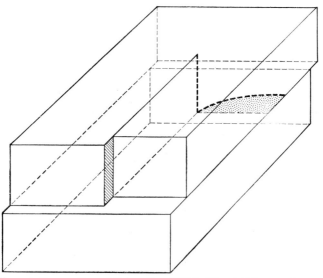

FIG. 6.4 The rotating section of dislocation (*CD* in Fig. 6.1) has made one complete revolution and swept over the whole slip plane—thus producing one unit of slip. (Note the visible offset, or slip line.) Now the shaded area represents the area which has slipped by two units since the dislocation started to move.

As CD rotates it does not remain straight; Sec. 6.3 will show that CD winds itself up into a spiral. However, in typical cases, the maximum curvature (near D) is about 1 (micron)$^{-1}$. Thus, over a distance of many atoms from D, CD can be considered approximately straight. Before discussing the exact form of CD, we consider the atoms near the pivot point.

Motion of the Atoms. Figures 2.7 to 2.9 show the atoms near D on each side of the slip plane of CD. In the area that CD has swept out, the atoms above the slip plane (open circles) are offset relative to the atoms below the slip plane (solid circles). At this point, the reader may wish to review the description of Figs. 2.6 to 2.9 in Sec. 2.5. As exercises draw the displacement of each atom as CD moves from one position to the next. Continue the sequence of drawings and show the 180° and 270° positions of CD. Observe that, after rotating 180°, CD is again pure edge but a negative edge; the extra plane of atoms is *below* the slip plane. By tracing the atomic displacements, show how the extra plane ceases to be *extra* when CD rotates away from the pure edge orientation.

6.3 The Rotating Spiral. This section shows why CD winds itself up into a spiral as it rotates.

If CD remained straight, the normal velocity at every point would be proportional to the distance from D. However the applied force is the same all along CD. Therefore CD cannot remain straight but must become curved. Section 5.8 showed that, in steady-state motion, the normal velocity (toward the center of curvature) increases with curvature. Or, when the applied force acts away from the center of curvature, the normal velocity in the direction of the applied force decreases with curvature. This requirement determines the steady-state form of CD, which is readily calculated subject to certain simplifying assumptions [such as Eq. (5.7)—see Prob. 5]. It will be more instructive, however, first to find the steady-state shape by tracing its development through the transient stage.

Initially the normal velocity is the same all along CD except at the point D, which is fixed. The restraining effect of D spreads along CD, and a curvature develops near D. Figure 6.5 shows seven successive positions of the rotating section of dislocation; the plane of the figure is the slip plane. In position 2, notice the curvature developing near the fixed pivot point. Observe also that the points near D have a shorter distance to go to make one revolution about D than do the points farther away; thus the inner sections can make more revolutions in a given time. Positions 1 to 5 show the beginning of the spiral. The spiral becomes more tightly wound as the inner sections make more revolutions than the outer ones (positions 6 and 7). However, associated with the developing curvature is a restoring force (Secs. 5.7 and 5.8). In Fig. 6.5 the restoring force opposes the motion. The curvature, and therefore the restoring force, decreases with distance from the pivot point. The net force in the direction of motion therefore increases with distance from the pivot point. Consequently the normal velocity increases with distance from the pivot point. As the spiral becomes more tightly wound, the inner sections

FIG. 6.5 Seven successive stages in the development of a spiral. The plane of the figure is the slip plane. The lines represent successive positions of a dislocation that leaves the slip plane at the point D. Under an applied stress, the initially straight section of dislocation (position 1) rotates about the fixed point D and winds itself up into a spiral. In the steady state, the spiral (position 7) rotates without change in shape.

continue to slow down until the outer sections can keep up with them. Finally a steady state is reached, in which all the points on CD move around D with the same angular velocity; in other words the spiral rotates as a whole without change in form.

The Frank-Read mechanism (as described above) explains (1) why a large amount of slip occurs on a single plane, as observed in slip bands, and (2) why the total length of dislocation in a specimen increases during deformation. The development of a spiral, however, is not the only way of increasing the length of dislocation. The following section shows how another form of the Frank-Read mechanism produces an unlimited number of closed loops of dislocation.

6.4 Formation of New Dislocation Loops—The Frank-Read Source.

This section discusses what is called a Frank-Read source, generator, or dislocation mill, which produces closed dislocation loops that expand and (1) sweep out the whole slip plane or (2) get tangled up with other dislocations and harden the specimen. The Frank-Read spiral and source are distinguished as follows: The basic mechanism requires a section of dislocation that lies in a slip plane and leaves that plane at a point in the interior of the crystal (as the section CD leaves its slip plane $ABCD$ at the interior point D). Now a length of dislocation lying entirely in a single slip plane can connect

1. Two points on the external surface (as in Fig. 2.4)
2. One surface and one interior point (as in Figs. 2.6 and 6.1 to 6.5) or
3. Two interior points

The Frank-Read spiral, discussed in the preceding section, corresponds to 2. The source corresponds to 3; its operation, which is described in the following paragraph, involves the same principle as the spiral.

A length of dislocation that leaves a given slip plane at two points inside the crystal can be visualized as follows: Imagine the crystal in Fig. 2.6 joined onto its mirror image on its right-hand external surface, so that the dislocation is $EDCD'E'$ where CD' is a continuation of DC and $D'E'$ is parallel to DE. The stress shown in Fig. 6.1 (upper left) produces a force τb on DD'; there is no force on DE or $D'E'$. Figures 6.1 to 6.3 joined onto *their* mirror images (across the right-hand surface) show the beginning of the motion.

What happens when the slipped area in Fig. 6.3 meets its mirror image on the right? Figure 6.6 gives the answer; the plane of the drawing is the slip plane of DD'; five successive positions of DD' are shown; the area swept out by DD' is shaded.

In Fig. 6.6, we assume the stress τ has been applied gradually. DD' bulges out to maintain static equilibrium. As Sec. 5.7 showed, the applied stress is a maximum for the semicircular form, which is shown in Fig. 6.6b. If the stress is raised above the critical value (see Prob. 1) corresponding to the semicircular form, then the dislocation becomes statically unstable and expands indefinitely; the work done by the applied stress goes into energy of motion or is dissipated. In Fig. 6.6c the unstable loop is beginning to expand and double back on itself. In Fig. 6.6d the shaded area (where slip has occurred since the dislocation started to move) has almost doubled back on itself; the two parts of the slipped area are about to join up behind the original position of DD'. Finally the two parts of the slipped area join (Fig. 6.6e); the sections of dislocation that meet annihilate one another and leave (1) a closed loop of dislocation, which continues to expand under the applied stress, and (2) a section of dislocation DD', which rapidly straightens out (under the applied stress

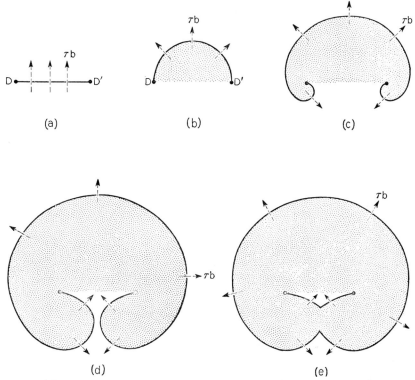

(a)   (b)   (c)

(d)   (e)

FIG. 6.6 The plane of the figure is the slip plane of a section of dislocation DD'; the dislocation leaves the plane of the figure at the fixed points D and D'. An applied stress produces a normal force τb on the dislocation and makes the dislocation bulge. The initially straight dislocation a acquires a curvature proportional to τ. If τ is increased beyond a critical value corresponding to position b, where the curvature is a maximum, the dislocation becomes unstable and expands indefinitely. The expanding loop doubles back on itself, c and d. Unit slip occurs in the (shaded) area swept out by the bulging loop. In e the two parts of the slipped area have joined; now there is a closed loop of dislocation and the section DD' is ready to bulge again and give off another closed loop.

and line tension) and is ready to go through the same process all over again. It can go on indefinitely giving off expanding loops of dislocation; every loop that expands over the slip plane produces unit slip in the area swept out. This self-perpetuating source of dislocations is the Frank-Read source, generator, or mill. We can think of the source as two oppositely winding spirals joined together. If the distance DD' were large enough, or if a supercritical stress were suddenly applied, then DD' might make several turns around each pivot point before giving off a closed loop.

Both forms of the Frank-Read mechanism have emerged naturally from a step-by-step development of basic three-dimensional concepts. The mechanism, of course, does not predict how much slip should occur on any single plane; the question of what hardens a slip plane and causes slip on it to stop is probably the least understood problem in plastic deformation. Sections 6.7 to 6.9 will discuss some of the things that can harden a slip plane.

6.5 Anchoring of the Pivot Point. So far we have assumed that the pivot point is fixed. It is sufficient, however, if the pivot is only partially anchored, so that it drags. Such anchoring may occur in various ways. For example, the pivot point might be a node where three dislocations meet; if the three dislocations have different slip planes, then the node cannot move freely by slip. (Draw three intersecting dislocations with different slip planes and show how the motion is restricted.) Mott (1952) assumes the pivot point is such a fixed node.

In certain crystals, such as the hexagonal close packed, the lower mobility of dislocations in non-close-packed planes may provide enough drag. Even for equal mobilities, the different forces on the two arms of an L-shaped dislocation might make one move faster and spiral around the other. Or a local stress concentration might anchor the pivot point. Chapter 9 will show how impurity atoms can lock a section of dislocation in place. We thus conclude that there are several possible methods of anchoring. The exact method that applies in any particular case is at present a subject of speculation. Some other speculative questions regarding the Frank-Read mechanisms are the following:

1. How do Frank-Read sources originate? How many are there per cubic centimeter in a well-annealed crystal—in a severely cold-worked crystal? (See Mott, 1952, and Orowan, 1953.) Which are more important, sources in the as-grown crystal or sources produced in plastic deformation? (Section 6.10 discusses one of the ways in which generators could form in plastic deformation.)

2. Are the significant sources well inside the crystal (two pivot points, as in Fig. 6.6) or near the external surface (so that the dislocation runs from the pivot point to the surface, as in Figs. 6.1 to 6.4)? For experimental evidence, see Barrett (1953)[1]—see also Prob. 2.

---

[1] Barrett has evidence that dislocation loops generated inside the crystal are prevented from escaping by an oxide layer at the surface. When the oxide layer is removed from a plastically twisted specimen, the specimen continues to twist in the absence of applied stress.

3. Is the stress field of the expanding dislocation loops what finally stops the source? (Show by a simple physical argument that the expanding loops *do* produce a stress at the source that opposes the applied stress.) Is the kinetic energy of the source responsible for the fact that a large number of loops are generated before the reverse stress of the loops stops the source (on the second and subsequent trips around, the source has a running start)? See Fisher, Hart, and Pry (1952) and Mott (1952).

6.6 The Same Mechanism in Climb. The Frank-Read mechanism applies also to climb as the following argument shows: First transform Figs. 2.6 and 6.1 to 6.6 so that the moving dislocation is pure edge; this simply means taking the Burgers vector parallel to DE. Now DE is pure screw and CD pure edge. $ABCD$ in Figs. 2.6 and 6.1 is the extra plane of atoms that ends on CD. If atoms are added onto the edge CD of the incomplete atomic plane, then the plane grows and covers the shaded area. Thus the edge dislocation CD climbs in the plane normal to its Burgers vector and rotates about the screw dislocation DE. The geometry is the same as for a gliding dislocation, and again a spiral develops. (What driving force favors this motion and what is the macroscopic deformation? See the following paragraph for the answer.)

Now let us look at the Frank-Read mechanism in climb from a three-dimensional viewpoint. Join the crystal in Fig. 2.2 onto a perfect crystal of the same orientation by setting the perfect crystal down on the upper surface. The joining is perfect except along the step AB—which becomes an edge dislocation. Again we have an L-shaped dislocation. If atoms are added to AB, AB advances and rotates about the fixed point A. Figure 6.5 now represents the successive positions of AB as viewed along the slip vector. Observe that every revolution of AB about A adds one more atomic plane to the crystal, or rather one more level to the spiral ramp. In other words, atoms are being added to the crystal; so it is growing. We have here really an example of the internal growth of a crystal, which can perhaps be appreciated better after the discussion in Chap. 10 of Frank's theory of crystal growth. As an exercise, show how Fig. 6.6 applies to the climb of an edge dislocation connecting two screws and how the crystal grows as the dislocation moves.

Since climb changes the shape of the crystal, it may be involved in some cases of plastic flow such as the Kirkendall effect. Bardeen and Herring (1952) have shown how an excess or deficiency of vacancies or interstitial atoms (over the equilibrium value) gives a driving force for climb. They have also interpreted the Kirkendall effect by the Frank-Read mechanism operating in climb.

6.7 Intersection of Dislocations. The preceding sections discussed *one* dislocation whose slip surface consisted of *two* intersecting plane sections. This section deals with *two* dislocations—one on each of two intersecting slip planes. When a dislocation moves on its slip plane, it must intersect other dislocations on other slip planes. The intersection of dislocations is important in work hardening because of the following facts:

1. Energy is required to make the dislocations cut. We shall show by a purely geometrical argument that, in general, the cutting increases the length—and therefore the energy—of one or both dislocations. Thus intersecting dislocations interfere with one another's motion and thereby contribute to work hardening.

2. In general, the point on a dislocation where it was cut cannot glide freely with the rest of the dislocation; instead it drags and impedes the motion.

We begin with a simple example where a dislocation is cut by slip on an intersecting slip plane; for the present it does not matter how the intersecting slip took place. Figure 6.7 shows the effect of intersecting slip on a closed loop of edge dislocation. Figure 6.7*a* shows an incomplete plane of atoms lying in the plane of the drawing and bounded by the closed loop of pure edge dislocation $ABCD$. The circles represent atoms in the extra plane; the Burgers vector of $ABCD$ is normal to the figure.

Consider what happens if slip occurs on a plane that cuts through $ABCD$. For example, let the slip vector of the intersecting slip system be $\mathbf{b}_i$, which lies in the plane of $ABCD$ as shown in Fig. 6.7*b*; the intersecting slip plane cuts the plane of the drawing along the dashed line. Figure 6.7*b* shows how the intersecting slip cuts $ABCD$ in two and displaces the two halves by $\mathbf{b}_i$. The sections of dislocation AD and BC have acquired what are called *jogs* at the points where they were cut by the intersecting slip. The jogs PP' and QQ' are short segments of dislocation equal in magnitude and direction to the slip vector $\mathbf{b}_i$ of the intersecting slip systems. Section 4.6 discussed jogs as sources and sinks for vacancies and interstitial atoms.

Now consider the dislocation associated with the intersecting slip. Figures 6.8 and 6.9 illustrate the intersection in three dimensions. The section AD of edge dislocation is shown in its slip plane P_{AD}. The Burgers vector $\mathbf{b}$ of AD is shown in Fig. 6.8 ($\mathbf{b}$ is normal to Fig. 6.7). The edge dislocation XY with slip vector $\mathbf{b}_i$ (shown) glides over its slip plane P_{XY}. In the area swept out by XY, the two sides of the slip plane are offset by $\mathbf{b}_i$; consequently AD is cut in two and its two halves are displaced by $\mathbf{b}_i$ as shown in Fig. 6.9. Since a dislocation cannot end inside the crystal, the two halves of AD must be connected by a short section of dislocation—in other words, by a jog. Thus again we have the jogged section $APP'D$, as in Fig. 6.7*b*. The cutting has increased the total energy of the dislocations by the energy of the jog; hence, there is resistance to the cutting and we have a mechanism of hardening.

The energy of a jog is the order of Gb^3 where G = shear modulus. (The line tension of a dislocation is roughly Gb^2, and a jog is a section of dis-

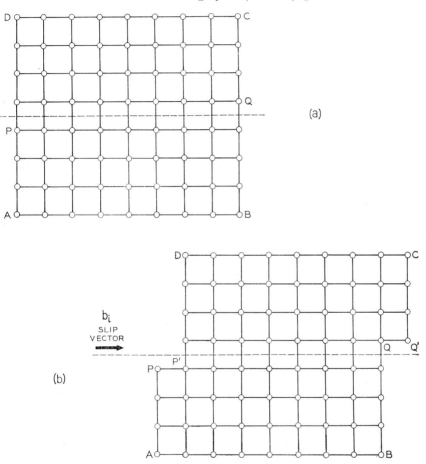

FIG. 6.7 (a) The circles represent an incomplete plane of atoms lying in the plane of the figure. The boundary $ABCD$ is a closed loop of edge dislocation (Burgers vector normal to the figure). Unit slip occurs on a slip plane that is inclined to the plane of the figure and intersects the latter along the dashed line. (b) The intersecting slip creates jogs PP' and QQ' in the dislocation; these jogs are segments of edge dislocation equal in length and direction to the slip vector $\mathbf{b}_i$ of the intersecting slip system.

location of length b.) As an exercise suppose there are a number of dislocations parallel and similar to AD equally spaced on P_{AD}; find the shear stress required to make XY cut through them as a function of their spacing.

Figures 6.8 and 6.9 show one edge dislocation cutting another. In the

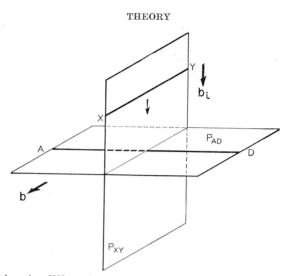

FIG. 6.8 A dislocation XY moving on its slip plane P_{XY} is about to cut the dislocation AD. The Burgers vector of XY is $\mathbf{b}_i$. AD has Burgers vector $\mathbf{b}$ and lies on the slip plane P_{AD}.

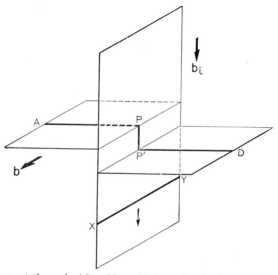

FIG. 6.9 XY has cut through AD. Now AD has a jog PP' (as in Fig. 6.7). PP' has the direction and magnitude of $\mathbf{b}_i$.

following paragraph, we consider the intersection of an edge and a screw. After that it will be a short step to a general theorem about cutting and jogs.

Let the screw dislocation be the dislocation in Fig. 2.2, where the crystal is one continuous atomic plane in the form of a helicoid, or spiral ramp. Figure 6.10 represents the same crystal by a helical surface; the atoms are considered to lie between successive layers of the helical surface. To reveal the interior of the crystal, the upper half is not shown in Fig. 6.10; however, it joins continuously onto the lower half along the jagged line.   The spiral ramp continues upward and ends in a step AB on the upper surface (Fig. 2.2).   The vertical line in Fig. 6.10 is the screw dislocation; its slip vector (not shown) is parallel to it.

Next consider a dislocation whose slip plane is normal to the screw dislocation in Fig. 6.10—for example, the dislocation EF in Fig. 6.10, which lies on the spiral surface.   Assume that EF is pure edge and that its slip

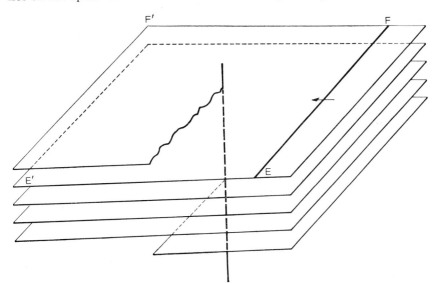

Fig. 6.10 Part of a crystal containing a screw dislocation (vertical line).   The crystal consists of a single atomic plane in the form of a helicoid, or spiral ramp.   The atoms lie between successive layers of the spiral surface shown.   This is part of the crystal in Fig. 2.2; the upper part of the crystal is not shown, but it joins continuously onto the lower part along the jagged line.   The line EF is another dislocation, which is gliding to the left on the spiral surface.   The point E moves to E'; F moves to F'.

vector is normal to the screw dislocation.   Then the spiral surface is the slip surface of EF.   Suppose EF glides over the spiral surface from right to left (as shown by the arrow). E goes to E' and F to F'.   However, E' and F' are not in the same slip plane.   Thus $E'F'$ must have a jog where it jumps from one level of the ramp to the next, and it must have acquired that jog when it cut the screw dislocation.   Figure 6.11 shows the jog, which is equal in magnitude and direction to the slip vector of the vertical screw dislocation.   The slip vector shown in Fig. 6.11 is the slip vector of the moving edge dislocation EF.

Figure 6.11 illustrates a point that will be discussed further in Sec. 6.8. When the moving dislocation EF in Fig. 6.10 cuts through the screw dislocation and acquires a jog, its slip surface is changed.   Before the cutting, *EF* could glide on an (approximately) plane slip surface.   After the cutting, its slip surface is stepped; the jog glides on the step and sweeps out the area which is shown shaded in Fig. 6.11.   In Fig. 6.11, where the moving dislocation is pure edge, the jog can glide freely in the direction of motion of the dislocation.   The motion of the jog, however, forms the subject of Sec. 6.8.

We have now considered two examples of dislocation intersection—an edge cutting an edge and an edge cutting a screw.   From these examples,

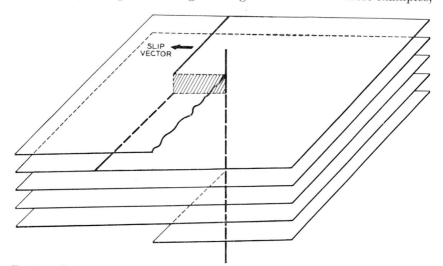

FIG. 6.11 Same as Fig. 6.10 after the moving dislocation (*EF* in Fig. 6.10) has cut the vertical screw dislocation and acquired a jog.   Now the moving dislocation glides on a stepped slip surface; the jog glides on the step and sweeps out the shaded area.   The slip vector of the moving dislocation is shown and is normal to the dislocation—therefore parallel to the direction of motion of the jog.

it is a short step to a general theorem.   First however consider an important distinction that can be illustrated by the following problem: In the first example (Fig. 6.9) only the stationary dislocation acquired a jog; in the second example (Fig. 6.11) a jog appeared only in the moving dislocation.   Why?   (The reader may wish to solve this problem for himself before going on to the answer, which is given in the following paragraph.)

The answer is that a jog must be normal to the slip plane of the dislocation; a jog lying *in* the slip plane would immediately be eliminated since the dislocation would straighten out by pure glide.   As an exercise apply this result to the preceding two examples—Figs. 6.8 to 6.11.   Observe how the slip surface in Fig. 6.7 is changed by the intersection; construct a diffusion process that would restore the original condition, shown in Fig. 6.7a.

Now we are in a position to state the general theorem about intersections and jogs: *When one dislocation cuts another, each dislocation acquires a jog equal to the component normal to its own slip plane of the other dislocation's Burgers vector.* Thus the energy of the two dislocations is increased—by the jog energy—unless each Burgers vector lies in both slip planes.

The following section shows how jogs slow up a moving dislocation. First however, a word about the so-far-neglected forces between the intersecting dislocations. Each dislocation lies, for a short distance, in the region of high elastic stress around the other dislocation. Thus, near the point of closest approach, the dislocations exert high local forces on one another. The only effect of such forces is to distort the shape of the dislocations locally. For example, suppose the dislocations repel, so that the moving dislocation stops as it approaches the other. However, since the forces are local, the sections of moving dislocation far from the obstruction keep moving. Show how the moving dislocation goes by and leaves a bulge around the other, and how the bulge is pinched off and contracts to nothing. The net result is independent of how the dislocations deform before cutting; hence no generality is lost in the simple picture of straight dislocations.

6.8 Motion of a Jog.[1] This section shows that, in general, a jog in a moving dislocation produces a drag that slows down the dislocation. Also, the moving jog leaves behind a trail of lattice vacancies or interstitial atoms except in the special case where the moving dislocation is pure edge (as was the case for both examples in Sec. 6.7).

To approach the general case, return to Figs. 6.10 and 6.11 and consider again how the slip surface of the moving dislocation changes when the dislocation acquires a jog. After intersecting the screw dislocation, the slip surface of *EF* has a step, which is shown shaded in Fig. 6.11. The step is in all cases parallel to the slip vector, which in the special case of Fig. 6.11 is normal to the dislocation. Thus in Fig. 6.11 the jog can glide along with the dislocation and still have the same normal velocity as the rest of the dislocation. This is always true of a jog in an edge dislocation. However, it is not true in general, as the following argument will show.

Take the opposite extreme, where the moving dislocation *EF* in Fig. 6.10 is pure screw. After it cuts the vertical screw dislocation, it acquires a jog, as before. Now, however, the jog can *glide* only in the direction *parallel* to the moving dislocation (since its slip vector is parallel to the moving dislocation). Thus the jog can move along with the moving dis-

<hr>

[1] The ideas presented in this section were developed in private communication with F. C. Frank and discussed briefly by Read and Shockley (1952a). Similar ideas have been discussed by F. Seitz (1952).

location *only if it climbs.* Figure 6.12 shows the climbing jog in three dimensions. The figure is the same as Fig. 6.11 except that the slip vector of the moving dislocation is rotated through 90° as shown. The two sides of the step are displaced by the slip (Burgers) vector, *which now is normal to the step.* Thus, the moving jog leaves behind a void, which is shown by the shaded volume in Fig. 6.12. Actually, it is more convenient to think of the void as a close-packed row of vacancies. If the slip vector of the moving dislocation were reversed, the vacancies would be replaced by a close-packed row of interstitial atoms.

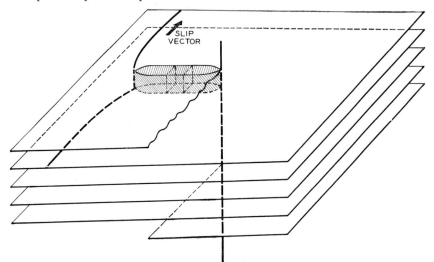

SLIP VECTOR

Fig. 6.12 Same as Fig. 6.11 except that the moving dislocation (*EF* in Fig. 6.10) was originally pure screw; now the Burgers vector is normal to the direction of motion of the jog; the jog, therefore, moves by climb and leaves behind a void in the crystal consisting of a row of vacancies (shaded volume).

We now show how the jog produces a drag on the moving dislocation. Energy is required to create the vacancies left behind by the jog. The jog therefore cannot move so rapidly as the rest of the dislocation (which moves by pure glide). Consequently the jog drags behind and forms the tip of a cusp in the moving dislocation, as Fig. 6.12 shows. The line tension in the two sections of cusp provides an added force on the dragging jog. The cusp becomes deeper and sharper, and the force on the jog increases until the jog can keep up with the moving dislocation. The force of the cusp on the jog must be sufficient to furnish the energy for creating the trail of vacancies. The following paragraph proves that, when there is only a single jog, the cusp can always drag the jog along with the moving dislocation no matter how fast the latter is moving. (The reader may wish to prove this as an exercise before going on.)

Assume that the cusp angle is zero. Then, at the tip of the cusp, we have two parallel opposite edge dislocations on different levels of the spiral ramp. These opposite sections of dislocation attract and therefore line up one directly above the other. Such a configuration, however, *is* a trail of vacancies. Actually, the cusp angle would not have to be zero since distortional energy is released as the two branches of the cusp approach one another, and some of this energy could go into forming vacancies. (Throughout this section it is understood that, when the slip vector of the moving dislocation is reversed, vacancies are replaced by interstitial atoms.)

Finally, consider the case where the moving dislocation *EF* in Fig. 6.10 is between the edge and screw orientations. We can distinguish the following two geometrically possible motions, of which the first appears to be physically unreasonable:

1. Suppose the jog moves by pure glide. If the dislocation makes an angle α with its slip vector, then the slip plane of the jog is a step inclined at an angle α to the dislocation. Thus, in Fig. 6.11, where the dislocation is pure edge, the step (shaded) is normal to the moving dislocation; so the jog can move with the moving dislocation and have the same normal velocity as the latter. In the general case, however, the jog has to move with csc α times the normal velocity of the dislocation. For a fast-moving dislocation and small α this might require the jog to move faster than sound—which is impossible. For any α except $\alpha = 90°$, the jog would have a component of velocity tangential to the dislocation; however, there is no driving force for such a component (see Prob. 6 for a further discussion of the gliding jog). Thus we conclude that, although it is geometrically possible for a jog to move by pure glide, it seems physically unlikely that it would do so except for $\alpha = 90°$.

2. Suppose that the jog moves along the normal to the moving dislocation—as in Figs. 6.11 and 6.12. The jog then moves partly by climb and partly by glide and leaves behind a trail of vacancies. As an exercise, show that the vacancies are spaced at intervals of sec α atomic spacings. Thus in Fig. 6.11 ($\alpha = 90°$) there are no vacancies (infinite spacing), and in Fig. 6.12 there is a closed-packed trail—one vacancy per atomic distance moved by the jog. The drag of the jog (work done per unit displacement) will be equal to the energy of a vacancy times the density of vacancies, which is proportional to cos α. Thus the drag due to jogs is a maximum for screw dislocations and is zero for pure edge dislocations. We have already seen that a moving screw dislocation can drag the jog along with it (so that the jog moves along the normal to the moving dislocation). Since the drag is a maximum for a pure screw ($\alpha = 0$), we conclude that the moving dislocation can always drag the jog along with it.

The fact that jogs exert a greater drag on screws than on edges has applications to plastic deformation, as the following section shows.

6.9 Application to Plastic Deformation. This section shows how dislocation intersections and moving jogs can play a significant role in plastic deformation and produce effects that one can measure.

A dislocation gliding across a slip plane intersects other dislocations and acquires jogs. For example, suppose a circular loop of dislocation has expanded to a radius R on its slip plane. It will have on the average $\pi R \rho / 2$ jogs per unit length where ρ is the number of other dislocations that cut unit area of its slip plane and have Burgers vectors that do not lie in that slip plane. As R increases, the drag due to the jogs may become sufficient to prevent the dislocation from moving under the applied stress.

Since jogs cause a much greater drag on screw dislocations than on edge dislocations, we would expect screws to move more slowly (other things being equal). Chen and Pond (1952) appear to have evidence that screws *do* move more slowly. Their evidence comes from moving pictures of slip lines as viewed (1) along the slip vector and (2) almost at right angles to the slip vector. As an exercise, describe what Chen and Pond would see if expanding loops of dislocation are generated by a Frank-Read source inside the crystal and the edge sections move faster than the screw sections. (The answer is what Chen and Pond do, in fact, observe.)

The vacancies and interstitial atoms left behind by a moving jog have short-range stress fields which may impede the motion of other dislocations and contribute, in a very small way, to work hardening.

Seitz (1952) has suggested that there is experimental evidence for the generation of vacancies by moving dislocations: Gyulai and Hartly (1928) observed that the electrolytic conductivity of silver chloride increased during plastic deformation.

6.10 Formation of L-shaped Dislocations by Intersection. This section illustrates one of several simple ways whereby the Frank-Read multiplication mechanism could originate in plastic deformation.

Figure 6.13 shows two dislocations AB and CD on different slip planes. However they have the *same* Burgers vector. Let the signs of the two Burgers vectors be the same when AB is considered to go from A to B and CD from C to D. The two slip planes P_{AB} and P_{CD} intersect along a line parallel to the slip vector **b** as shown. Apply a shearing stress τ on P_{CD} as shown; τ exerts a force on CD urging it to glide to the left; there is no force on AB.

As CD glides it intersects AB at the point P, Fig. 6.14. Now there are four dislocations going into the intersection point P. The total length of dislocation can be reduced and Burgers vectors conserved as follows: Let AP join onto PD; and CP, onto PB; now there are two L-shaped disloca-

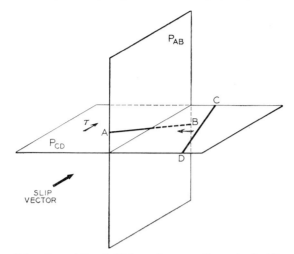

FIG. 6.13 Two dislocations AB and CD have the same slip vector but lie on intersecting slip planes P_{AB} and P_{CD}. Dislocation CD is moving to the left under the force due to the applied shear stress τ, which acts on the plane P_{CD}.

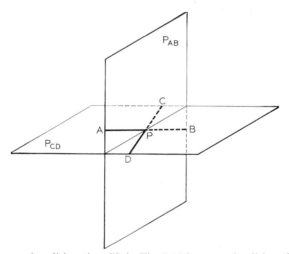

FIG. 6.14 The moving dislocation CD in Fig. 6.13 has met the dislocation AB at the point P.

tions, which separate and contract under their line tensions as Fig. 6.15 shows. Each of the two L-shaped segments can spiral; $P'D$ spirals around AP' and CP'' spirals around $P''B$.

L-shaped dislocations, which can spiral, are produced whenever the applied stress is sufficient to move dislocations far enough to intersect one another. This may be the origin of Frank-Read mechanisms in actual crystals.

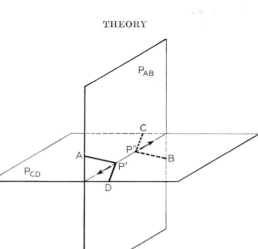

Fig. 6.15 The section of dislocation AP in Fig. 6.14 joins onto PD; CP joins onto PB. Now there are two L-shaped dislocations that separate and contract under their line tension. Either of the two L-shaped dislocations $AP'D$ and $CP''B$ can produce slip by the Frank-Read mechanism.

PROBLEMS

1. Use the approximation $T = Gb^2$ (Sec. 5.7) to find the approximate length of Frank-Read sources whose critical stress is equal to the observed yield stress in typical well-annealed metal crystals. Do the same for severely cold-worked crystals.

2. Consider a length of dislocation lying in a slip plane and running from an interior point to a free surface. Using the constant-line-tension approximation, show that the dislocation begins to operate as a Frank-Read source (of semicircular loops) at one-half the critical stress for a source consisting of the same length of dislocation connecting two interior points. See Fisher (1952) for the answer. Fisher suggests that the lower critical stress for surface sources may account for the fact that crystals flow more easily after a hardened surface layer (such as a layer of oxide or alloy) has been removed.

3. An alternative way of looking at Figs. 6.11 and 6.12 is as follows: Consider that there is no jog—rather the two sections of moving dislocation (on different levels of the ramp) are connected by a hairpin loop of dislocation going around the axis of the ramp. The two branches of the loop are parallel opposite dislocations one directly above the other on neighboring slip planes. This alternative description is physically equivalent to the moving-jog concept of the text. What would happen if each branch of the hairpin loop kept gliding under the applied stress? (According to Frank's dynamic multiplication mechanism, this might happen if the two branches had sufficient kinetic energy to overcome their strong mutual attraction.)

4. Imagine that the crystal in Fig. 2.2 contains a closed loop of pure edge dislocation in addition to the screw dislocation shown in the figure. Let the edge and screw have the same Burgers vector; the edge then lies in a plane normal to the screw. Initially the edge dislocation does not encircle the screw. However the closed loop of edge dislocation is expanding (by climb) as vacancies condense. What happens when the expanding loop of edge dislocation intersects the screw dislocation? Show how the edge dislocation can be quickly eliminated by pure slip, so that only the screw remains after the intersection. (HINT: Use the ideas illustrated in Figs. 6.14 and 6.15.)

5. Let the form of the rotating steady-state Frank-Read spiral be expressed in cylindrical coordinates r, θ. Derive the differential equation for $r = r(\theta)$ from Eq. (5.7).

6. Consider a moving dislocation containing a dragging jog ($\alpha \neq 90°$). Let the dislocation approach a straight line at infinite distances from the jog. Use the results of Prob. 9a in Chap. 5 to show that, in steady-state motion, the cusp must be symmetrical. Use the result of Prob. 9c to draw the cusp for a cusp angle of 30°.

CHAPTER 7

PARTIAL DISLOCATIONS

7.1 Introduction. This chapter describes partial dislocations and their effect on slip lines and work hardening. Section 3.9 defined a partial dislocation as the high-energy boundary (within a crystal) of a low-energy fault. At present the most important faults appear to be the stacking faults in close-packed structures. Section 7.2 discusses stacking orders in close-packed structures and introduces a notation for describing them. Sections 7.3 to 7.13 deal entirely with the face-centered cubic structure (hereafter denoted by *f.c.c.*).

Sections 7.3 to 7.5 discuss stacking faults in f.c.c. If a stacking fault ends inside the crystal, its boundary is either a Frank partial (also called sessile) dislocation or a Shockley partial. (We shall frequently use *partial* to mean *partial dislocation.*) Section 7.6 describes the Shockley partial and Sec. 7.7, the Frank partial. The motion of a partial in f.c.c. (Sec. 7.8) is restricted to a plane—a fact which is used to explain why slip lines are relatively straight in f.c.c. metal crystals. A total dislocation lying in a {111} plane can split into a so-called extended dislocation, which is a pair of parallel Shockley partials connected by a strip of fault. Section 7.10 discusses the effect of faults and extended dislocations on slip lines and work hardening. Section 7.11 considers the possible origins of Frank dislocations. Section 7.12 discusses other possible partials associated with plane faults and introduces the Cottrell dislocation, which involves a bent fault. The Cottrell dislocation is shown to provide a simple mechanism of work hardening in f.c.c. crystals.

A twin boundary that is not quite coherent contains a type of partial dislocation known as a twinning dislocation (Sec. 7.13), which may play a significant role in twinning.

Section 7.14 covers the same subjects for hexagonal crystals (Zn, Cd, . . .). Many of the results carry over almost exactly—in particular, Shockley partial and extended dislocations are similar in the two structures; Frank partials are somewhat different.

Section 7.15 generalizes the analysis of faults and partials to any type of fault.

7.2 The Stacking Order in Close-packed Structures. This section reviews briefly the possible close-packed structures and the ways of describing them.

92

Face-centered cubic and hexagonal close-packed structures are two simple examples of spheres stacked in close packing. Imagine the stacking as follows: First lay down a close-packed layer; call it the *A* layer. The second layer can go in either of the two sets of hollows on the first layer; call these the *B* and *C* positions, respectively. Figure 7.1 shows the three positions *A*, *B*, and *C*; the letters denote the centers of the spheres as projected in the plane of the figure, which is parallel to the

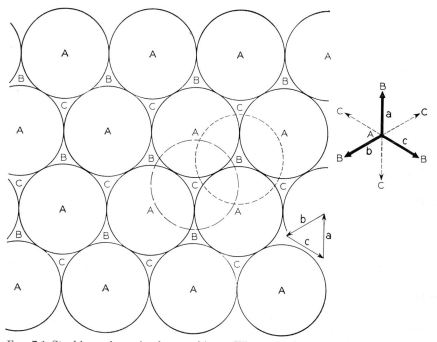

Fig. 7.1 Stacking spheres in close packing. When one close-packed layer has been laid down (the *A* layer), the next layer can go into either of the two sets of hollows (*B* or *C*) on the first layer. *A*, *B*, and *C* denote the centers of the spheres in the three possible positions. The vectors **a**, **b**, and **c** connect an *A* position with the three surrounding *B* positions (as projected in the plane of the figure).

close-packed planes of spheres. Every layer in the stack has to lie in one of the three positions—*A*, *B*, or *C*—if the stack is close packed. Any sequence of *A*'s, *B*'s, and *C*'s is called a stacking order; it represents a close-packed structure provided it contains no examples of *AA*, *BB*, or *CC*. The normal f.c.c. sequence is . . . *ABCABCABC* . . . ; here there are straight close-packed rows of atoms running both in *and at an angle* to the planes of Fig. 7.1. The normal hexagonal close-packed stacking sequence is . . . *ABABABAB* . . . ; here the only close-packed rows of atoms lie in the plane of the figure, which is the basal plane. At an angle to the basal plane, the nearest neighbor sequence is zigzag.

Frank has a convenient notation for describing any stacking sequence: he uses two symbols, ∇ and Δ, to represent the transition between two planes; ∇ means a transition in the ABC direction; Δ, in the reverse, CBA, sequence. Thus ABC is $\nabla\nabla$; ABA is $\nabla\Delta$. The f.c.c. structure is $\dots\nabla\nabla\nabla\nabla\nabla\dots$, or $\dots\Delta\Delta\Delta\Delta\Delta\dots$; an f.c.c. twin is $\dots\nabla\nabla\nabla\nabla\Delta\Delta\Delta\dots$. The normal hexagonal structure is $\dots\nabla\Delta\nabla\Delta\nabla\Delta\dots$.

7.3 Stacking Faults in Face-centered Cubic. A fault is a deviation from the normal stacking sequence. In f.c.c., where $\dots\nabla\nabla\nabla\nabla\dots$ represents the stacking order, any fault must involve replacing a ∇ with a Δ. This section discusses three simple operations that produce stacking faults in f.c.c.: (a) slip on a close-packed plane, where the slip vector is in the $<112>$ direction and is therefore not a **t** vector; (b) removing a close-packed plane and closing the gap; and (c) inserting a close-packed plane. The first two produce a $\dots\nabla\nabla\nabla\Delta\nabla\nabla\nabla\dots$ fault; the third produces a $\dots\nabla\nabla\nabla\Delta\Delta\nabla\nabla\nabla\dots$ fault. Sections 7.6 and 7.7 show that the three simple ways of producing a fault define three partial dislocations in f.c.c. We now look at a, b, and c in more detail:

a. Slip. Let the A, B, and C planes be (111) and let slip occur in the $[11\bar{2}]$ direction between an A and a B layer. The slip carries the B plane into an adjacent set of hollows, so that it becomes a C plane. For all the atomic planes on one side of the slip plane, $A \rightarrow B \rightarrow C \rightarrow A$. Thus the stacking sequence becomes $\dots B\ C\ A\ B\ C\ A \downarrow C\ A\ B\ C\ A\ B\dots$, where $\downarrow$ marks the slip plane. In the other notation it is $\dots\nabla\nabla\nabla\Delta\nabla\nabla\nabla\dots$. The left side of Fig. 7.2 shows an example of this fault viewed edge on and at right angles to the slip vector. The same fault appears in Fig. 7.4.

b. Removing a Plane. Exactly the same fault is produced by removing a B plane and closing up the gap by bringing the A and C planes together without offset. (By *offset* we mean *tangential displacement*.)

c. Inserting a Plane. Cut the crystal between a B and a C plane and insert an A plane. This gives $\dots ABCABACABCA\dots$. In the other notation, it is $\dots\nabla\nabla\nabla\Delta\Delta\nabla\nabla\nabla\dots$. Observe that this gives the same fault as doing a on each of two neighboring planes.

Before considering the partial dislocations associated with a, b, and c, let us look at the energies of the faults.

7.4 Energies of Stacking Faults. Shockley (private communication) estimates fault energies by counting next-nearest neighbor violations. In f.c.c., every sequence of three atomic planes *not* in the ABC or CBA order is a violation; for example, ABA is one. Shockley's scheme is an approximation—valid when *next-next*-nearest neighbor (and higher order) interactions are relatively unimportant energywise. As unit energy,

Shockley takes the energy of a coherent twin boundary (which has been measured for some metals). A twin in f.c.c. is . . . $ABCABCBACBA$ . . . or . . . $\nabla\nabla\nabla\nabla\triangle\triangle\triangle$ . . . ; it has one next-nearest neighbor violation, BCB. Note that the faults in Sec. 7.3 have two such violations. We can think of all stacking faults in f.c.c. as twins one or more atomic planes thick. If . . . $\nabla\nabla\nabla$ . . . is the normal sequence, each $\triangle$ represents one atomic layer of twin. Illustrate this by drawing the atoms in a $(\bar{1}01)$ plane (as in Fig. 7.2). The faults in Sec. 7.3 were one- and two-layer twins; in each case there were two twin boundaries—hence an energy of 2 on Shockley's scale.

Fullman (1951) obtained 19 ergs/cm² for the coherent twin boundary of copper. For aluminum he gets a larger value, of the order of 100 to 200 ergs/cm². (What he measured was the ratio of twin-boundary energy to average grain-boundary energy; the latter is not known for aluminum; it is probably around 500 to 1,000 ergs/cm². Fullman obtained a ratio of 1:5—which makes the twin energy 100 to 200 ergs/cm².)

7.5 Geometry and Crystallography of Faults, f Vectors. This section defines what we call **f** vectors; **f** vectors describe faults in much the same way that Burgers vectors describe dislocations. In a single crystal, the orientation is the same on the two sides of a fault; one-half of the crystal is simply translated relative to the other; the translation vector is defined as the **f** vector of the fault.

Before giving some examples of **f** vectors, we introduce a notation for vectors in the cubic systems: Take, for example, the **t** vector in f.c.c. whose components are $\frac{1}{2}$, $\frac{1}{2}$, 0—the cube edge being unit length. In the notation we are going to use, we write

$$\mathbf{t} = [\tfrac{1}{2}\,\tfrac{1}{2}\,0] = \tfrac{1}{2}[110]$$

The *class* of **t** vectors in f.c.c. is written as $\frac{1}{2}<110>$. Now consider the vectors that describe faults.

Suppose the plane of Fig. 7.1 is the (111) plane in f.c.c. The vector $\mathbf{n} = \frac{1}{3}[111]$ is normal to the plane of the figure and equal in magnitude to an interplanar spacing. The vectors **a**, **b**, and **c** lie in the plane of the figure and connect an A position with the three surrounding B positions (they also connect a B with the three surrounding C's, etc.). Thus

$$\mathbf{a} = \tfrac{1}{6}[\bar{2}11]$$
$$\mathbf{b} = \tfrac{1}{6}[1\bar{2}1]$$
$$\mathbf{c} = \tfrac{1}{6}[11\bar{2}]$$

The f.c.c. stacking sequence in the $+\mathbf{n}$ direction is. . . $ABCA$ . . . (**n** is out of the plane of the figure in Fig. 7.1, and up in Fig. 7.2). In Fig. 7.1, $\mathbf{n} + \mathbf{a}$ connects an atom in the A plane with an atom in the B plane just above. The **t** vectors in f.c.c. are $\pm(\mathbf{a} - \mathbf{b})$, $\pm(\mathbf{n} + \mathbf{a})$, and so on for all permutations of **a**, **b**, and **c**. (Show that **n** − **a** *is not* a **t** vector.)

What are the **f** vectors for the faults in Sec. 7.3? To define the sign of **f**, let **f** be the displacement of the atomic plane on the +**n** side of the cut or slip plane relative to the material on the −**n** side. Take operations (*a*), (*b*), and (*c*) in order.

a. Slip. Here we have pure slip on a close-packed plane; **f** equals **a**, **b**, or **c** (they all give the same fault). Observe that **f** could not equal

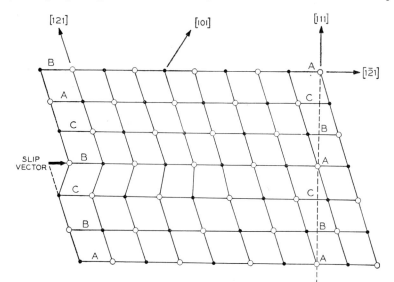

Fig. 7.2 A Shockley partial dislocation in the edge orientation in face-centered cubic. The plane of the figure ($\bar{1}$01) is normal to the dislocation. The slip vector $\frac{1}{6}[1\bar{2}1]$ is shown. Note the fault on the left of the partial dislocation. The open and solid circles represent atoms in different elevations.

−**a**, −**b**, or −**c**; if it did there would be an *AA*-type sequence, which violates *nearest* neighbor requirements.

b. Removing a Plane. The part of the crystal above the missing plane drops directly down to close the gap; so **f** = −**n**. The fault is the same as in *a*—which illustrates the following general theorem: *Two **f** vectors describe the same fault if they differ by a **t** vector.* Note that

$$\mathbf{a} - (-\mathbf{n}) = \mathbf{a} + \mathbf{n}$$

which is a **t** vector.

c. Inserting a Plane. The upper half crystal is raised up to make room for the inserted plane; so **f** = +**n**.

Sections 7.6 and 7.7 show how *a*, *b*, and *c* lead to three partial dislocations when the fault ends inside the crystal.

Many of the properties of partial dislocations follow from the properties of faults. A particularly important property of stacking faults is that *a given stacking fault can lie on only one plane* ("given" here means "given **f** vector"). The most general form of a stacking fault is a plane surface. For example, a fault with $\mathbf{f} = \mathbf{a} = \frac{1}{6}[1\bar{2}1]$ could exist only on the (111) plane. On any other plane, it would be, not a low-energy fault, but a high-energy misfit surface with nearest neighbors severely disturbed. For example, draw $\mathbf{f} = \frac{1}{6}[1\bar{2}1]$ on the $(\bar{1}01)$ plane.

Partial dislocations and their properties are easily derived from the properties of faults.

7.6 Shockley Partial Dislocations. If a fault ends inside the crystal, its boundary is a partial dislocation. Section 3.9 discussed partial dislocations briefly. Along a partial dislocation, nearest neighbor relations are violated; the maximum misfit energy per atom is higher than for a fault and lower than for a total dislocation. This section and Sec. 7.7 take up again the three ways—*a*, *b*, and *c*—of making a fault; now, however, the slipped area, or the missing or inserted atomic plane, does not go completely through the crystal.

a. Nonuniform Slip. Figure 7.2 shows a (111) plane viewed edge on looking in the $[\bar{1}01]$ direction, which is normal to the figure. Slip has occurred over part of the (111) plane. The slip vector is $\frac{1}{6}[1\bar{2}1]$, which is *not* a **t** vector. Hence the slipped area (on the left) is faulted. The boundary of the slipped area runs normal to the figure; this boundary is, by definition, a partial dislocation. In the next paragraph, we find the Burgers vector.

We have to redefine *Burgers vector* for a *partial* dislocation since a partial dislocation is not completely surrounded by good material. Frank (1951) gives the following procedure: begin the Burgers circuit on the fault and go into good material, making a sequence of steps along **t** vectors such that the same sequence would close in a perfect crystal. Now however, the last step will not be an atom-to-atom step; in other words, the closure failure (= Burgers vector) is not a **t** vector. As an exercise, make a Burgers circuit in Fig. 7.2 and find the Burgers vector. (HINT: make a closed circuit in a perfect crystal and show how introducing the dislocation opens it.) The Burgers vector is always a possible **f** vector of the fault—but *not* vice versa. (Remember that any fault has a number of **f** vectors; if **f** is one, **f** + **t** is another where **t** is a **t** vector.)

In Fig. 7.2 the Burgers vector $\frac{1}{6}[1\bar{2}1]$ lies in the plane of the drawing: so the partial dislocation is in the edge orientation.

Since a stacking fault has to lie in one plane, the partial dislocation must also lie in that plane. A total dislocation can follow any *space* curve, but a partial dislocation must be a *plane* curve.

Consider how to eliminate a partial dislocation. The procedure is essentially the same as for a total dislocation: make a cut and displace its sides by the Burgers vector. Now, however, we cannot choose the cut arbitrarily: the cut must be on the fault. This limits the ways—at least the simple ways—of making or eliminating a partial dislocation.

It is hardly necessary to prove that the conservation of Burgers vectors holds for partial dislocations. The boundary (within the crystal) of a fault closes on itself, ends on the external surface, or joins other dislocations (total or partial) at a node.

The dislocation in Fig. 7.2 is one example of a type introduced by Heidenreich and Shockley (1948). A *partial dislocation whose Burgers vector lies in the plane of the fault is called a Shockley partial.*

A Shockley partial can form any curve in the plane of its fault; the angle α between the dislocation and its Burgers vector can have any value. Figure 7.2 shows the edge orientation. It is easy to construct a drawing like Fig. 2.3 for a Shockley partial in the screw orientation. Figure 7.3 shows a Shockley partial running at an angle of 30° to its Burgers vector; the dislocation is horizontal in the drawing. In the general case, the orientation varies along the dislocation line. As an exercise, construct a figure like Fig. 2.5 for a curved Shockley partial which is pure screw at one end and pure edge at the other.

The Shockley partial is one of the three types of partial dislocations associated with plane faults in f.c.c. The other two (discussed in the following section) are Frank partial dislocations.

7.7 Frank Partial (Sessile) Dislocations. This section discusses the partial dislocations for operations b and c of Sec. 7.3. Now, however, we remove or insert only *part* of a plane.

b. Removing Part of a Close-packed Plane. Again we close up the gap without offset so that the adjoining planes come together along the normal (a B plane remains a B plane, etc.). Figure 7.4 shows the result. The fault is the same as in Fig. 7.2. The Burgers vector $-\mathbf{n}$ is normal to the fault. Again the dislocation can be any closed curve in the plane of the fault. However, it is always pure edge since the Burgers vector is normal to the fault. *A partial whose Burgers vector is not parallel to the fault is a Frank partial dislocation;* it is also called a sessile dislocation, for reasons that will become clear later. There are two kinds of Frank partials in f.c.c.: they differ in the sign of the Burgers vector $\pm\mathbf{n}$. The one in Fig. 7.4, where part of a plane has been removed, is a *negative* Frank partial. Part c of this section describes the positive Frank partial.

Observe that the atomic misfit in Fig. 7.4 is greater than in Fig. 7.2 but less than for a total dislocation. We have already mentioned that the energy of a dislocation varies (approximately) as the Burgers vector squared. Thus a Shockley partial has approximately $\frac{1}{3}$ the energy of a

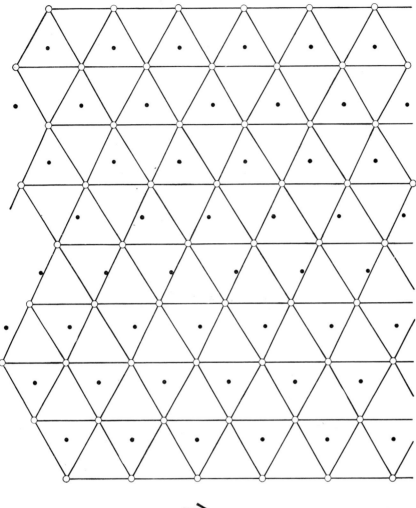

SLIP VECTOR

FIG. 7.3 A Shockley partial dislocation viewed along the normal to its slip plane, which is a close-packed plane. The open circles are atoms just above the slip plane, the solid circles, atoms just below. The dislocation runs horizontally across the figure at an angle of 30° to its slip vector. The material on one side of the dislocation is faulted. Since only two planes of atoms are shown, the fault could be on either side of the partial, and the figure could apply to either the face-centered cubic or hexagonal close-packed (or almost close-packed) structure.

total dislocation, and a Frank partial, $\frac{2}{3}$ (taking the cube edge as unit length, $\mathbf{a}^2 = \mathbf{b}^2 = \mathbf{c}^2 = \frac{1}{6}$, $\mathbf{n}^2 = \frac{1}{3}$, $\mathbf{t}^2 = \frac{1}{2}$).

c. Inserting Part of a Plane. Here we cut the crystal, move the two halves apart without offset, and insert a close-packed plane. If the inserted plane ends inside the crystal, its boundary is a *positive* Frank partial; the Burgers vector is $+\mathbf{n}$. It also is pure edge and can have any shape in the plane of the fault. As an exercise construct a drawing like Fig. 7.4 showing a positive Frank partial.

The sign of $\pm\mathbf{n}$ for a Frank partial has a real physical significance. The positive Frank partial has a *two*-layer twin on the *compression* side; the negative Frank partial has a *one*-layer twin on the *tension* side. The

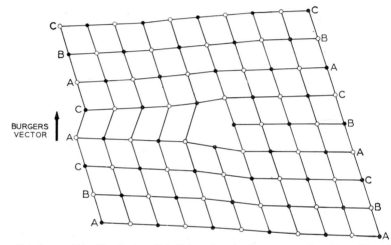

BURGERS VECTOR

Fig. 7.4 A negative Frank (sessile) dislocation in face-centered cubic. The plane of the drawing is (10$\bar{1}$), and the dislocation runs normal to the figure. Note that the fault is the same as in Fig. 7.2.

negative total edge dislocation, by contrast, is simply the positive turned upside down; the difference is only a matter of convention.

As an exercise show that two negative (or two positive) Frank partials can combine and annihilate one another and that a positive and a negative Frank dislocation would not necessarily annihilate one another if they combined. The answer is in the following paragraph.

The Burgers vector of a Frank partial has been defined with respect to the fault. The direction of the Burgers vector in a fixed reference system, however, would be reversed if the fault were changed from the left side of the partial to the right side. For example, consider two parallel negative Frank partials; one partial is on the right of its fault (as in Fig. 7.4); the other partial is on the left of *its* fault (Fig. 7.4 turned upside down). If the two faults lie on the same (111) plane, the two partials can move together (by climb) and annihilate one another. Thus we conclude that the two partials have opposite Burgers vectors even though both are negative Frank partials. An alternative is to say that they have the same Burgers vector but run in opposite directions.

7.8 Partial Dislocations in Motion. The motion of a partial is restricted to the plane of its fault. Thus a Shockley partial can glide but not climb and a Frank partial can climb but not glide. Consider first the Shockley partial. Everything that Chap. 4 said about glide of a total dislocation applies to a Shockley partial: it glides easily, causes a macroscopic deformation, and experiences a force in a stress field. However it cannot climb. A Shockley partial in the pure screw orientation cannot glide on any plane except the plane of the fault.

As an exercise, show how the atoms move when the dislocations in Figs. 7.2 and 7.3 glide.

A Frank partial can move only by climb—as atoms are added to or removed from the edge of the incomplete atomic plane. Illustrate this for the Frank dislocation in Fig. 7.4.

A dislocation which cannot glide, but has to move by some form of mass transport, is called **sessile.** Frank dislocations are always sessile and are often called sessile dislocations. Dislocations that can move by pure slip, such as the Shockley partial and all total dislocations, are called **glissile.**

A stress produces a force on a partial dislocation just as it does on a total dislocation; the components of force are given by exactly the same formulas.

We next consider the origin of partial dislocations and their role in deformation.

7.9 Extended Dislocations. Heidenreich and Shockley (1948) showed how a total dislocation on a $\{111\}$ plane can split into what is called an extended dislocation. An extended dislocation is two partials connected by a section of fault. This section discusses the extended dislocation; the following section shows why it is important in plastic deformation.

Consider a total dislocation with Burgers vector $\frac{1}{2}[\bar{1}10]$ and slip plane (111). This dislocation is equivalent to two superposed Shockley partials having Burgers vectors $\frac{1}{6}[\bar{2}11]$ and $\frac{1}{6}[\bar{1}2\bar{1}]$, respectively. The partials could move apart by pure glide on the (111) plane. When the partials are exactly superposed, the fault of one cancels the fault of the other, since the two **f** vectors add up to a **t** vector. If they move apart, there is a striplike region between them where the fault of one is not canceled by the fault of the other. The two parallel Shockley partials connected by a strip of fault form an *extended* dislocation.

It may be helpful to imagine the extended dislocation in terms of slip. First suppose the total dislocation is the boundary of a slipped area on a (111) slip plane. In the slipped area, an atom originally in an A position has slipped into the next A position; call the two positions A_1 and A_2. As the dislocation sweeps by, it shifts an atom from A_1 to A_2. Now suppose the dislocation splits and becomes an extended dislocation. As the extended dislocation sweeps over the slip plane, the first partial slips the same A atom into a B position, thus producing a fault; the second partial slips it from the B position into the next A position, thus terminating the fault. Here the sequence is $A_1 \rightarrow B \rightarrow A_2$, instead of $A_1 \rightarrow A_2$ as it would be for a total dislocation.

An extended dislocation is called edge or screw according to its orientation with respect to the resultant $\frac{1}{2} <110>$ Burgers vector. Show that, in an extended edge or screw dislocation, neither of the two partials can be either edge or screw. As an exercise, draw a pure screw total dislocation and show how it splits into Shockley partials that are part screw and part edge. The left half of the drawing is already done in Fig. 7.3; complete the right-hand side by showing the transition between the faulted and completely slipped regions. Note that the fault could terminate (on the right) in either of two Shockley partials. Thus Fig. 7.3 could represent the left half of either of two extended dislocations.

This takes care of *how* dislocations split. We now consider *why*. If energy is proportional to Burgers vector squared, then each Shockley partial has one-third the energy of a total; the splitting therefore seems to be energetically favorable. An exact treatment of this will have to wait until Chap. 9, where the stress field around a partial is calculated. It turns out that, at least in the isotropic case, the pair of parallel partials always exert repulsive forces on one another. The repulsive force falls off inversely as the separation. The surface tension (= energy per unit area) of the connecting fault holds the partials together. The partials move apart until their mutual repulsion is equal to the constant surface tension of the fault. Note that surface tension, energy per unit area, and force on a dislocation have the same dimensions, dynes/cm = ergs/cm^2.

The equilibrium separation of the partials is called the width of the extended dislocation; it varies with orientation. Chapter 9 shows that, in the isotropic case, the width varies by a factor of approximately 2 from the edge to screw orientations. The calculation has not been made for anisotropic elasticity. There might be some orientations in highly anisotropic crystals where dislocations on close-packed planes would *not* split.

Recently, J. F. Nye (unpublished) noticed extended dislocations in some of the early photographs of three-dimensional bubble rafts.

The next section discusses some of the reasons why extended dislocations are important in plastic deformation.

7.10 Faults and Extended Dislocations in Plastic Deformation. The following are a few examples of why faults and extended dislocations are important in slip and work hardening.

a. Straight vs. Wavy Slip Lines. Extended dislocations affect the form of slip lines. In α iron and other crystals where slip lines are wavy, screw dislocations gliding through the crystal evidently shift freely from one slip plane to another. Extended dislocations in f.c.c. can*not* do this because every partial is confined to a single plane. If an extended screw dislocation wants to shift from one plane to another, it must first collapse into a single dislocation, then split into a second pair of partials on the second plane. For example, a dislocation with $\frac{1}{2}[110]$ Burgers vector can split into an extended dislocation on either $(\bar{1}11)$ or $(1\bar{1}1)$. On $(\bar{1}11)$ the Burgers vectors of the partials are $\frac{1}{6}[211]$ and $\frac{1}{6}[12\bar{1}]$, respectively; on the $(1\bar{1}1)$ plane they are $\frac{1}{6}[21\bar{1}]$ and $\frac{1}{6}[121]$. Note that, in each case, the two Burgers vectors lie on the slip plane and add up to the original Burgers vector.

The strong repulsion between the two partials prevents their coming together. The dislocation therefore remains on one slip plane and produces a straight slip line. This may be the reason why slip lines are relatively straight in f.c.c. metals (Read and Shockley, 1952a). At present there is no reason to suppose that dislocations in body-centered cubic have anything to gain by splitting; if they *do not* split, the screws can glide in any direction and produce wavy slip lines, like the ones in α iron. However, if a screw dislocation is not symmetrical, there will be an activation energy for it to change slip planes (see end of Sec. 4.3).

b. Slip on {111} Planes in Face-centered Cubic. Face-centered-cubic metals have a decided preference for slip on the close-packed planes. We can explain this as follows: Extended dislocations have less energy than others, and they lie on {111} planes; therefore dislocations should form more easily on {111} planes. For example, the critical stress for the Frank-Read mechanism is proportional to dislocation energy; the mechanism should therefore operate preferentially on {111} planes.

c. Critical Resolved Shear Stress Law. It seems physically reasonable that an f.c.c. crystal would slip more easily in a $<112>$ direction than in a $<110>$ direction. (To see this, try sliding one close-packed plane of ball bearings over another in the two directions.) Yet slip is governed by the resolved shear stress in a $<110>$ direction. Mathewson (1951) calls this *incongruent shear*. If slip starts in a $<112>$ direction, it must proceed by closely coupled $<112>$ movements which add up to $<110>$ slip. The extended dislocation explains why these movements are closely coupled: the two partials are held together by the connecting strip of fault.

d. Faults and Work Hardening. Consider a fault that extends completely through the crystal, and let slip take place on a plane that intersects the fault. If the slip vector is not parallel to the fault, the intersecting slip cuts the fault into two halves, which are displaced parallel to the slip vector. Now each of the halves has a boundary within the crystal. These boundaries, by definition, are partial dislocations. The slip that cuts the fault has to supply the energy to create the partials. Therefore a fault is a barrier to slip on an intersecting plane. This agrees with Barrett's (1952b) observation that pronounced faulting (in Cu-Si alloys) hardens the crystal.

Before leaving this example, let us see what happens to the two new partials created by cutting the fault. These two must have equal and opposite Burgers vectors. Probably the new partials will be Shockley partials rather than Frank partials—since the former appear to have a lower energy. Each partial can glide in the plane of its fault and leave behind good crystal. This is like cutting a soap film in two; the two halves shrink under their surface tension. Each partial experiences a force due to the surface tension of its fault. Initially the partials are held close together by a strong attraction. (Chapter 9 will show that opposite dislocations always attract; this can be seen from the fact that they would annihilate one another if they combined.) As slip on the intersecting plane continues, the slip planes of the partials are moved farther apart and the mutual attraction decreases; when the attraction has become less than the surface tension of the faults, the two halves of the fault shrink and disappear as the partials glide over the faulted area.

e. Extended Dislocations and Hardening. Section 6.9 showed how dislocations can harden intersecting slip systems. The slip has to cut through the dislocations and produce jogs. An extended dislocation is hard to cut; where it jogs, the partials have to come together. Thus an extended dislocation has to unsplit before it can be cut. The mutual repulsion of the partials resists this.

7.11 Origin of Frank Partial Dislocations. This section discusses the possible origins of Frank dislocations and their role in deformation.

Frank dislocations could form in the following three ways: (*a*) by splitting of a total dislocation, (*b*) by condensation of vacancies or interstitial atoms, (*c*) by combination of a Shockley partial with a total dislocation. We now discuss these in order and consider the conditions where each might happen.

a. Splitting. A total dislocation with $\frac{1}{2}[110]$ Burgers vector might lie on any one of the four {111} planes; of these, two are possible slip planes. Section 7.9 showed how extended dislocations could form on the two slip planes. This section shows how a total dislocation could become extended on any of the four {111} planes. First, however, it will be convenient to describe what are called dislocation reactions: a combination of two or more dislocations or a splitting of a dislocation into several dislocations is known as a dislocation **reaction.** A reaction is represented by an equation relating the Burgers vectors; for example,

$\frac{1}{2}[110] = \frac{1}{6}[211] + \frac{1}{6}[12\bar{1}]$ represents the splitting of a total dislocation into two Shockley partials. The accompanying table gives the four possible reactions in which a total dislocation on a $\{111\}$ plane can become extended. The plane of the fault—or plane on which the reaction occurs —is listed in each case.

Plane	Reaction
$(\bar{1}11)$	$\frac{1}{2}[110] = \frac{1}{6}[211] + \frac{1}{6}[12\bar{1}]$
$(1\bar{1}1)$	$\frac{1}{2}[110] = \frac{1}{6}[21\bar{1}] + \frac{1}{6}[121]$
$(11\bar{1})$	$\frac{1}{2}[110] = \frac{1}{3}[11\bar{1}] + \frac{1}{6}[112]$
(111)	$\frac{1}{2}[110] = \frac{1}{3}[111] + \frac{1}{6}[11\bar{2}]$

Thus there are two kinds of extended dislocations a Shockley-Shockley and a Shockley-Frank; we have already discussed the Shockley-Shockley and seen that it can glide freely. The Shockley-Frank extended dislocation (third and fourth examples above) cannot glide although the splitting itself requires only glide.

When any total dislocation splits into a Frank and a Shockley partial, the Frank partial must be negative. Why? Illustrate this case by showing how the fault in Fig. 7.2 could end in a Frank partial like the one in Fig. 7.4 but with the fault on the right of the dislocation.

Energywise, the third and fourth cases are doubtful. The Burgers-vector-squared measure of energy shows no energy change. Isotropic elasticity (Chap. 9) gives zero force between the partials. However, a more exact analysis, using anisotropic elasticity, might show a repulsive force in some cases—perhaps a strong enough force to overcome the surface tension of the fault.

We have not yet considered the question whether all dislocations in f.c.c. *do* split into extended dislocations; they can all be resolved into segments in $\{111\}$ planes; however, if the segments are only a few atoms long, they would not have room to split. Thus an arbitrarily curved dislocation is probably not extended; a straight dislocation longer than the width of an extended dislocation probably is extended.

b. Condensation of Vacancies or Interstitials. The simplest way to form a Frank partial is to remove or insert part of a close-packed plane. Physically, this means the condensation of vacancies or interstitial atoms on a (111) plane. The result would be a close loop of Frank dislocation.

Begin with vacancies and consider first the kinetics. Brooks (unpublished) shows that the condensation of vacancies in a cluster on one plane is a nucleation problem, similar to the nucleation of new atomic layers on a growth face (Chap. 10). Whether or not stable clusters would develop depends critically on the concentration of vacancies in excess of the equilibrium value. Brooks's analysis of the kinetics concludes that it is doubtful whether the vacancies would condense even in the most favorable case, where the excess of vacancies is equal to their equilibrium concentration at the melting point (such supersaturation would occur in sudden freezing). Of course, the excess vacancies will freeze out eventually, probably by diffusing to edge dislocations.

Assuming that there *are* conditions where vacancies condense in a cluster, let us look at the crystallography. The vacancies form a disklike void on a {111} plane. When enough vacancies have accumulated, the adjoining atomic planes come together and close up the void. The closing can happen in the following two ways:

1. As discussed in *b* of Secs. 7.3, 7.5, and 7.7 the two adjoining planes can come together without offset and produce a one-layer fault surrounded by a negative Frank partial.
2. The two atomic planes could come together with an offset so that their relative displacement is $\frac{1}{2}<110>$. This means, for example, removing a *B* plane and shifting all the planes above it so that $C \rightarrow B \rightarrow A \rightarrow C$. Now there is no fault and the missing plane is surrounded by a closed loop of total dislocation which can glide on a cylindrical slip surface inclined at an angle to the missing {111} plane.

Now consider the energies in the two cases. For a small loop the energy of the loop dominates and case 1 has less energy. For a large loop, the energy of the fault dominates and case 2 is favored. We conclude that 1 is the initial condition and that as the missing atomic plane grows 2 becomes the low-energy form. However, the change from 1 to 2 has a high activation energy, since it requires the formation of a closed loop of Shockley partial which glides over the entire area of the fault (thus eliminating the fault) and combines with the Frank partial to form a total dislocation (see Prob. 2). In view of the energy necessary to create the Shockley partial, we conclude that, if the vacancies *do* condense in a cluster, they probably form a closed loop of negative Frank partial.

The same argument holds for condensing interstitial atoms except that case 2 produces a *positive* Frank partial around a *two*-layer fault; now *two* Shockley partials are required to change 1 to 2. If only one layer is eliminated, the remaining layer is surrounded by a partial having a $\frac{1}{6}<411>$ Burgers vector—we discuss this in *c* below.

c. Combination of a Shockley Partial with a Total Dislocation on an Intersecting Slip Plane. Frank partials can be formed indirectly by combination of a total dislocation with a Shockley partial. This is the converse of one of the splits discussed in Sec. 7.10. An example of the combination—in terms of Burgers vectors—is

$$\frac{1}{2}[110] \quad + \quad \frac{1}{6}[1\overline{1}2] \quad = \quad \frac{1}{3}[11\overline{1}]$$

(Total dislocation) + (Shockley partial) = (Frank partial)

According to the Burgers-vector-squared rule, this combination reduces the total dislocation energy by a factor of 2. Thus whenever the total dislocation and the Shockley partial come close together, they could combine. Pure glide can therefore produce a Frank partial. However, if the Shockley partial is part of a Shockley-Shockley extended dislocation, the above combination gives a Shockley-Frank extended dislocation; and, as we have seen, this may not be stable; it might collapse into a total dislocation under the surface tension of the fault.

Could a positive Frank partial also originate in pure slip? To answer this, take a Shockley partial and add its Burgers vector to each of the t vectors; physically each addition represents a combination of the Shockley partial with a total dislocation. Use the Burgers-vectors-squared energy criterion to find the energetically favorable combinations and show that all of them have already been discussed except

$$\tfrac{1}{2}[110] + \tfrac{1}{6}[1\bar{2}1] = \tfrac{1}{6}[411]$$

or, in the other notation,

$$(\mathbf{n} + \mathbf{b}) + \mathbf{a} = \mathbf{n} - \mathbf{c}$$

The sum of the Burgers vectors squared on the left is $\tfrac{1}{2} + \tfrac{1}{6} = \tfrac{2}{3}$; and on the right, $\tfrac{1}{2}$—an energy reduction of 16.7 per cent. The vector $\mathbf{n} - \mathbf{c} = \tfrac{1}{6}[411]$ has the same length as a t vector. We have mentioned this partial before—there is a one-layer fault on the compression side. It is the same as a positive Frank partial superposed on a Shockley partial—just as a total dislocation may be the same as a *negative* Frank partial superposed on a Shockley partial. The $\tfrac{1}{6}\langle411\rangle$-type partial is also a sessile since its Burgers vector is inclined at an angle to its fault. As an exercise illustrate this partial by a drawing similar to Figs. 7.2 and 7.4.

What happens if the $\tfrac{1}{6}\langle411\rangle$ partial splits and the Shockley partial glides away from the fixed Frank partial? The Shockley partial leaves behind a two-layer fault connecting it with the Frank partial (draw this, as an exercise). On the other side of the Shockley partial is a one-layer fault. Since these two faults have the same energy, the surface tensions produce no net force on the Shockley partial. Again both the Burgers-vectors-squared energy criterion and isotropic elasticity show no force between the two partials. Thus, we cannot tell under what conditions—if any—a $\tfrac{1}{6}\langle411\rangle$ partial would split. Conclusion: If positive Frank partials do not form in pure slip (by combination), then $\tfrac{1}{6}\langle411\rangle$-type partials do.

7.12 Other Partials in Face-centered Cubic—Cottrell's Dislocation. So far we have considered only single plane faults. In this section we shall (1) show that we have already considered all the possible partials corresponding to plane stacking faults one or two layers thick, and (2) discuss Cottrell's extended dislocation, which consists of two Shockley partials connected by a *bent* fault, the bend itself being a new type of partial.

1. A given fault can end only on a partial dislocation whose Burgers vector is an **f** vector of the fault. When one **f** vector is known, all the others can be found by adding that one to each of the **t** vectors. Thus we can find all possible partial dislocations corresponding to a one-layer twin by combining a Shockley partial with each of the total dislocations; the result either is unstable or is one of the partials already considered. We can obtain the same result for a two-layer twin by combining a positive Frank partial with each of the total dislocations.

2. Cottrell's extended dislocation forms when two Shockley extended dislocations on different {111} planes combine. Let A and B be the two Shockley extended dislocations. A lies on the $(1\bar{1}1)$ plane and has split into Shockley partials A_1 and A_2 having Burgers vectors $\frac{1}{6}[121]$ and $\frac{1}{6}[21\bar{1}]$, respectively. B lies on the (111) plane and has split into partials B_1 and B_2 with Burgers vectors $\frac{1}{6}[1\bar{2}1]$ and $\frac{1}{6}[\bar{1}12]$, respectively. Both A_1 and A_2 attract both B_1 and B_2. Show that the attraction between A_2 and B_2 is the strongest. When A_2 and B_2 combine, they form a partial C whose Burgers vector is $\frac{1}{6}[101]$. We now have a V-shaped fault consisting of two plane sections that join along C; in other words, C *is* the sharp bend in the V-shaped fault. The two plane sections of fault connect C with A_1 and B_1, respectively. We call the three dislocations (A_1, B_1, and C) and the two connecting sections of fault a *Cottrell extended dislocation*. It was proposed by Cottrell (1952) following a suggestion of Lomer (1951).

Consider next the stability of Cottrell's dislocation: Use the Burgers-vector-squared criterion to show that A_1 and B_1 attract one another and would like to come together at C and form a total dislocation. However show that, if A_1, B_1, and C *did* combine, the total energy would increase. In other words A_1 and B_1 are more strongly repelled by C than they are attracted to one another. Hence the Cottrell extended dislocation is stable.

Now consider the motion of Cottrell's dislocation and its role in work hardening. It is easily seen to be a supersessile dislocation; it cannot move even by climb. It provides a simple mechanism of work hardening in f.c.c. crystals because (1) it forms during plastic deformation and (2) it is a fixed source of internal stress. The fact that it forms during slip on intersecting planes agrees with the fact that f.c.c. crystals work harden more than hexagonal close-packed crystals.

This concludes the discussion of faults and partial dislocations in f.c.c. single crystals. The next section deals with partial dislocations in f.c.c. twin boundaries.

7.13 Twinning Dislocations. A stacking fault that ends inside the crystal on a Shockley partial is a one-layer twin. An N-layer twin is N stacking faults, one above the other; suppose they all end on Shockley partials; the row of partials is a noncoherent twin boundary (twin boundary that does not coincide with the twinning plane).

Another way of looking at it is this: Resolve the noncoherent twin boundary into plane sections of coherent twin interface connected by steps; each step goes from one (111) plane to the next parallel plane. When the twin boundary is almost parallel to the twinning plane, the steps are widely spaced. Figure 7.5 shows one such step. The plane of

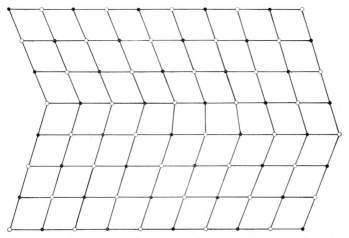

FIG. 7.5 A twinning dislocation in face-centered cubic. The plane of the figure ($\bar{1}01$) is normal to the dislocation. The twinning dislocation is a sidewise step in an otherwise coherent twin interface.

the drawing is ($\bar{1}01$), as in Figs. 7.2 and 7.4. The twin interface is viewed edge on; the step runs normal to the drawing. Observe that the step in the otherwise coherent twin boundary is similar to a Shockley partial (compare Figs. 7.2 and 7.5). Frank and van der Merwe (1949), who discovered this dislocation, named it a twinning dislocation. Section 3.9 discussed it briefly.

Frank defines the Burgers vector of a twinning dislocation as the closure failure of a circuit that would close in a perfect (coherent) twin. A twinning dislocation can glide on the twin interface; every twinning dislocation that does so changes one atomic plane from the untwinned to the twinned state—or vice versa.

As an exercise, draw a twinning dislocation that terminates at a point in the twin interface; show that this point is a node where the twinning dislocation joins two total dislocations coming in from the twinned and untwinned sides, respectively. Apply the conservation of Burgers vectors to show that the two $\frac{1}{2}<110>$ Burgers vectors are related by the shear transformation characteristic of the twinning. Observe that the twin interface here is shaped like the upper surface of the crystal in Fig. 2.2. Cottrell and Bilby (1951) show how the twinning dislocation can rotate about the node and glide up the spiral ramp so that the twinned region grows at the expense of the untwinned. This is similar to the Frank-Read mechanism except that the rotating dislocation runs up the spiral ramp as it glides. In the steady state, a rotating spiral develops and glides up the spiral ramp. Illustrate this by a drawing similar to Fig. 6.10. For a more complete discussion, see Cottrell and Bilby (1951).

7.14 Faults and Partial Dislocations in Hexagonal Crystals. Many of the results in the previous sections carry over to hexagonal crystals. This section reviews the similarities and brings out the differences between the f.c.c. and hexagonal cases. Figure 7.1 and the ABC and $\nabla\Delta$ notations apply also to hexagonal crystals. The normal sequence is . . . $ABABABAB$ . . . or . . . $\nabla\Delta\nabla\Delta\nabla\Delta\nabla\Delta$ . . . ; a fault involves three or more planes in the ABC order characteristic of f.c.c., or two or more ∇'s or Δ's together.

Consider the nearest-neighbor relations in the normal hexagonal case, other than those in the basal plane. Suppose we go from an atom in an A plane to an atom in the adjoining B plane. If we continue in the same straight line, we do *not* come to another atom in the next plane, which is an A plane. A path consisting of steps between nearest neighbors is zigzag, unless it lies in a basal plane. When there is a fault, and three or more planes follow the ABC order, then we can move in a straight line connecting nearest neighbors and there will be as many atoms on that line as there are planes in the ABC order. Faults are classified by the number of planes in the ABC sequence. If there are m planes in the ABC order, then there are $m - 2$ violations of next-nearest neighbor requirements. Again we use the number of such violations as a measure of fault energy.

The vectors $\mathbf{a}$, $\mathbf{b}$, $\mathbf{c}$, and $\mathbf{n}$ (Fig. 7.1) also apply to the hexagonal case. The $\mathbf{t}$ vectors (other than those in the basal planes) are $\pm 2\mathbf{n}$. No $\mathbf{t}$ vector connects atoms in adjoining basal planes. An atom in a B plane has nearest neighbors at $\pm\mathbf{n} + \mathbf{a}$. An atom in an A plane has neighbors at $\pm\mathbf{n} - \mathbf{a}$, and not at $\pm\mathbf{n} + \mathbf{a}$.

All stacking faults in hexagonal crystals are on basal planes; so any given partial dislocation is confined to a basal plane.

The following paragraphs discuss (in order) four simple operations that produce faults and partial dislocations. All the arguments in this section apply to both close-packed and non-close-packed hexagonal crystals; the arguments hold for any value of the ratio (spacing between basal planes)/(nearest neighbor spacing in the basal planes).

a. Slip, $A \to B \to C \to A$. This is similar to Sec. 7.3*a* in the f.c.c. case. In the slipped area, the stacking order becomes . . . $A\ B\ A\ B\ A \downarrow C$ $B\ C\ B\ C$ . . . where $\downarrow$ marks the slip plane; in Frank's notation, . . . $\triangle \triangledown \triangle \triangledown \triangle \triangle \triangle \triangledown \triangle \triangledown \triangle$ . . . . Here four planes $BACB$ are in the straight-line, f.c.c., order. There are two violations of next-nearest neighbor requirements, BAC and ACB; so the relative energy is 2.

If the fault ends inside the crystal, its boundary is a partial dislocation whose Burgers vector is **a**, **b**, or **c**; all these are possible **f** vectors of the fault and are parallel to the fault. Thus, by definition, the boundary of the fault is a Shockley partial. Shockley partials in hexagonal and f.c.c. crystals are very similar. Figure 7.3 could represent either (since it shows only two planes). As an exercise construct a figure like Fig. 7.2 showing a Shockley partial in the edge orientation in a hexagonal close-packed crystal.

As in f.c.c., the Shockley partial can have any shape in the plane of its fault and can glide in that plane; but it cannot climb or shift onto another slip plane. A total dislocation lying in a basal plane can split into an extended dislocation consisting of a pair of Shockley partials connected by a strip of fault. Again the hexagonal and f.c.c. cases are very similar. However in the hexagonal case, any given total dislocation can split into an extended dislocation on only one plane—the basal plane.

b. Removal of a Basal Plane—With Offset. This is *not* analogous to Sec. 7.3*b* in the f.c.c. case because the planes adjoining the missing plane cannot come together without offset to close the gap. If they did, the stacking order would have an AA sequence. In addition to coming together, the two A planes adjoining the gap must have an offset that shifts one A plane into either the B or the C hollows on the other A plane. For example, we can remove a B plane and, above the gap, shift $A \to B \to C$. Now we have . . . $A\ B\ A\ B\ A \downarrow B\ C\ B\ C\ B\ C\ B$ . . . ; so there are only three planes in the ABC order, hence, one violation of nearest neighbor requirements and one unit of energy on the relative scale.

Recall that in f.c.c. removing part of a {111} plane and bringing the adjoining planes together *with offset* produced a closed loop of total dislocation and no fault. In the hexagonal case, it produces a fault surrounded by a partial dislocation whose Burgers vector is one of the six vectors $-\mathbf{n} \pm \mathbf{a}$, $-\mathbf{n} \pm \mathbf{b}$, $-\mathbf{n} \pm \mathbf{c}$, which are possible **f** vectors of the fault. This dislocation is the negative Frank partial in the hexagonal case. It can climb but not glide. In a hexagonal close-packed crystal, the Burgers vector of a negative Frank partial is equal in magnitude to an interatomic spacing. Thus, as measured by Burgers vectors squared, the negative Frank partial has the same energy as a total dislocation and three times that of a Shockley partial. However the associated fault has only one-half the energy of the Shockley partial's fault.

As an exercise draw a figure like Fig. 7.4 for a negative Frank partial in a hexagonal crystal.

c. Inserting a Basal Plane—No Offset. Now insert a C plane between an A plane and the adjoining B plane where the latter are moved apart *without offset.* The stacking order becomes . . . $ABABABCABAB$ . . . ; which has five planes $ABCAB$ in the ABC order; three violations of next-nearest neighbor requirements ABC, BCA, and CAB; and a fault energy of three on the relative scale. The boundary (within the crystal) of the fault is a partial dislocation whose Burgers vector is $+\mathbf{n}$, which is an **f** vector of the fault. The partial is *one type* of positive Frank partial in a hexagonal crystal. The following introduces the other type.

d. Inserting a Basal Plane—With Offset. Again insert a C plane, but now give all the planes above the inserted plane an offset so that $A \to B \to C$, as in b (above). Now instead of . . . $ABABCABAB$ . . . we have . . . $A\ B\ A\ B\ C^{\downarrow}B\ C\ B\ C$ . . . where $\downarrow$ marks the offset— just above the inserted C plane. Observe that this is exactly the same fault as in b. But it terminates inside the crystal on a different partial: namely, on a positive Frank partial whose Burgers vector is $\mathbf{n} \pm \mathbf{a}, \mathbf{n} \pm \mathbf{b}$, or $\mathbf{n} \pm \mathbf{c}$; these vectors are all possible **f** vectors of the fault; they differ from the **f** vectors in b by **t** vectors; for example, $\mathbf{n} + \mathbf{a} - (-\mathbf{n} + \mathbf{a}) = 2\mathbf{n}$.

Now we compare the negative Frank partial and the two positive Frank partials; call the latter the **n** and **n** + **a** types, respectively. The **n** + **a** type has the same dislocation energy and the same fault as the negative Frank partial. Physically the two differ in that the fault is on the compression side in one case and on the tension side in the other.

Next consider the difference between the two positive Frank partials. The **n** + **a** type is equivalent to the **n** type superposed on a Shockley partial. We cannot (at present) say whether the combination is stable; the Burgers vectors are orthogonal. However the **n** type has a fault with three units of energy; the **n** + **a** type's fault has only one unit of energy. If the **n** + **a** Frank partial splits into an **n** type Frank partial plus a Shockley partial, and the Shockley partial glides away, it leaves behind a three-units-of-energy fault connecting it with the **n** partial. (Draw this, taking the Shockley partial in the edge orientation and normal to the plane of the drawing.) On the other side of the Shockley partial is a one-unit-of-energy fault. In other words, the fault of the Shockley partial cancels part of the fault of the **n** partial where the two faults overlap; what is left over is the unit-energy fault characteristic of an **n** + **a** partial. Between the partials (where the two faults do not overlap) there is a three-units-of-energy fault whose surface tension pulls the partials together. Thus the **n** + **a** partial *does* appear to be stable.

To conclude this section, consider the possible origins of Frank partials. They cannot form by simple slip or by splitting of a total dislocation.

There is no combination that appears to be energetically favorable in which Frank partials could originate. Thus condensation of vacancies or interstitials or other accidents of growth appear to be the logical possibilities. Section 7.11's discussion of vacancies condensing applies here. The result would be a fault surrounded by a negative Frank partial. The condensation of interstitials would produce a closed loop of **n**-type positive Frank partial surrounding a three-units-of-energy fault. As condensation continues and the loop grows, the **n** + **a**-type surrounding a unit-energy fault becomes the low-energy form. However the change would require creating a closed loop of Shockley partial, and this would have a very high activation energy.

Frank partials would play a relatively important role in work hardening since they constitute fixed sources of internal stress.

7.15 Other Possible Faults and Partials. We have seen how all the partial dislocations can be found for any given fault. The foregoing sections have found the partials for stacking faults in f.c.c. and hexagonal crystals. If other types of faults are discovered and found to be important in real crystals, then a new class of partial dislocations will emerge.

It may be that there are faults that can lie on more than one plane. Cottrell and Bilby (1951) have discussed a possible fault on the {112} planes in body-centered cubic. Here the **f** vector ($= \frac{1}{6}<111>$) lies in the fault. This fault can lie on a bent surface made up of sections parallel to two different {112} planes. Cottrell and Bilby showed how such a fault could grow into a deformation twin by a variation of the Frank-Read process.

PROBLEMS

1. Consider two parallel negative Frank partials whose faults lie on adjacent (111) planes in f.c.c. The fault is on the left of one partial and on the right of the other. A small excess of vacancies causes the two partials to climb toward one another. Draw the final equilibrium configuration when the dislocations meet; show that the two partials form a step in a one-layer stacking fault, and that the step repells vacancies. Apply the result to the case of vacancies condensing in a cluster on a (111) plane that intersects a screw dislocation.

2. In Sec. 7.11b, we showed how vacancies condensing in a cluster on a (111) plane could form (1) a closed loop of Frank partial surrounding a fault, or (2) a loop of total dislocation and no fault. Take E_s as the energy per unit area of the fault and

$$E_\perp = \frac{1}{2} Gb^2 R \ln \frac{R}{R_0}$$

as the energy of a circular loop of dislocation of radius R and Burgers vector b; R_0 is a constant roughly equal to an interatomic spacing. Calculate the critical radius R_c at which (2) becomes the stable form, and find the activation energy required to change from (1) to (2).

3. Show that in Sec. 7.14b the Burgers vector can be $-\mathbf{n} + \mathbf{a}$ or $-\mathbf{n} - \mathbf{a}$ no matter which plane (A or B) is removed, but that in Sec. 7.14d the sign of **a** in $\mathbf{n} \pm \mathbf{a}$ depends on where the extra plane is inserted.

CHAPTER 8

THE STRESS AROUND A DISLOCATION

A dislocation is surrounded by an elastic stress field that produces forces on other dislocations and interferes with their motion, thereby hardening the crystal. This chapter discusses the stress distributions for a number of cases where exact calculations have been made. Chapter 9 uses the results to find the forces between dislocations in various cases of practical interest.

8.1 Elastic Strain and Atomic Misfit. The distortion associated with a dislocation consists of (1) severe atomic misfit in the bad material, (2) elastic strain in the surrounding good material. The elastic strain in the immediate vicinity of the dislocation depends on the interaction of the good material with the bad. However, as we move away from the dislocation, elasticity theory gives the strain with increasing accuracy. For a straight dislocation, the stress varies inversely as the distance from it. At a distance of 1 micron from the dislocation, the stress is about 10^7 dynes/cm^2, which is approximately the yield stress for typical well-annealed single crystals of metals. This gives an idea of the range over which dislocations will interfere with one another's motion under the applied stress.

This chapter deals with straight dislocations. The stress field of an arbitrary curved dislocation can be expressed by integrals taken over the dislocation line or over surfaces terminating on the dislocation; see Burgers (1939) or Peach and Koehler (1950). Except in special cases, the calculation is laborious and has not yet been done. The stress around a straight dislocation will be a good approximation to that around a curved dislocation at distances that are small compared with the radius of curvature. The known stress fields around straight dislocations have had wide application. We have already seen examples in Chap. 7 in connection with the forces between partials in extended dislocations. Another important application is to the quantitative theory of grain-boundary energies.

This chapter deals first with edge and screw dislocations in elastically isotropic crystals, then discusses briefly the general anisotropic case and presents several useful results for special anisotropic cases where calculations have been made. Finally, the stored elastic energy of a straight dislocation is found.

114

8.2 Dislocations in Elastically Isotropic Crystals. Begin with the isotropic case, where the stress field is much simpler and easier to calculate. The results will be good approximations for almost isotropic crystals, such as tungsten and aluminum.

This chapter uses both the rectangular xyz and cylindrical $r\theta z$ coordinate systems; the z axis is along the dislocation. For a straight dislocation, nothing varies with z. Let u, v, and w be the x, y, and z components of the displacement of a material point from its position in the unstressed state. Consider in order (1) a screw dislocation, (2) an edge, and (3) a dislocation making an arbitrary angle with its Burgers vector.

Screw Dislocation. The helical form of the crystal in Fig. 2.2 suggests the deformation

$$u = 0$$
$$v = 0 \tag{8.1}$$
$$w = \frac{b}{2\pi} \tan^{-1} \frac{y}{x} = \frac{b}{2\pi} \theta$$

where b is the magnitude of the slip vector and θ has a range of 2π; we take the discontinuity in θ on the (arbitrary) slip plane.

The derivatives of u, v, and w give the strain components, which give the stresses. In rectangular coordinates, the stress has only two nonvanishing components:

$$\tau_{xz} = G\left(\frac{\partial w}{\partial x} + \frac{\partial u}{\partial z}\right) = -\frac{Gb}{2\pi} \frac{y}{x^2 + y^2} \tag{8.2}$$

$$\tau_{yz} = G\left(\frac{\partial w}{\partial y} + \frac{\partial v}{\partial z}\right) = \frac{Gb}{2\pi} \frac{x}{x^2 + y^2} \tag{8.3}$$

where G is the shear modulus. In cylindrical coordinates, there is only one nonvanishing component

$$\tau_{\theta z} = \frac{G}{r} \frac{\partial w}{\partial \theta} = \frac{Gb}{2\pi r} \tag{8.4}$$

$\tau_{\theta z}$ acts in the slip direction on all the possible slip ($\theta = $ constant) planes. Observe that the stress vanishes at infinity, as required.

The Appendix shows that this stress satisfies the condition of equilibrium and is therefore a possible state of stress in the elastic region. However, it is not a unique solution but only the first term of an infinite series. The Appendix shows that the higher order terms depend on the interaction of the elastically strained material with the bad material on the z axis. In the expressions for stress, the higher order terms add second and higher order powers of b/r, where each power is multiplied by a trigonometric function of θ. As we move away from the dislocation, the first term becomes an increasingly good approximation.

Edge Dislocation. Take the x axis along the Burgers vector of the dislocation so that xz is the slip plane, as before. The discontinuity in displacement has the components $\Delta u = b$, $\Delta v = \Delta w = 0$. The solution for a screw suggests $u = b\theta/2\pi$. This together with $v = (b/2\pi) \ln r$ satisfies the equations of equilibrium. However the corresponding surface stresses on any cylinder surrounding the z axis give a resultant force on the cylinder; this is a real physical force exerted on a material mass—as distinct from the force on a configuration. Since there is no net force on a mass in the interior of the crystal, the solution has to be modified. This is a critical point in the mathematical theory of dislocations since the solution for a net force is similar to that for a dislocation. In both cases, the stress varies as b/r.

A solution that satisfies all the requirements is

$$u = \frac{b}{2\pi}\left[\tan^{-1}\frac{y}{x} + \frac{1}{2(1-\nu)}\frac{xy}{x^2+y^2}\right] = \frac{b}{2\pi}\left[\theta + \frac{\sin 2\theta}{4(1-\nu)}\right] \tag{8.5}$$

$$v = \frac{-b}{8\pi(1-\nu)}\left[(1-2\nu)\ln(x^2+y^2) + \frac{x^2-y^2}{x^2+y^2}\right]$$

$$= -\frac{b}{2\pi}\left[\frac{1-2\nu}{2(1-\nu)}\ln r + \frac{\cos 2\theta}{4(1-\nu)}\right] \tag{8.6}$$

where ν is Poisson's ratio. The third component w vanishes.

Note that for a pure screw $u = v = 0$, and for an edge $w = 0$; in other words the displacements parallel and normal to the dislocation are separable; this is what makes the isotropic case easy.

Figure 8.1 illustrates the deformation of a circle around the edge dislocation. The difference in displacement of any two points on the circle depends only on θ, not on r; in addition, the circle has a rigid body translation proportional to $\ln r$. The figure arbitrarily takes the discontinuity in displacement on the slip plane—as in Fig. 3.1a.

The stress components in the xy plane are

$$\sigma_x = -\frac{\tau_0 by(3x^2+y^2)}{(x^2+y^2)^2} = -\frac{\tau_0 b}{r}\sin\theta\,(2+\cos 2\theta) \tag{8 7}$$

$$\sigma_y = \frac{\tau_0 by(x^2-y^2)}{(x^2+y^2)^2} = \frac{\tau_0 b}{r}\sin\theta\cos 2\theta \tag{8.8}$$

$$\tau_{xy} = \frac{\tau_0 bx(x^2-y^2)}{(x^2+y^2)^2} = \frac{\tau_0 b}{r}\cos\theta\cos 2\theta \tag{8.9}$$

where

$$\tau_0 = \frac{G}{2\pi(1-\nu)} \tag{8.10}$$

The shearing stresses components τ_{xz} and τ_{yz}, which involve w and $\partial/\partial z$, vanish.

The stress-strain relations together with $\partial w/\partial z = 0$ give

$$\sigma_z = \nu(\sigma_x + \sigma_y)$$
$$= 2\nu \frac{\tau_0 b y}{r^2} = -2\nu \frac{\tau_0 b}{r} \sin \theta \tag{8.11}$$

As an exercise verify that these stresses give zero net force and torque on any closed surface about the z axis. The force and torque on any volume of good material necessarily vanishes since the solution satisfies the equations of equilibrium (see Timoshenko, 1934, p. 195).

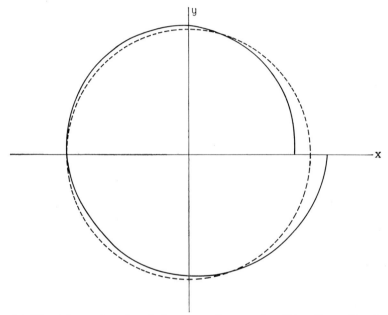

FIG. 8.1 The deformation of a circle surrounding an edge dislocation. The dashed line shows the unstrained circle; the solid line represents the same circle after a dislocation has been introduced at the center of the circle. Note the discontinuity in displacement on the slip plane.

Figure 8.2 pictures the stress; the components change sign on the eight lines separating the eight regions shown in the figure.

Equations (8.7) to (8.10), like the corresponding equations for a screw, represent only the first term in an infinite series; they become an increasingly good approximation as we move away from the dislocation.

Arbitrary Orientation. For an arbitrary angle α between the dislocation and its Burgers vector, the solution is equal to the sum of (1) the solution for a screw, with b replaced by $b \cos \alpha$, plus (2) the solution for an edge, with b replaced by $b \sin \alpha$. As an exercise show that the shearing stress τ on the slip plane and in the slip direction is given by $\tau = \tau_0 b/r$ where

$$\tau_0 = \frac{G}{2\pi(1-\nu)} \, (1 - \nu \cos^2 \alpha) \tag{8.12}$$

We next consider the isotropic case, where the stress depends on the orientation of the dislocation with respect to *both* its Burgers vector and the crystal axes.

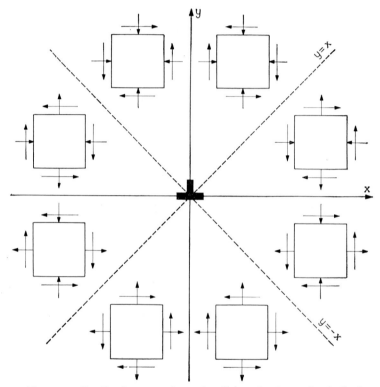

FIG. 8.2 The stress distribution around an edge dislocation in an elastically isotropic crystal. The stress components change sign on the boundaries of the eight regions shown.

8.3 General (Anisotropic) Case. Many of the results of the last section are true for any straight dislocation in a crystal with arbitrary (anisotropic) elastic constants C_{ij}. The stress is an infinite series in powers of b/r; the Burgers vector, elastic constants, and orientation of the dislocation determine uniquely the first term. Except near the dislocation, the first term dominates and stress varies as b/r times a periodic function of θ.

One of the most important quantities in dislocation theory is the shearing stress τ on the slip plane and in the direction of the Burgers vector; τ is always given by

$$\tau = \tau_0 \frac{b}{r} \tag{8.13}$$

plus higher order terms. Hereafter we shall forget about the higher order terms; it is understood that all solutions apply only where such terms are negligible.

The parameter τ_0 in Eq. (8.13) is basic in energy calculations, especially in the theory of grain-boundary energies. Equation (8.4) gives $\tau_0 = G/2\pi$ for a screw dislocation in the isotropic case; Eq. (8.10) gives τ_0 for an edge; both are special cases of (8.12).

Now consider specifically the anisotropic case: first some general results, then some special cases of practical value where solutions have been worked out.

Eshelby, Read, and Shockley (1953) have treated straight dislocations in the general anisotropic case; they find that the stress is given by the sum of three terms, where each term has the form

$$\frac{b(Ax + By)}{(x + py)^2 + q^2 y^2} \tag{8.14}$$

b is the magnitude of the Burgers vector, and A, B, p, and q are constants that depend on the elastic constants C_{ij} and the orientation of the dislocation and Burgers vector with respect to the crystal axes. The evaluation of the constants in particular cases is straightforward but laborious. For example, the three values of p and q are the real and imaginary parts of three complex conjugate pairs of roots of a sixth-order polynomial.

The displacements are linear combinations of three terms having the form

$$\ln\left[(x + py)^2 + q^2 y^2\right] = \ln r + \ln\left[(\cos\theta + p\sin\theta)^2 + q^2\sin^2\theta\right] \tag{8.15a}$$

and another three of the form

$$\tan^{-1}\frac{qy}{x + py} = \tan^{-1}\left(\frac{q}{p + \cot\theta}\right) \tag{8.15b}$$

The latter give the discontinuity in displacement. Observe that, as in the isotropic case, the stress varies as $1/r$ times a function of θ, and the displacement is equal to a function of θ plus a constant times $\ln r$.

Since the stress depends on periodic functions of θ, it is not affected by where we take the discontinuity in θ; that is, it does not matter whether the range of θ is 0 to 2π, $-\pi$ to π, etc. This is the mathematical expression of the arbitrariness of the cut, discussed in Sec. 3.7.

In the general anisotropic case, a pure screw involves all three components u, v, and w of displacement and all six components of stress. The same is true of a pure edge. Nothing is gained, therefore, by treating the edge and screw components separately as in the isotropic case. However, there are special cases where w is separable from u and v, for example, when the dislocation runs in a $<100>$ or $<110>$ direction in a cubic crystal. Eshelby, Read, and Shockley (1953) have solved these cases. The following are a few of their results that have practical applications, for example, to the prediction of grain-boundary energies. Here we list only the parameter τ_0:

For a dislocation in an $<001>$ direction with its Burgers vector in either a $\{100\}$ or $\{110\}$ plane containing the dislocation

$$\tau_0 = \frac{1}{2\pi}\left[C_{44}\cos^2\alpha + \sin^2\alpha\,(C_{11}+C_{12})\sqrt{\frac{C_{44}(C_{11}-C_{12})}{C_{11}(C_{11}+C_{12}+2C_{44})}}\right] \quad (8.16)$$

where α is the angle between Burgers vector and dislocation. The elastic constants C_{11}, C_{12}, C_{44} are tabulated for cubic crystals by Schmid and Boas (English translation, 1950, pp. 18, 19). Since the dislocation lies in an $<001>$ direction, α can have only certain values; these depend on the crystal structure. For simple cubic, either $\alpha = 0$ or $\alpha = \pi/2$. For face-centered cubic, $\alpha = \pi/2$ or $\alpha = \pi/4$. For body-centered cubic, $\alpha = \cos^{-1}(\frac{1}{3})^{\frac{1}{2}}$.

For a pure screw dislocation parallel to $<110>$ in face-centered cubic,

$$\tau_0 = \frac{1}{2\pi}\sqrt{\frac{C_{44}(C_{11}-C_{12})}{2}} \quad (8.17)$$

and the shear stress is the same on all planes containing the dislocation.

Eshelby (1949b) gives τ_0 for a pure edge dislocation parallel to $<110>$ in body-centered cubic.

8.4 Elastic Energy. The stored energy of distortion E_s for a single dislocation is the sum of (1) the energy of atomic misfit in the bad material, where elasticity does not apply, plus (2) the elastic energy in the good material. This section derives the elastic energy for a straight dislocation.

Elastic energy per unit volume is $\frac{1}{2}$ (stress) $\times$ (strain). Integrating the elastic energy density over the entire volume gives the total energy. However, there is a simpler procedure based on the method of forming a dislocation (Sec. 3.7): First cut the crystal on the slip plane; apply forces to the sides of the cut to maintain equilibrium; then slowly give the sides an offset **b**. The work done by the applied forces is the stored energy. Let us apply this procedure to find the elastic energy in the region between two cylindrical surfaces $r = R_1$ and $r = R_2$. Take R_1 large enough that the unknown higher order terms in the stress are negligible. The energy in the region is the work done on its boundary when the dislocation is formed. The *boundary* of an elastic region includes the two sides of the cut (which in this case is on the slip plane). Thus the boundary consists of the two cylinders plus the connecting section of slip plane. As an exercise show that the work done on one of the cylinders is the negative of that done on the other. (Include the fact that the net force on each cylinder necessarily vanishes; therefore no work is done in a rigid body translation of the cylinder.) We thus have to find only the work done on the slip plane, where the calculation is simple since the relative displacement (offset) of the adjoining planes is $\mathbf{b}$ = constant. The work is done by the shearing stress τ on the slip plane and in the slip direction; τ is given by Eq. (8.13). Thus the energy $E(R_1,R_2)$ in the region between the two cylinders is

$$
\begin{aligned}
E(R_1,R_2) &= \frac{b}{2} \int_{R_1}^{R_2} \tau(r)\, dr = \frac{b^2 \tau_0}{2} \int_{R_1}^{R_2} \frac{dr}{r} \\
&= \frac{b^2}{2} \tau_0 \ln \frac{R_2}{R_1}
\end{aligned}
\tag{8.18}
$$

Note that a single dislocation in an infinitely large crystal would have infinite elastic energy.

Show that the higher order terms contribute an energy which is localized near the dislocation and, therefore, independent of the size of the crystal provided the crystal is many atoms in extent. This localized elastic energy, added to the localized energy of atomic misfit, gives a total unknown energy $E(0,R_1)$ inside R_1. The total energy inside R_2 is therefore

$$
E(0,R_2) = \frac{b^2}{2} \tau_0 \ln \frac{R_2}{R_1} + E(0,R_1)
\tag{8.19}
$$

Thus the energy inside $R \gg b$ can be expressed by a single unknown parameter R_0:

$$
E(0,R) = \frac{b^2}{2} \tau_0 \ln \frac{R}{R_0}
\tag{8.20}
$$

R_0 can be estimated from measured grain-boundary energies; it is of the order of an atomic radius, as would be expected.

When many dislocations are present, their stress fields add. The total energy is the sum of the energy of each dislocation alone plus the energy of interaction; the latter can conveniently be represented by forces between dislocations, as Chap. 9 will show.

Thus far we have considered the energy rather than the free energy: Cottrell (1953) discusses the entropy of a dislocation and shows that the energy of a dislocation differs from the free energy by only a few kT

per atomic spacing along the dislocation (k = Boltzmann's constant, T = absolute temperature). The energy of a dislocation as given by Eq. (8.20) is several electron volts (per atomic spacing) for typical crystals and dimensions. At room temperature, $kT \approx \frac{1}{40}$ electron volt. Thus under most conditions the energy and free energy are approximately equal and the contribution of entropy to free energy can be neglected.

PROBLEMS[1]

1. Any state of plane strain ($w = \partial/\partial z = 0$) can be represented by what is called an Airy stress function $f(x,y)$ where

$$\sigma_x = \frac{\partial^2 f}{\partial y^2} \qquad \sigma_y = \frac{\partial^2 f}{\partial x^2} \qquad \tau_{xy} = -\frac{\partial^2 f}{\partial x\, \partial y}$$

Show that for an edge dislocation

$$f = -\tau_0\, by \ln r$$

2. When $u = v = \partial/\partial z = 0$, show that the most general state of stress is given by $\tau_{xz} + i\tau_{yz} = F(Z)$ where $i^2 = -1$, $Z = x + iy$, and F is an arbitrary function. Find $F(Z)$ for a screw dislocation.

3. Derive the results of the Appendix by requiring $F(Z)$ in the preceding problem to represent a single-valued analytic state of stress that vanishes at infinity—and has a singularity at $x = y = 0$.

4. Show that, for an edge dislocation,

$$\tau_{xy} = \tau_0\, \mathrm{Re}\, \frac{\partial}{\partial y} \frac{y}{Z}$$

where Re means *real part of* and $Z = x + iy$, as in the preceding problems.

5. In the Peierls-Nabarro analysis (Sec. 2.7), the relative displacement δ across the slip plane varies with x according to the relation $x = a \tan \pi \left(\frac{\delta}{b} - \frac{1}{2} \right)$ where $2a = b$ for a screw dislocation and $2(1 - \nu)a = b$ for an edge. Show that the shear stress τ on the slip plane is given by

$$\tau = \frac{G}{2\pi} \frac{ax}{a^2 + x^2}$$

Consider the work done on the slip plane in forming the dislocation. Show that, in addition to the work done in deforming the two (elastic) halves of the crystal, an amount of work $Ga/2\pi$ is done against the nonlinear forces acting across the slip plane (where the sine law holds).

6. If $u = v = 0$, $w = w\,(x,y)$ represents a stationary screw dislocation, show that $u = v = 0$ and

$$w = w\left(\frac{x - vt}{\sqrt{1 - \dfrac{v^2}{c^2}}}, y \right)$$

represents a screw dislocation moving in the x direction with velocity v, where c is sound velocity. For the proof see Cottrell (1953) or Frank (1949). This is the relativistic effect discussed in Sec. 4.8.

[1] Use isotropic elasticity in all problems.

7. Consider a screw dislocation at the center of a cylinder of radius R. Show that the stress field of the dislocation—as given by the equations in this chapter—produces a couple of magnitude $\frac{1}{2}GbR^2$ acting about the dislocation and on a plane normal to the dislocation. Show that we can remove this couple by adding a distribution of stress that vanishes as R approaches infinity and is negligibly small for $R \gg b$. For the solution see Cottrell (1953).

8. Show that the displacement $\mathbf{u}(x,y,z)$ due to an arbitrary dislocation with Burgers vector $\mathbf{b}$ is given by

$$\mathbf{F} \cdot \mathbf{u} = - \int_S \mathbf{b} \cdot \mathbf{P} \cdot d\mathbf{S}$$

where the dyadic $\mathbf{P}$ represents the stress that would be produced by an arbitrary force $\mathbf{F}$ acting at the point x,y,z (inside the crystal) and S is any surface bounded (within the crystal) by the dislocation; $d\mathbf{S}$ is normal to the surface S at each point and equal in magnitude to dS. *Hint:* Consider the interaction energy of the dislocation and the point force. (The author wishes to thank J. D. Eshelby for this problem.)

CHAPTER 9

FORCES BETWEEN DISLOCATIONS

9.1 Introduction. Chapter 5 showed how a dislocation experiences a force in a stress field; Chap. 8 found the stress fields around various dislocations. This chapter combines the two and finds the forces that dislocations exert on one another. It also discusses briefly Cottrell's analysis of the forces between dislocations and impurity atoms; Cottrell's theory explains the yield point observed in certain single crystals, and correctly predicts the time law of strain aging.

Section 9.2 proves, by physical arguments, that the formulas of Chap. 5 give the force on a dislocation in a stress field where that stress field is due to another dislocation. Section 9.3 shows how the work done by the force between dislocations comes from the stored energy E_s.

Section 9.4 calculates the forces between parallel screw dislocations and parallel edge dislocations. Section 9.5 shows how a simple two-dislocation model of a crystal can display many effects observed in actual crystals, for example, permanent plastic deformation, work hardening, lattice rotation, and change of elastic constants and internal friction during cold work. The model is also used to illustrate various types of energy exchange.

Section 9.6 calculates the width of an extended dislocation using isotropic elasticity. The width is found to vary by a factor of about 2 with dislocation orientation.

Section 9.7 discusses dislocations on intersecting slip planes. Section 9.8 shows how dislocations are attracted to an external surface; this effect in some cases can be represented by an image dislocation, similar to the image charge in electrostatics. Section 9.9 deals briefly with the nonuniform forces between nonparallel dislocations. Section 9.10 discusses Cottrell's analysis of the interaction of dislocations with impurity atoms.

9.2 Applied vs. Internal Stress. Chapter 5 derived the force on a dislocation in an externally applied stress field; that force depends only on the local value of the stress at the dislocation. This section will show that exactly the same formulas give the force in terms of the local stress when the local stress is an internal stress, such as the stress around another dislocation or other type of imperfection. This result is physically reasonable from the following intuitive argument. Since the force depends on the *local* stress at the dislocation, it should not matter whether the stress

124

is due to applied loads or to another dislocation. The following paragraph gives a rigorous proof, still using only physical arguments.

Chapter 5 considered a single dislocation and found the force from the work W done on the external surface by the applied stress. Now consider a crystal with two dislocations but no applied stress. Call the dislocations D_1 and D_2. Imagine the crystal divided into two halves C_1 and C_2, where C_1 contains only D_1, and C_2, only D_2. The two halves exert stresses on one another across the imaginary C_1-C_2 boundary. Focus attention just on C_2 and suppose D_2 moves so as to sweep out an area dA_2; this causes a macroscopic deformation of C_2, in which the stresses exerted on C_2 by C_1 do work dW_{12}. dW_{12} is mechanical work done on the surface of the half crystal C_2 by an external source of energy, namely, the other half crystal C_1. Therefore we can apply to dW_{12} the same argument applied to dW in Chap. 5 and obtain the same formulas for the force. Thus formulas (5.2) to (5.5) give the force on a dislocation in terms of the local stress field independently of the source of the stress. In the general case, the local stress is the sum of the applied stress and one or more internal stress fields. The force due to several superposed elastic stress fields is the sum of their individual forces (since superposed elastic stresses add).

9.3 Stored Energy and the Force between Dislocations. If a dislocation moves in the absence of an externally applied stress, then its energy of motion comes out of the stored elastic energy E_s and the force on the dislocation is, by definition, the change in E_s per unit area swept out by the dislocation in its motion. Thus, by definition, $\mathbf{F} = -\nabla E_s$ (∇ = gradient of). When there are *both* externally applied and internal stress fields, $\mathbf{F} = \nabla(W - E_s)$. This section takes a simple example of two parallel dislocations A and B with no applied stress and derives the formulas of Chap. 5 from $\mathbf{F} = -\nabla E_s$.

Take A and B parallel to the z axis. A is at 0, 0 and B is at x, y. Let B's slip plane be parallel to the xz plane. The stored energy E_s of the pair of dislocations is the sum of the following three terms:

E_A is the energy of A alone. It is called the self-energy of A.

E_B is the self-energy of B.

E_{AB} is the energy of interaction. It is equal to the work done by A's stress field in the deformation associated with B, or vice versa. If the dislocations are far enough from the external surface, the self-energies do not change if the dislocations move. $E_{AB}(x,y) = E_{BA}(x,y)$ depends on the relative position of the dislocations. If B moves, the force of A on B does work dW_{AB}. This work comes from the stored elastic energy $E_s = E_A + E_B + E_{AB}$ of the pair of dislocations. Thus

$$dW_{AB} = -dE_s = -dE_{AB}$$

dW_{AB} goes into B's energy of motion or is dissipated at B. From the definition $\mathbf{F} = -\boldsymbol{\nabla}E_s$, we have

$$F_x = -\frac{\partial E_{AB}}{\partial x}\,(x,y) \tag{9.1}$$

$$F_y = -\frac{\partial E_{AB}}{\partial y}\,(x,y) \tag{9.2}$$

According to Eq. (5.2) of Chap. 5, the x component of the force of A on B is

$$F_x = b_B \tau_{AB} \tag{9.3}$$

where $\mathbf{b}_B$ is B's Burgers vector and τ_{AB} is the component of A's stress field in the direction of $\mathbf{b}_B$ and on B's slip plane. The following argument derives (9.3) from (9.1).

By definition, E_{AB} is the work done by the stress field of A in the deformation associated with B. Imagine that B is created by making a cut along its slip plane and giving the two sides of the cut an offset $\mathbf{b}_B$. To be exact and take account of the width of the dislocation, let $\delta(x' - x)$ be the relative displacement of the two sides of the cut at a point x', where x is at the center of the dislocation. The exact form of the function δ is not known; however, except within a few atoms of the dislocation, it is constant; on the unslipped side of B, $\delta = 0$ and on the slipped side, $\delta = b_B$. The work done by the stress field of A in the process of forming B is (stress) $\times$ (displacement) integrated over the slip plane. Thus

$$E_{AB}(x,y) = \int_{-\infty}^{\infty} \tau_{AB}(x',y)\,\delta(x' - x)\,dx' \tag{9.4}$$

Differentiating gives

$$\frac{\partial E_{AB}(x,y)}{\partial x} = -\int_{-\infty}^{\infty} \tau_{AB}(x',y)\,\frac{d\delta}{dx'}\,(x' - x)dx'$$

If the dislocations are many atomic spacings apart, τ_{AB} will not vary appreciably over the width of a dislocation (where δ is changing from 0 to b_B). Thus

$$\frac{\partial E_{AB}(x,y)}{\partial x} = -\tau_{AB}(x,y)\int_{-\infty}^{\infty} \frac{d\delta}{dx'}\,(x' - x)dx' \tag{9.5}$$

$$= -\tau_{AB}\int_{0}^{b_B} d\delta = -b_B\tau_{AB}$$

Equations (9.5) and (9.1) give (9.3)—thus completing the proof.

If the dislocations are so close together that τ_{AB} *does* vary appreciably over the width of a dislocation, then the interaction will depend on the (at present) unknown interatomic forces in the overlapping bad regions, and the present derivation does not apply.

As an exercise go through the same argument for Eq. (9.2), either by using Eq. (9.3), together with the equilibrium equations, or by taking the cut on the yz plane. The result will be the same as the second of Eqs. (5.4) where $\mathbf{b}$ is the slip vector of B and the stress is due to A.

It is now a short step to the theorem: Equations (5.4) give the force that one dislocation exerts on another; the stress components refer to the stress field of the dislocation *exerting* the force and b and α refer to the dislocation *experiencing* the force. The following sections derive the force for several simple cases.

Observe that the force of A on B is equal and opposite to the force of B on A. (Recall that $E_{AB} = E_{BA}$.) Thus Newton's third law holds for dislocations.

9.4 Examples of Parallel Dislocations in the Isotropic Case. This section discusses (1) parallel screw dislocations, and (2) parallel edge dislocations on parallel slip planes. Consider only the isotropic case, so we can use Eqs. (8.1) to (8.11).

Parallel Screws. Take the two dislocations and their Burgers vectors parallel to the z axis. First find the component of force F_r in the plane containing the two dislocations. This plane is one of the possible slip planes of the dislocations. Taking dislocation A at the origin, the radial component of force on dislocation B is

$$F_r = b_B \tau_{\theta z} = \frac{G\mathbf{b}_B \cdot \mathbf{b}_A}{2\pi r} \tag{9.6}$$

where $\mathbf{b}_A$ and $\mathbf{b}_B$ are the two Burgers vectors. In general $\mathbf{b}_A = \pm \mathbf{b}_B$ so that

$$F_r = \pm \frac{Gb^2}{2\pi r} \tag{9.7}$$

where the force is repulsive if $\mathbf{b}_A$ and $\mathbf{b}_B$ are parallel and attractive if they are antiparallel. Since the sign of the Burgers vector depends on the direction of the dislocation, we can arbitrarily take $\mathbf{b}_1$ and $\mathbf{b}_2$ parallel; then the sign of the force depends on whether the *dislocations* are parallel or antiparallel.

The other component of force in polar coordinates $F_\theta = b\tau_{rz} = 0$. The force between parallel screws is therefore central and varies inversely as their separation—just like the force between parallel charged wires. In this analogy, the charge and Burgers vector are equal in magnitude and sign and the dielectric constant is proportional to $2\pi/G$.

If the two parallel screws can glide freely, there is no equilibrium configuration. They either combine and annihilate or move apart indefinitely.

Parallel Edge Dislocations on Parallel Slip Planes. Take one dislocation along the z axis with slip plane in the xz plane, as in Fig. 8.2. The force on the other dislocation is found from Eq. (5.4) with $\alpha = \pi/2$; the components are $F_x = \pm b\tau_{xy}$, $F_y = \mp b\sigma_x$, where the sign depends on whether the Burgers vectors are parallel. Equations (8.8) and (8.9) give the stress components. The signs of the force components in and at right angles to the slip plane are readily visualized with the aid of Fig. 8.2.

For two like edge dislocations (Burgers vectors parallel), the force F_x in the slip plane is repulsive when $x^2 > y^2$. The y axis, however, is a position of metastable equilibrium for pure glide. This is the basis for the stability of polygonized boundaries and other symmetrical small-angle-of-misfit grain boundaries, which are rows of like edge dislocations one above the other (Chap. 11).

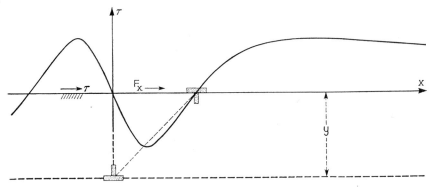

FIG. 9.1 Opposite edge dislocations on parallel slip planes. The positive dislocation at the origin exerts a force $F_x = -b\tau$ on the negative dislocation at x, y. The variation of τ with x on the slip plane of the negative dislocation is shown. Note that the position shown is stable for pure slip.

Figure 8.2 shows that, if both glide and climb are permitted, two like edge dislocations will move as far apart as possible. On the other hand, two opposite edge dislocations will try to come together and annihilate one another. Physically this annihilation consists of a joining up of the two extra planes, which are, respectively, above and below the slip plane. If only slipping motions can occur, then the two opposite edge dislocations will lock into a stable position at $x = \pm y$ and give rise to certain effects discussed in the following section.

9.5 Simple Two-dislocation Model. This section shows how a hypothetical crystal with only two dislocations displays some of the properties of real crystals. The two-dislocation model consists of opposite edge dislocations on parallel slip planes. Figure 9.1 shows the two dislocations in the $x = y$ position, which is stable for pure slip. The figure shows also the distribution of shearing stress $\tau = \tau_{xy}$ that the positive dislocation at the origin produces on the slip plane of the negative dislocation at x, y. Associated with τ is a force $F_x = -b\tau$ in the slip plane as shown in the figure. Consider first how the separation y of the slip planes affects the distribution of τ: Changing y simply changes the τ and x scales. The amplitude of the τ vs. x curve varies as $1/y$; the x scale is proportional to y. Thus the total area under any part of the curve is independent of y; this means, for example, that the energy required to separate the dislocations (and move one to $x = \infty$) is independent of y.

As an exercise show that the maximum positive and negative values of τ are equal within $\frac{1}{2}$ per cent to one another and to $\tau_m = \tau_0 b/4y$. Assume that initially the dislocations were far apart and were brought within effective range of one another's stress fields by an applied stress which moved the negative dislocation to the left and the positive dislocation to the right. Associated with this motion is a macroscopic deformation in which the crystal yields to the applied stress. If y is small enough that the applied stress cannot force the dislocations past the position of maximum opposing force $b\tau_m$, the dislocations become stuck in a stable position and the deformation stops. Now remove the applied stress; the dislocations remain stuck in the $x = y$ position and do not return to their original positions. Thus the motion of the dislocations has produced a permanent deformation. To force the dislocations past one another and cause further deformation, the applied stress must be increased above τ_m; thus the crystal is work hardened. A stress lower than the critical stress τ_m simply shifts the equilibrium position so that the force between dislocations is just equal to the force due to the applied stress. When the applied stress is small compared to τ_m, the displacement of the dislocations is proportional to the applied stress, and so is the associated macroscopic deformation. This deformation—which is reversible—is added to the elastic strain that would occur in the absence of dislocations. Thus the dislocations increase the linear reversible strain for a given stress; this lowers the measured values of the elastic moduli.

Under a small alternating stress, the dislocations oscillate about the position $x = y$ and dissipate energy in the form of heat and acoustical waves. Thus the dislocations contribute to the internal friction.

Draw the atomic arrangement for the pair of dislocations in the $x = y$ position; show that the material between the dislocations is relatively unstrained but is rotated about the z axis in respect to the rest of the crystal.

Finally suppose we anneal the crystal at a temperature where appreciable diffusion occurs; the attractive force F_y at right angles to the slip plane causes the dislocations to climb. The resultant force is always attractive; so the dislocations move together along $x = y$ by a combination of climb and glide and annihilate one another.

To summarize the consequences of the simple two-dislocation model: permanent plastic deformation is associated with work hardening, local rotation of the lattice, and changes in the measured elastic constants and internal friction; these effects disappear after annealing. Naturally a detailed quantitative theory of plastic deformation would have to be based on a much more complicated model involving many dislocations. The simple model only shows, in a qualitative way, how elements of a theory of deformation emerge from the interaction of a pair of dislocations.

We conclude this section by using the two-dislocation model to illustrate the types of energy exchange that occur when dislocations move. At first, the dislocations were so far apart that the force between them was negligible. Under the applied stress the dislocations begin to move. Now the applied stress is doing work in the deformation of the crystal, and this work is being dissipated at the dislocation or going into its energy of motion, that is, $\delta W = \delta E_d + \delta E_s$.

When the two dislocations are stuck in the equilibrium $x = y$ position, and the external stress is applied so slowly that equilibrium is maintained, the work done by the applied stress goes into stored elastic energy: $\delta W = \delta E_s$, $\delta E_d = \delta E_m = 0$. When the applied stress is suddenly released, the dislocations move back toward the equilibrium position and the stored elastic energy goes into energy of motion or energy dissipated: $-\delta E_s = \delta E_m + \delta E_d$. If the dislocations could move without dissipating energy, they would oscillate indefinitely with $E_s + E_m = $ constant. This is analogous to the oscillation of a spring and mass. The energy flows back and forth between distortional energy E_s and kinetic energy E_m.

9.6 Parallel Dislocations on Parallel Slip Planes. Width of an Extended Dislocation. In the isotropic case, a screw dislocation exerts no force on a parallel edge dislocation; thus the force between parallel dislocations with arbitrary Burgers vectors is found by treating the edge and screw components separately. As an exercise, derive the general expression for the force between two parallel dislocations on parallel slip planes where the Burgers vectors make angles α_1 and α_2 with the dislocations; determine the positions of stable equilibrium for various examples in actual crystals. In general, there are one or more stable positions if only glide is permitted, and there is no stable position for both climb and glide.

Now, as a practical example, we find the width of an extended dislocation. As Chap. 7 showed, a dislocation in a face-centered cubic or hexagonal crystal can lower its energy by dissociating into a pair of parallel Shockley partials connected by a strip of stacking fault. The equilibrium separation w of the partials (= width of fault) is given by the condition that the force of repulsion between the partials be equal to the surface tension (energy per unit area) of the connecting fault. Here the two partials are on the same slip plane ($y = 0$). Calculating the force of repulsion from the formulas of Chap. 8, we find that, in an elastically isotropic crystal, w is given by

$$w = w_0 \left(1 - \frac{2\nu}{2 - \nu} \cos 2\alpha\right) \tag{9.8}$$

where α is the angle between the dislocations and the resultant Burgers vector of the extended dislocation (sum of the Burgers vectors of the partials). The mean width w_0 is given in terms of the surface energy E_f of the fault by

$$w_0 = \frac{Gb^2}{8\pi E_f} \frac{2 - \nu}{1 - \nu} \tag{9.9}$$

where b is the magnitude of the Burgers vector of a Shockley partial. The width is a minimum when the extended dislocation is pure screw, $\alpha = 0$, and a maximum when the extended dislocation is pure edge, $\alpha = \pi/2$. Thus the width varies by a factor of $(2 + \nu)/(2 - 3\nu)$ with the orientation of the dislocation line; this is a factor of about 2 in typical cases.

The corresponding calculation for anisotropic elasticity has not yet been made; it would be a useful result and would show whether there are some orientations in real crystals where the partials would attract one another, so that an extended dislocation would not form.

9.7 Parallel Dislocations on Intersecting Slip Planes. Here the dislocations can glide into any relative position; so the equilibrium position for pure slip is the same as for slip plus climb; in both cases the resultant force must vanish. For example, if the slip planes are orthogonal and dislocation A exerts a force F_C on B normal to B's slip plane, then A experiences a force $F_S = -F_C$ in its slip plane. In other words, the slipping motion of one has the same effect on relative position as the climbing motion of the other.

In general there is no stable position when the two slip planes intersect; the two dislocations either try to come together or move far apart. An approximate rule is that the dislocations attract if the angle between their Burgers vectors is greater than 90° and repel if the angle is less than 90°. This rule follows from the fact that the energy of a dislocation is roughly proportional to the square of its Burgers vector; the dislocations attract and try to combine if the sum of the squares of their Burgers vectors is greater than the square of the sum (so that energy is released in the combination). For example, we would expect two dislocations with Burgers vectors $\frac{1}{2}[110]$ and $\frac{1}{2}[\bar{1}01]$ in face-centered cubic to attract since the combination would be a single dislocation with Burgers vector $\frac{1}{2}[011]$. The rule is not exact, however, unless the two dislocations have crystallographically equivalent orientations in respect to their Burgers vectors as, for example, in the case of pure edge dislocations.

The question of forces between dislocations on intersecting slip planes is closely related to the stability of large dislocations—Sec. 3.10 defined a large dislocation as a total dislocation whose Burgers vector was the sum of two or more t vectors (in other words, a lattice translation vector but *not* of minimum length).   The most interesting of the possible large dislocations is a dislocation with [100] Burgers vector in body-centered cubic; Frank (private communication) pointed out that, according to the Burgers-vector-squared energy criterion, such a dislocation should be stable— and not split into two total dislocations with Burgers vectors $\frac{1}{2}$[111] and $\frac{1}{2}$[11$\bar{1}$], respectively.   As an exercise show that, in the isotropic case, a [100] large dislocation parallel to the [011] direction is *definitely* stable—at least as far as elastic energy is concerned; in other words, if the large dislocation does split, the two $\frac{1}{2}<111>$ dislocations will not move farther apart than the distance where the first term in the series expression for elastic stress becomes a good approximation.   Eshelby (1949b) has carried out the same calculation for anisotropic elasticity; he made numerical calculations using the elastic constants for α iron and found that there the large dislocation is stable.

Figure 8.2 shows that, in the isotropic case, two edge dislocations with orthogonal Burgers vectors line up along the line which bisects the angle between the two extra planes; along this line there is no force of attraction or repulsion at any point.

9.8 Image Forces.   We have mentioned earlier that a dislocation experiences a force of attraction to an external surface.   Physically this means that, as the dislocation moves closer to the surface, more of its elastic stress field is cut off and the energy correspondingly reduced. Mathematically the image force arises from the boundary conditions on stress at the surface; for example, the surface stress must vanish on a free surface.

As an example consider a pure screw dislocation along the z axis in an isotropic medium; let the plane x = constant be a stress-free external surface.   The formula for the stress field around a screw dislocation in an infinite medium gives a stress $\tau_{zz} = \tau_0 by/(x^2 + y^2)$ on the plane x = constant.   Thus the boundary conditions are not satisfied, and it is necessary to superpose a distribution of stress $\tau'_{zz} = -\tau_{zz}$ on the free surface.   This could be done by placing an imaginary opposite screw dislocation at an equal distance on the other side of the free surface.   The stress field of the image dislocation exerts an attractive force on the real dislocation.

The corresponding case of an edge dislocation is more complicated; here both τ_{xy} and σ_x have to be neutralized on the stress-free surface (x = constant).   An opposite edge dislocation at the image position takes care of σ_x; however, it doubles τ_{xy}—see Eqs. (8.7) to (8.9). Fortunately, there are standard, and fairly simple, methods that give the stress field produced by an arbitrary distribution of stress on a plane surface. Calculation shows that the opposite image dislocation *does* give the correct force on the real dislocation even though it does not satisfy the boundary conditions on the stress-free surface. The proof of this forms Prob. 4. Problem 5 concerns the force on a dislocation when the slip plane makes an arbitrary angle with the external plane surface.

9.9 Nonuniform Forces. In the previous sections, the force has been the same all along the dislocation. This section discusses briefly forces that vary along the length of a dislocation. An example is the force between nonparallel dislocations; in general, each dislocation experiences both a net force and a torque. [The torque on a dislocation is defined as (force per unit length) $\times$ (lever arm) integrated over the length of the dislocation.] Problem 1 concerns the forces and torques between pairs of orthogonal straight dislocations. If the dislocations are free to move, they will not *remain* straight under the nonuniform force. Instead, they bend until the forces arising from each dislocation itself balance the force due to the other dislocation. The exact calculation of the equilibrium shapes of several interacting dislocations is generally laborious. Sometimes the one-dimensional soap-film approximation is helpful here.

Chapter 6 showed that the intersection of two dislocations produces a jog unless the Burgers vector of each dislocation lies in both slip planes. The energy of the jog comes from the applied force tending to move one dislocation through the other. In addition to creating the jog, this force must be able to overcome the high local stress fields where the dislocations intersect. For example, consider a dislocation moving across its slip plane under an applied stress. As it moves, it intersects other dislocations and, at some points, experiences high local forces that oppose its motion. Thus the dislocations accumulating inside the crystal harden it. Interstitial and impurity atoms, vacancies, and hard precipitates also have stress fields that contribute to work hardening.

9.10 Cottrell's Treatment of Impurity Atoms. Cottrell's analysis of the forces between impurity atoms is basic in dislocation theories of yield point and strain aging. Cottrell explains the yield point, observed in iron and other crystals, as a breaking away of dislocations from surrounding impurity atoms. In one of the decisive triumphs of dislocation theory, Cottrell and Bilby (1949) correctly predicted the time law of strain aging from the rate of diffusion of impurity atoms to dislocations.

As a simple example, consider a substitutional impurity atom that is slightly larger than the matrix; it produces a symmetrical dilation of the matrix. This oversized atom is attracted to regions of hydrostatic ten-

sion and repelled from regions of compression. It therefore diffuses to
the tension side of an edge dislocation. An undersized substitutional
impurity is attracted to the compression side.

Suppose the impurity atom occupies a volume δV greater than the volume of a matrix atom; its energy of interaction with the local stress field
is $P\delta V$ where $P = -\frac{1}{3}(\sigma_x + \sigma_y + \sigma_z)$ is the hydrostatic pressure. Thus
the force on the impurity atom (= work done per unit displacement) is
$-\delta V \nabla P$. As an exercise plot the flow lines and equipotential surfaces
for an edge dislocation.

The net force of the impurity on a dislocation is equal and opposite to
the force of the dislocation on the impurity; however, the impurity exerts
a nonuniform force on the dislocation. As an exercise, show that the
impurity atom exerts a torque that tends to twist the dislocation locally
into the edge orientation. [Timoshenko (1934, p. 325) gives the elastic
stress field around a center of dilation.] The impurity exerts no net force
on a screw dislocation. However, if it twists the screw dislocation locally
toward the edge orientation, it then interacts with the edge component.

Cottrell (1953) shows how interstitial impurities that distort the structure nonsymmetrically are attracted to regions of shear stress; hence
there will be a strong interaction even with pure screw dislocations.

Cottrell and Bilby (1949) calculated the rate of diffusion of impurities
in the stress field of an edge-dislocation; from this they predicted the time
law of strain aging in a cold-worked metal. Harper (1951) verified their
prediction for the case of carbon atoms in iron single crystals.

Cottrell explains the yield point as the breaking away of dislocations
from the short-range forces of the surrounding "atmosphere" of impurity
atoms. Once the dislocations have broken away, a lower stress can keep
them moving—hence, the drop in the stress-strain curve.

At this point we leave the problem of interacting impurities and dislocations—not because the work in this area of metal physics does not
deserve a longer treatment, but because Cottrell (1953) has already
covered the subject in a way that is both introductory and complete.

PROBLEMS[1]

1. Consider two orthogonal dislocations in an infinite medium; let each dislocation
and each Burgers vector be parallel to one of the axes of a rectangular coordinate
system. The distance of closest approach of the two dislocations is many atomic
spacings (so that each dislocation lies in the known elastic stress field of the other).
Find the force per unit length, the net force, and the net torque on each dislocation in
the following cases:

a. Both dislocations are screws: show that the force per unit length on each dislocation acts in the direction that is normal to both dislocations; there is a net force of
magnitude $\frac{1}{2}Gb^2$ but no net torque.

[1] Use *isotropic* elasticity in all problems.

b. One dislocation is edge, and the other screw and the two have the same Burgers vector: show that the net force vanishes; an infinite torque acts on each dislocation trying to rotate the dislocations into the antiparallel orientation.

c. One dislocation is edge and the other screw, and the Burgers vectors are orthogonal: show that there is no net force on either dislocation and no net torque on the screw; however the screw exerts an infinite torque on the edge tending to make the edge rotate in its slip plane. Explain why Newton's law of action and reaction does not apply to the torques that two dislocations exert on one another.

d. Both dislocations are edge: Distinguish three different cases; show that each dislocation experiences a force per unit length normal to its slip plane. Prove the following: there is no net force unless the slip planes are parallel; if the slip planes are parallel, the net force is $Gb^2\nu/(1-\nu)$; there is no torque if the slip planes are parallel, and if they are not parallel there is an infinite torque tending to rotate one or both dislocations toward the parallel-slip-planes orientation. When is there an infinite torque on one dislocation and no torque on the other?

2. Extend formulas (9.8) and (9.9) for the width of an extended dislocation to the case where an applied shear stress τ acts on the slip plane and at right angles to the resultant Burgers vector of the extended dislocation.

3. Show that the energy of interaction (per unit length) of an edge dislocation with an externally applied stress field is

$$b \frac{\partial f}{\partial y}(x,y)$$

where the y axis is normal to the dislocation's slip plane, the dislocation is parallel to the z axis, and f is the Airy stress function of the applied stress field (Prob. 1, Chap. 8). It is assumed that the applied stress does not vary along the dislocation.

4. A stress-free external surface is normal to the Burgers vector of a straight edge dislocation. Show that an opposite *image* dislocation (image with respect to the stress-free surface) gives the correct force on the dislocation in the crystal (see Timoshenko, 1934, pp. 82–89).

5. Find the force on a straight dislocation that runs parallel to a plane stress-free external surface for the general case where the dislocation makes an angle α with its Burgers vector and its slip plane makes an angle ϕ with the external surface.

6. Find the width of the two plane sections of V-shaped fault in the Cottrell extended dislocation (Sec. 7.12).

7. Consider a circular loop of dislocation of radius R lying in its slip plane; a screw dislocation runs normal to that plane. Show that the loop cannot be maintained at a radius $R > b$ by the stress field of the screw dislocation; the loop will shrink to nothing (or at least to a radius $R \sim b$ where the elasticity theory does not apply). Use the expression in prob. 2, chap. 7, for the energy $E_\perp$ of a circular loop of dislocation.

PART II

APPLICATIONS

CHAPTER 10

APPLICATION TO CRYSTAL GROWTH

10.1 Applications: Crystal Growth and Grain Boundaries. The purpose of Part II is to discuss the application of dislocation theory to two problems of metal physics, or physical metallurgy, namely, crystal growth (from the vapor or dilute solution) and small-angle-of-misfit grain boundaries. These problems are less urgent from a practical engineering standpoint than problems of plastic flow. They are, however, especially important from a research viewpoint. They represent two of the most clear-cut applications of dislocation theory to real crystals.

Part I showed how dislocation theory accounts, in a general way, for the mechanical properties of crystals. The strength and weakness of dislocation theory is its flexibility and versatility. One reason for taking dislocations seriously is that they seem to have the flexibility required to explain the wide variety of phenomena observed in real crystals. In general, this means that definite predictions about a *particular crystal* can be made only if special assumptions are introduced. Chapter 1 mentioned that the special assumptions consist of postulating a dislocation model and that by choosing the right model almost any observation could be explained—usually in many different ways. The theories of crystal growth and grain boundaries are not subject to this difficulty because of the following two facts: (1) The dislocation model is not important in crystal growth. It is sufficient to have one dislocation with a screw component meeting the close-packed growth surface, where the theory applies. The presence of other dislocations does not change the picture much. (2) In grain-boundary theory, the dislocation model is basic; but it is known from geometry. Thus in one case the model is unimportant; in the other it is known. In most problems of physical metallurgy, and especially in plastic deformation, the dislocation model is *both important and unknown*. Theories are therefore largely speculative and easily altered to fit observations.

Before starting the discussion of crystal growth, it may be helpful to explore further the comparison between the crystal-growth and grain-boundary theories: Both involve crystal geometry and how dislocations modify it. In crystal growth, only surface geometry is involved; dislocations affect the problem if they end on the surface. Figure 2.2

showed how a screw dislocation alters the shape of a crystal surface on which it ends. The theory of grain boundaries has little connection with specifically surface effects.

We have already mentioned that the crystal-growth theory depends on the properties of individual dislocations; the arrangement of dislocations, or dislocation model, is relatively unimportant, while the properties of grain boundaries involve both the properties of individual dislocations and their arrangement.

The grain-boundary theory is both static and dynamic; it concerns both the structures and energies of stationary boundaries and the motion of a boundary under applied stress. Theory shows that there are only certain special boundaries that will glide freely under applied stress. The motion of such a boundary was predicted by Shockley in 1948 and observed by Parker and Washburn in 1951. To date this is the most fundamental observation made in dislocation dynamics. Chapter 14 shows how the Parker-Washburn experiment provides a powerful tool for studying the atomic mechanism of plastic deformation.

Although moving dislocations are not involved in crystal growth, observations of growth surfaces have revealed that specific dislocations have moved from one point to another over a specific path. This too is a powerful tool. Thus both the crystal-growth and grain-boundary studies open up promising approaches to the important practical problems of plastic deformation.

The quantitative theory of dislocations is used in grain-boundary theory: forces between dislocations play an important role, and a major triumph of the theory has been the calculation of grain-boundary energy. So far, in crystal growth, only the geometry of dislocations is involved; dislocation stress fields and energies play no significant role. The quantitative theory of growth is highly developed and basic in the theory—but it is surface kinetics, not dislocation theory. Whenever results from surface kinetics are required, this chapter simply states them without proof. For a complete account, see the original papers by Burton, Cabrera, and Frank.

This chapter does not attempt to give either a complete or well-rounded account of crystal growth; it simply shows, mostly by pictures, why dislocations are important in crystal growth. The reason why four chapters are devoted to grain boundaries and one to crystal growth is that more of Part I is used in the grain-boundary theories; also little else is needed.

Frank introduced dislocations into crystal-growth theory in 1949. Frank's dislocation theory together with Burton and Cabrera's analysis of the atomic nature of a growth surface explained the otherwise mysteriously high rate of growth on densely packed faces at low supersaturations. The theory also predicted the form of growth surfaces. Griffin, Verma, and others subsequently verified these predictions by observing steps one cell constant in height on growth surfaces; the steps had the shape predicted by Frank's theory.   To date, this work represents the most direct and clear-cut verification of dislocation theory and the most convincing experimental evidence for the existence of dislocations in real crystals.

We shall present Frank's theory in terms of growth from the vapor; an essentially similar argument applies to growth from a dilute solution.   A theory of growth from the melt would probably be quite different.

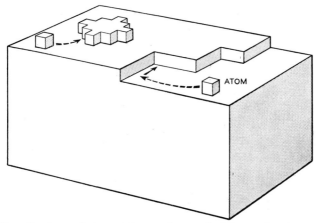

FIG. 10.1 Growth of a perfect crystal on a close-packed face.   One incomplete layer and one small monolayer, or nucleus, are shown.   The boundary of an incomplete layer is a step containing kinks (reentrant corners).   Atoms adsorbed from the vapor diffuse over the surface and are most likely to stick at kinks.   Continued growth requires the nucleation of new layers as old layers grow into complete atomic planes.

Section 10.2 discusses the growth of a perfect crystal and leads to predictions that contradict experiment.   Frank's theory removes the contradiction (Sec. 10.3) and predicts the form of growth surfaces (Sec. 10.4), which were later observed (Sec. 10.5).   Section 10.6 discusses evidence for the motion of dislocations.

10.2 Growth of a Perfect Crystal.   Figure 10.1 shows a simple cubic crystal in contact with its vapor.   The upper surface contains a *step* with several reentrant corners called *kinks*.   A surface of any macroscopic orientation can be constructed from such kinked steps, with the proper orientation and density of kinks and steps.   The crystal surfaces that coincide with densely packed planes are the only surfaces that are planar in the sense that all the surface atoms lie on a plane.   All other surfaces are made up of densely packed plane sections connected by kinked steps. This is true for any crystal structure; all the arguments of this chapter apply for any crystal structure; the hypothetical simple cubic is used for simplicity.

Now consider the effect of vapor pressure. Atoms from the vapor are adsorbed on the crystal surface. The quantitative theory of surfaces shows that surface diffusion is so rapid that an adsorbed atom diffuses a considerable distance before reevaporating. Suppose the atom hits a step as it diffuses over the surface (Fig. 10.1). An atom is more tightly bound to the crystal at a step; for example, in Fig. 10.1 an atom at a step has two nearest neighbors in the crystal instead of one. Now the atom diffuses along the step. If it hits a kink, it is in contact with the crystal on three of its six sides and is still more tightly held. In equilibrium vapor, atoms join and leave the kinks with equal frequency.

Consider the effect of increasing the vapor pressure over the equilibrium value. Define supersaturation as the per cent excess of vapor pressure over the pressure which gives zero growth rate on a surface containing kinked steps. For positive supersaturation, more atoms arrive at the kinks than leave; so the step advances. (Rate of arrival is proportional to vapor pressure; rate of departure depends only on temperature.) As growth proceeds by the addition of atoms to the steps, the step finally advances to the edge of the crystal. This completes the atomic layer and eliminates the step.

When all the steps have been eliminated by advancing and forming complete layers, it is necessary to nucleate additional layers for growth to proceed. Figure 10.1 shows one such nucleus, or island monolayer. The nucleation of an island monolayer on a close-packed crystal face is similar to the familar problem of nucleating a water droplet. For a given supersaturation, there is a critical size of droplet such that any larger droplet will grow and any smaller droplet will evaporate. The reason is as follows: Associated with the surface energy of the droplet is a local equilibrium vapor pressure that increases with the curvature of the droplet. Analogously, in the case of an island monolayer, the line energy of the step is associated with a *local* equilibrium vapor pressure that increases with the curvature of the step. Thus, around a small nucleus, the excess of vapor pressure over the equilibrium vapor pressure is small or even negative. The critical size nucleus has a local equilibrium vapor pressure just equal to the existing vapor pressure. Any smaller nucleus will probably evaporate and any larger nucleus grow. The probability that a nucleus of critical size will form is very sensitive to supersaturation. In general, a critical supersaturation of 25 to 40 per cent is needed for nuclei to form fast enough that the growth rate is appreciable on the time scale of a laboratory experiment—for the calculation see Frank (1952). Above the critical supersaturation, there are always plenty of nuclei; so growth is not limited by nucleation, and the growth rate increases rapidly with supersaturation.

Figure 10.2 is a plot of some typical results. These were obtained by

Volmer and Schultze (1931) on iodine crystals grown from the vapor. Contrary to the above predictions, the growth rate increases almost in proportion to supersaturation for supersaturations as low as 3 to 4 per cent; only below 1 per cent is the growth rate negligible on the scale of millimeters per hour. In fact the curve is just the one that would be expected *if nucleation of island monolayers did not occur, but steps were always present on the surface,* and were never used up by growing into complete atomic planes. This raises the problem of how a surface can remain stepped no matter how far the steps advance. The following section shows how Frank's theory solves this problem.

10.3 Frank's Theory of the Growth of an Imperfect Crystal. Frank's theory is based on the idea that the growing crystal is not perfect (like the

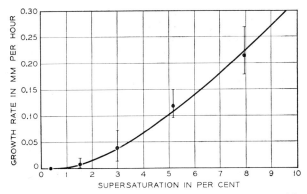

FIG. 10.2 Growth of iodine crystals from the vapor at 0°C as measured by Volmer and Schultze (1931) (after Frank, 1952). Measurable growth even at low supersaturation contradicts the surface nucleation theory.

one in the last section) but contains dislocations. Both X-ray analysis and the observed shearing strength indicate that most single crystals *do* contain some dislocations. Part I showed how even a single dislocation in a crystal can reduce the yield stress by many orders of magnitude. Frank's explanation shows that even a single dislocation can change the growth pattern and remove the necessity of nucleating steps on a crystal surface.

Figure 10.3 illustrates Frank's explanation. Here a screw dislocation (slip vector parallel to dislocation axis) meets the surface of the crystal at right angles; a step on the surface connects the end of the screw dislocation with the edge of the crystal. This is the same dislocation shown in Fig. 2.2. It can be visualized as the result of slip on a segmented slip surface. Since the dislocation is pure screw, it is independent of the shape of the (imagined) slip surface; the latter affects only the form of the step. Figure 10.4 shows the atomic arrangement at the terminal point of the step, where the screw dislocation intersects the surface. The strain

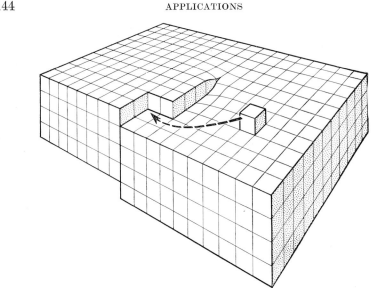

FIG. 10.3 Crystal containing a screw dislocation running normal to the upper surface (as in Fig. 2.2). The upper surface is now a spiral ramp; the step can*not* be eliminated by adding atoms to form a complete atomic layer; hence there is no necessity to nucleate new layers for growth to continue.

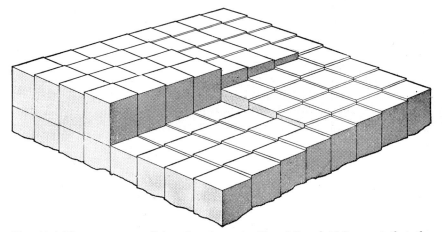

FIG. 10.4 The same screw dislocation shown in Figs. 2.2 and 10.3 except that the atoms are represented by undistorted cubes displaced tangentially relative to one another.

around a pure screw dislocation is mostly pure shear (Sec. 2.3 last paragraph); hence the atoms can be represented by undistorted cubes slipped over one another as shown in the figure.

As atoms are adsorbed on the surface, and diffuse to the step, the step advances. However, it can never grow so as to produce a completed atomic layer since the upper surface is a spiral ramp. Recall that the crystal of Figs. 10.3 and 10.4 is not a stack of atomic planes one above the other; it is rather a single atomic plane in the form of a helicoid, or spiral staircase. Hence the step can advance indefinitely and the crystal grow to any size without nucleation of new layers.

Figure 10.5 shows the step after it has advanced several atoms. Since the end point of the dislocation remains fixed, the step tends to rotate around that point. The geometry of the process is very similar to the

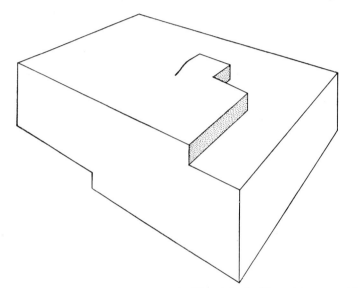

FIG. 10.5 As atoms are added to the step in Fig. 10.3, the step advances and begins to spiral around the point where the screw dislocation meets the upper surface.

Frank-Read mechanism (Sec. 6.3); again a spiral develops; the outer sections have farther to go to make one complete revolution; so the inner sections make more revolutions in a given time. Figure 10.6 shows the spiral beginning to take shape. The rate of advance of any section of the step is proportional to the excess of vapor pressure over the local equilibrium vapor pressure, where the latter increases with curvature. As the spiral develops, the sections of step near the dislocation acquire a higher curvature. This increases the local equilibrium vapor pressure; now the inner sections advance more slowly than the outer sections. Finally a steady state is reached in which (rate of advance)/(distance from dislocation) = (angular velocity) = (revolutions per unit time) is the same for all points on the step. In the steady state, the form of the spiral remains constant; the whole spiral rotates uniformly about the dislocation. Figure 6.5 applies to the development of a growth spiral, as well as to a slip spiral.   Now the lines represent a step on a growth surface instead of a dislocation on a slip plane.

The spacing between turns of the steady-state spiral is proportional to the diameter of the critical nucleus for growth on a perfect crystal, which is inversely proportional to supersaturation.

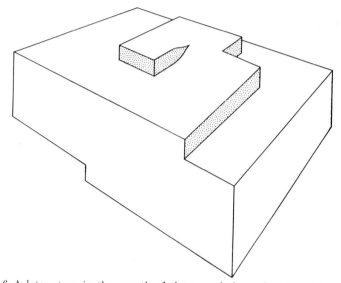

FIG. 10.6 A later stage in the growth of the crystal shown in Figs. 10.3 and 10.5. Finally the step winds itself up into a spiral (on a macroscopic scale) that rotates (around the end of the screw dislocation) without change in form.

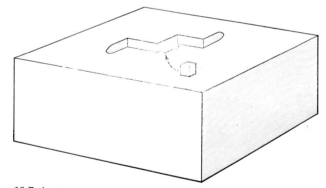

FIG. 10.7 A step connecting the ends of two opposite screw dislocations.

The following section discusses the varieties of growth steps, one of which is similar to the Frank-Read source, or double spiral.   In fact, Frank's theory of crystal growth suggested the Frank-Read slip mechanism.   Frank discovered the growth mechanisms in 1949.   The applica-

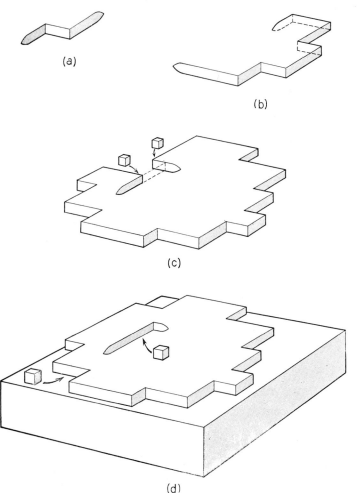

FIG. 10.8 Growth by motion of a step connecting opposite screw dislocations. (*a*) The step connecting two opposite screws, as in Fig. 10.7. (*b*) As atoms are added to the step, the step advances and bulges (the ends of the step are held fixed at the screw dislocations). (*c*) The bulging step doubles back on itself; the two sections of advancing step are about to meet (dashed line) as atoms fill in the valley between them. (*d*) The step has doubled back on itself to form a closed loop of step and a section of step connecting the ends of the screw dislocations; the latter is ready to bulge again and give off another closed loop. The closed loops continue to expand and form complete layers.

tion of the same principle to slip was discovered independently and simultaneously (within a few hours) by Frank and Read in May, 1950.

10.4 Other Forms of the Growth Steps. The spiral in Fig. 6.5 is drawn as a smooth curve (spiral of circular symmetry). Growth spirals have this shape (except on an atomic scale) if growth proceeds at equal rates in all directions. However, at lower temperatures, the portions of the step parallel to close-packed directions grow more slowly and we have a "polygonal" spiral; the sides of the polygon are parallel to close-packed directions.

Another, similar, growth mechanism is analogous to the Frank-Read source, or double spiral. Figure 10.7 shows two screw dislocations that have equal and opposite slip vectors. Both dislocations end on the upper surface of the crystal; the two end points are connected by a step one atomic spacing in height. In supersaturated vapor, the step advances as

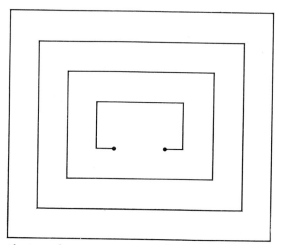

FIG. 10.9 Growth steps of square symmetry. The lines represent steps viewed normal to the growth surface. Several closed steps have already been formed. The section of step connecting the ends of two opposite screw dislocations is about to double back on itself. Steps having square, or polygonal, symmetry are associated with unequal growth rates for different orientations of steps; the sides of the polygon are normal to directions of slow growth.

adsorbed atoms diffuse to it and stick at the kinks. Figure 10.8 shows the growth of this step in three dimensions. Figure 10.8a shows a step similar to the one in Fig. 10.7; it connects two screw dislocations of opposite sign. As adsorbed atoms join the step, it advances, Fig. 10.8b. Figure 10.8b and c show how the step bulges out and doubles back on itself. Figure 10.8c shows how the two sections of step join up. In Fig. 10.8d the step has returned to approximately its original position; now it is ready to start again. The surrounding closed step, or ring, continues to grow. As successive rings develop, the surface of the crystal becomes a pyramid. Figure 6.6 also applies to the development of growth step of circular symmetry; the shaded area represents the region where growth has occurred since the step started to move. D_1 and D_2 are the end points of screw dislocations. The driving force now is the excess vapor pressure. For a given supersaturation, the step will *not* bulge beyond the semicircular position unless the distance D_1D_2 is greater than a critical amount, which is the diameter of a stable nucleus (Sec. 10.2).

If close-packed sections of step advance more slowly, then the closed loops are polygonal rather than circular. Figure 10.9 shows this for the case where there are two orthogonal directions of slow growth.

Frank (1952) has discussed intersecting and interlocking spirals centered on different dislocations. He distinguishes the following three cases:

1. If two similar dislocations are very close together, their spirals may join and form a single spiral step of multiple height. In some cases the growth steps are hundreds or thousands of atomic spacings high and are easily seen.

2. If two similar dislocations are somewhat farther apart but still closer than 2π times the critical radius of stable nuclei, then they generate a pair of interlocking nonintersecting spirals. They are now said to be cooperating.

3. Two dislocations separated by a distance large compared to the critical radius can be centers of two independent growth spirals, and there are two growth hills on the surface. If the supersaturation at the center of one spiral is slightly greater, then a single growth hill results; the one dislocation is then said to dominate the other; the second dislocation simply contributes turns to the spiral centered on the dominant dislocation.

Section 10.5 reviews observational examples of these different types.

A significant result of the theory is that the rate of growth is relatively independent of the number of dislocations meeting the surface; see Frank (1952).

10.5 Observations. Recently developed optical techniques, involving multiple-beam interferometry and phase-contrast microscopy, have made it possible to resolve small steps on a crystal surface. This section describes several phase-contrast micrographs showing growth steps. In phase-contrast microscopy, the lateral resolution (at right angles to the direction of observation) is that characteristic of light microscopy; therefore observations have to be made on almost perfect crystal faces (where the steps on the surface are sufficiently far apart to be resolved by a light microscope). Few crystals have surfaces which are atomically plane over such wide areas. This has restricted the experimental observations to a relatively few crystals. It is also desirable that the lattice translation vector (= step height) be large.

Figures 10.10 to 10.12 are some of Verma's (1951) phase-contrast

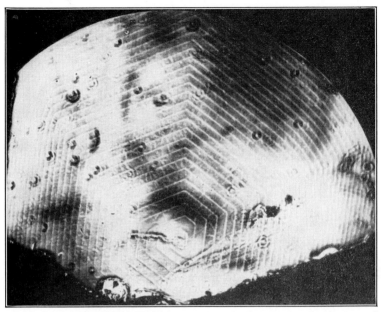

Fig. 10.10 One of Verma's (1951) phase-contrast micrographs showing two inter-locking growth spirals of hexagonal symmetry on carborundum.   The step height is 15 A, or one cell constant.

Fig. 10.11 "Circular" growth spirals on carborundum (Verma, 1951).

micrographs. They show the spiral growth steps on the surfaces of carborundum (SiC) crystal grown from the vapor. The step height here is 15 A, or one cell constant. Figure 10.10 shows two interlocking spirals centered on a cooperating pair of similar screw dislocations close together. Figure 10.11 shows a single circular spiral on the left; on the right is a double spiral with several turns wound around one dislocation of the pair and only one around the other. Figure 10.12 shows three dislocations of like sign, close together; observe the three nonintersecting interlocked spirals.

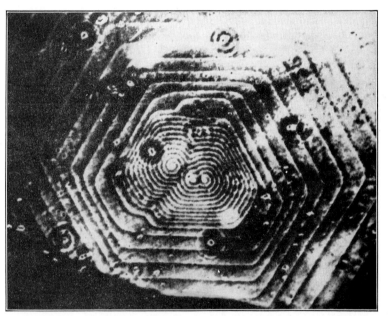

FIG. 10.12 Growth spirals on carborundum (Verma, 1951).

Figure 10.13a shows a spiral and Fig. 10.13b a pyramid, both of square symmetry, on faces of long-chain paraffin crystals grown from dilute solution. These figures are electron micrographs, taken by Dawson and Vand (1951). The monomolecular step height (about 50 A) is clearly visible after metal shadowing.

Griffin (1950) was the first to photograph steps only one cell constant high. Figure 10.14 is Griffin's original phase-contrast micrograph; it shows the face of a natural beryl crystal grown slowly over geological times. The face of this crystal is unusually perfect. The step height is 8 A, and the exceptionally fine resolution is probably due in part to some natural etching of the step. The growth steps here have a razor-blade shape, indicating one direction of slow growth. The figure shows one

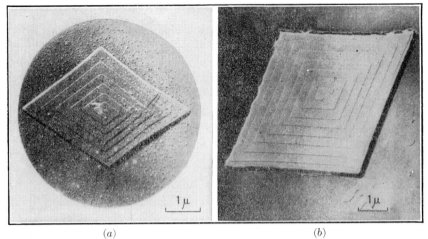

(a)   (b)

FIG. 10.13 Dawson and Vand's electron micrographs of growth steps on long-chain paraffin crystals. The monomolecular step height 50 A is visible after metal shadowing. (a) A single dislocation. (b) Two opposite screw dislocations connected by a step.

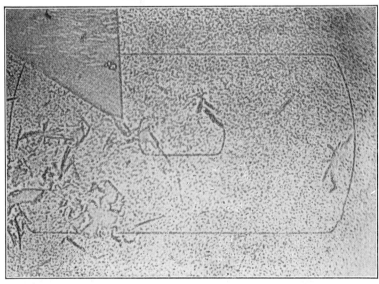

FIG. 10.14 Griffin's original (1950) phase-contrast micrograph of growth steps on a natural beryl crystal.

continuous step surrounding the step that connects two opposite screw dislocations.

Recently spiral growth steps have been seen on several metal crystals. Forty (1952) has photographed growth spirals on cadmium and magnesium crystals grown from their vapors; the step, which was one or two cell constants high, appeared after exposure to air and plasticine; this "decorating" is not yet understood.   It is believed, however, that in many cases the good visibility of small steps is due to foreign matter which accumulates at the steps—probably for the same reason that continued growth occurs at the steps.   Forty (1953) has also observed growth steps on silver crystals and has detected the motion of the screw dislocation by the associated unit "slip line" on the growth surface—the following section discusses this powerful technique for studying plastic deformation on an atomic scale.

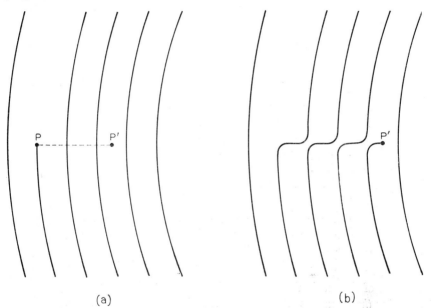

(a)   (b)

Fig. 10.15 (a) A dislocation meeting the surface at P contributes turns to a spiral centered on another dislocation.   When the dislocation moves from P to P′, it forms a step PP′.   (b) The sharp corners are rounded off leaving a visible trail.   Griffin (1952) has observed such evidence for dislocation motion.

10.6 The Movement of Dislocations.   Figure 10.15a shows steps (solid lines) on a crystal surface.   A screw dislocation intersecting the surface at the point P contributes turns to a spiral centered on another dislocation (the other dislocation dominates the dislocation at P).   Now let the dislocation move so that it intersects the surface at P′; the dotted line PP′ shows the path of motion.   The added section of step PP′ cuts across several other steps.   The sharp corners where PP′ intersects the other steps become rounded off in time (the local evaporation rate is high at a sharp corner).   Figure 10.15b shows the final result.   The path traced out by the dislocation in its motion is revealed by the offsets on the growth steps.

Griffin (1952) has observed a number of examples similar to Fig. 10.15*b* where the motion of a dislocation can be detected from anomalies in the observed growth pattern.   Griffin's observations, made on beryl crystals, gave evidence for both the movement of single dislocations over short distances and the production of a large number of dislocations from a source in the interior.   This suggests the possibility of studying the motions of dislocations under controlled stressing to check predictions from the dynamical theory of dislocations.

10.7 Summary of Crystal Growth. This sketchy and incomplete treatment of the dislocation theory of crystal growth may be summarized briefly as follows:

1. A screw dislocation ending on a surface provides a mechanism for crystal growth without nucleation and explains observed growth rates at low supersaturation.

2. Growth steps one lattice constant in height and of the form predicted by Frank's theory have been observed on nearly perfect surfaces of several crystals including beryl, carborundum, long-chain paraffin, magnesium, cadmium, and silver.   The point where a growth step ends on a crystal face is, by definition, a dislocation.   Thus the observed growth spirals are direct evidence for dislocations.   The observations on metal crystals are especially important since most of dislocation theory has been concerned with metals.

3. A moving dislocation of the type responsible for growth leaves behind a well-defined trail marked by offsets in the steps it cuts.   This suggests that dislocations could be made to move by application of known stresses to the crystal and the observed motions compared with the predictions of dislocation theory.   *This would provide a very powerful tool for studying the dynamics of plastic deformation on an atomic scale.*

CHAPTER 11

SIMPLE GRAIN BOUNDARY

11.1 Dislocation Models of Grain Boundaries. The theory of small-angle-of-misfit grain boundaries illustrates another way of making unique predictions from dislocation theory. Although many dislocations are present on a grain boundary, the geometry of the boundary limits the dislocation model to only a few possibilities. This chapter and the next show how to find the energy of a grain boundary from the dislocation model. Thus we can find which model of a given boundary has the lowest energy. Chapter 13 compares the calculated energies with experimental measurements on well-annealed samples.

Dislocation models of grain boundaries were proposed by Bragg (1940) and Burgers (1940). When the adjoining grains have a small difference in orientation, the dislocation model emerges naturally from the crystal geometry. From the known elastic stress field around a dislocation, we can calculate the elastic energy of any array of dislocations. This chapter and the next show that, if other quantities are held constant, the energy E per unit area of boundary varies with the orientation difference θ, according to the formula

$$E = E_0\theta[A - \ln \theta] \tag{11.1}$$

where E_0 and A are independent of θ. This formula was apparently derived independently at several places, including Cambridge University and the University of Bristol, and was first published and compared with experimental measurements by Read and Shockley (1950, 1952b).

The parameter E_0 depends only on the elastic distortion; it can be calculated from the dislocation model and the elastic constants of the material. In general, anisotropic elasticity is used for specific crystals. E_0 can also be measured experimentally; thus a *quantitative* comparison can be made between theoretical predictions and experimental measurements.

The parameter A depends on the nonelastic core energy of the dislocation. A enters the derivation as an unknown constant of integration; its evaluation would require a calculation of the forces between atoms in the bad material of the dislocation core.

The derivation of the formula from the dislocation model is valid only for small angles, where the regions of atomic disorder do not overlap.

Formula (11.1) is unique in the field of dislocation theory: it is the only energy relation that follows directly from the properties of a known array of dislocations without any additional assumptions which could be altered to fit experimental results.

The theory presented here and in the following chapters applies only to boundaries where θ is small. Large-angle-of-misfit boundaries are considerably more difficult to analyze, and the dislocation description no longer has a unique significance; the dislocations are so close together that their individual character is lost. Read and Shockley (1950) and Shockley (1952) have discussed large θ boundaries and conclude that, from a research standpoint, it is better to work with small-angle boundaries, where the theory is much better developed and is capable of further development as needed, and the interpretation of experiments is more direct. After small-angle boundaries and their properties are well understood, it may be easier to attack the more complicated problem of large-angle boundaries.

This chapter discusses a particularly simple boundary where the dislocation model is a row of identical dislocations. Section 11.2 shows how crystal geometry determines the dislocation model. Section 11.3 discusses the energy of the boundary in terms of the dislocation model, and Sec. 11.4 derives $E = E_0\theta[A - \ln \theta]$ from a simple physical argument that brings out the physical meaning of the formula; the latter is discussed further in Sec. 11.5. Section 11.6 outlines a simple procedure for testing the formula and reviews briefly some of the experimental data to be presented in Chap. 13. Section 11.7 gives an alternative derivation that shows why the formula is limited to small θ. The small-θ limitation is discussed in detail in Sec. 11.8. Chapter 12 extends the formula to more general grain boundaries, and Chap. 13 compares it with experimental measurements of both relative and absolute values of grain boundary energy. Chapter 14 deals with the dynamics of a small-angle grain boundary and shows how certain special boundaries can move under applied stress.

11.2 Dislocation Model of a Simple Grain Boundary. Figure 11.1a shows two simple cubic crystals that have a common cube [001] axis. Their difference in orientation is defined by a relative rotation through an angle θ about their common axis. The interface between the grains is a plane of symmetry; it is parallel to the mean (100) plane of the two crystals. In Fig. 11.1b, the two grains are joined to form a bicrystal. The misfit is accommodated in two ways: (1) by atomic misfit on the boundary, (2) by elastic deformation extending over areas many atomic spacings in extent. As much as possible of the misfit will be accommodated in the latter way; a severe stress concentration on the boundary would relieve itself by spreading over larger areas. However, elastic deformation alone cannot accommodate all the misfit; some of the (approximately) vertical planes of atoms must terminate on the boundary. Where a plane terminates, there is a line imperfection running straight through the crystal normal to the plane of the drawing. Along these lines, the atoms are not properly surrounded by neighbors; for example,

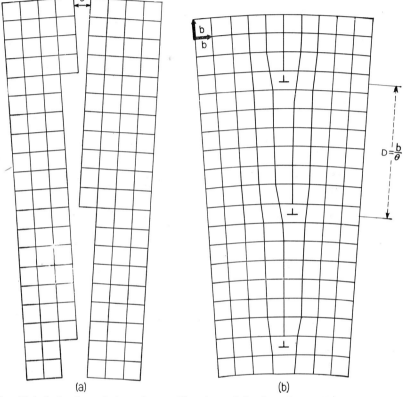

FIG. 11.1 A simple grain boundary. The plane of the figure is parallel to a cube face and normal to the axis of relative rotation of the two grains. (a) Two grains have a common cube axis and an angular difference in orientation θ. (b) The two grains are joined to form a bicrystal. The joining requires only elastic strain except where a plane of atoms ends on the boundary in an edge dislocation, denoted by the symbol ⊥.

the atoms on the edge of the terminating plane have only three, instead of four, nearest neighbors in the plane of the drawing. These imperfections are recognized as edge dislocations; they are denoted by the symbol ⊥ in Fig. 11.1b. To prove that the line imperfections are dislocations, surround one of them with a Burgers circuit; the closure failure of the circuit is equal to a [100] **t** vector. If the circuit encloses *N* line imperfections, then the closure failure is *N* **t** vectors. Thus, by definition, the line imperfections are dislocations.

The geometry of Fig. 11.1 shows that the spacing D between dislocations is given by

$$\frac{b}{D} = 2 \sin \frac{\theta}{2} \doteq \theta \qquad (11.2)$$

where the approximation holds for small angles.

The following conclusions follow directly from the geometry of Fig. 11.1:

1. There is no other physically reasonable way of joining the grains except by an array of dislocations.
2. The only dislocation array that will accomplish the joining is the array shown: namely, a row of edge type dislocations, all parallel to the common cube axis of the two grains and having [100] Burgers vectors. Of course, we could add dislocations of any type in pairs of opposite sign; but these could move together by slip and diffusion and annihilate one another; hence they would not exist in a well-annealed specimen.

For larger values of θ, the dislocations are closer together. When θ is so large that the dislocations are separated by only one or two atomic spacings, then practically all the misfit consists of atomic disorder on the boundary, and the elastic deformation of the grains is negligible. When there are no well-defined regions of good material on the boundary, the dislocation model has only a formal significance and some other way of describing the misfit may be preferable. The dislocation model represents a unique description only when θ is small enough that the dislocations are many atomic spacings apart, so that most of the material on the boundary is elastically deformed. In this case, the dislocation model emerges by geometrical necessity; it cannot be chosen arbitrarily to fit experimental results. This is one reason for restricting the formula to small angles.

We now discuss some direct experimental evidence for the structure of grain boundaries. It is known that the rate of etching is increased by strain energy; Lacombe and Yannaquis (1947), for example, found that large-angle grain boundaries in aluminum etch rapidly and appear as grooves on the surface; on the other hand twin boundaries (which have a low energy, since nearest neighbor relations are satisfied) resisted etch particularly well. Thus one would expect that, with sufficiently good resolution, a small-angle boundary would appear as a *row of discrete etch pits;* that is, the etch should attack the strained material at a dislocation more rapidly than the less-strained material between dislocations. Lacombe (1948) observed distinguishable etch pits on subboundaries in aluminum. Recently, Vogel, Pfann, Corey, and Thomas (1953) found striking evidence for the dislocation structure of small-θ boundaries in germanium. The boundary appeared as a row of tiny pits relatively evenly spaced—see frontispiece. The spacing between pits, which was about a micron, agreed with the spacing calculated from the measured difference in orientation of the grains.

11.3 Energy of the Grain Boundary. This section discusses the energy of the boundary in Fig. 11.1. Two types of energy are present, corresponding to the two ways of taking up the misfit: one is the energy of atomic disorder in the dislocation core, where the distortion is so severe that atoms are not properly surrounded by their neighbors and Hooke's law fails; the other is the energy of elastic deformation, which extends over distances comparable to the spacing between dislocations. A simple physical argument gives the grain-boundary energy E as a function of θ. (Note that grain-boundary energy is surface energy, ergs/cm².) Chapter 12 shows that the same formula holds for any small-θ grain boundary with a fixed arbitrary orientation of the boundary and axis of relative rotation of the adjoining grains.

Section 11.1 mentioned that the formula for E vs. θ contains two parameters; these correspond to the two types of energy. The parameter E_0 can be evaluated by considering only the energy in regions where the strain is elastic; the parameter A depends on the forces between atoms in the bad regions. However, *the form of the formula* depends only on the elastic strain, and *not* on the atomic misfit in the bad regions. By considering only elastic strain, we shall set up a simple differential expression for the change in energy with change in θ. In the integration of this simple differential expression, the unknown core energy enters as an undetermined constant of integration.

In the derivation we shall need one simple formula from anisotropic elasticity theory: the shearing stress τ on the slip plane and in the slip direction of a single straight dislocation. Chapter 8 and the Appendix, Eq. (A.12), showed that τ is given by an infinite series

$$\tau = \tau_0 \frac{b}{R} + \tau_1 \frac{b^2}{R^2} + \cdots \tau_n \frac{b^{n+1}}{R^{n+1}} \tag{11.3}$$

where R is the distance from the dislocation. Remember that τ_0 is uniquely determined by the Burgers vector, the elastic constants, and the orientation of the dislocation. The other coefficients depend on the (at-present) unknown interaction of the elastically strained material with the bad material at the core of the dislocation. For small θ we need to know the stress only where R/b is large enough to neglect the higher order terms and use the approximate Eq. (8.13)

$$\tau = \tau_0 \frac{b}{R} \tag{11.4}$$

Equations (8.16) and (8.17) gave τ_0 in terms of the (anisotropic) elastic constants for various special cases of practical interest.

11.4 Derivation of E vs. θ.   This section derives Eq. (11.1) from the dislocation model of the boundary.   The derivation is based on a simple physical argument that brings out the physical meaning of the formula. Section 11.7 will give an alternative derivation, which is shorter and a little more abstract and which clarifies the small θ limitation.

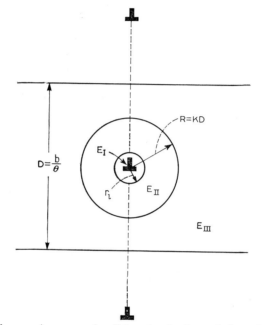

Fig. 11.2 The three regions around a dislocation in the grain boundary of Fig. 11.1. The energies in the three regions are E_I, E_{II}, and E_{III}, respectively.

Section 11.2 showed that the grain boundary in Fig. 11.1 consists of a vertical row of parallel edge dislocations; Fig. 11.2 shows three of the dislocations.   We are now going to find the grain-boundary energy per dislocation, which we shall call $E_\perp$; $E_\perp$ is energy per unit length of dislocation.

First divide the crystal into uniform parallel strips by drawing lines normal to the boundary and between dislocations, so that one dislocation is at the center of each strip.   One such strip is shown by the horizontal lines in Fig. 11.2.   Assume that the strip is infinitely long in the horizontal dimension; later we shall find that it need only be long in comparison with D.   The energy in a strip is $E_\perp$. $E_\perp$ includes both the atomic-misfit energy in the bad material and the elastic energy in the good material.   The following derivation is based on a further subdivision of the elastic energy into two parts; thus $E_\perp$ has three parts, which we now distinguish and define with the aid of Fig. 11.2:

E_I is the unknown energy of atomic misfit in the bad material; the bad material lies within a circle of radius r_l about the dislocation.

E_{II} is one of the two parts of the elastic energy; it is the energy in the (good) material outside the circle of radius r_l and inside a circle of radius $R = KD \gg b$; K is a constant less than unity. The actual value of K is not important, but it must be small enough that the stress field inside R is approximately equal to the stress field of the enclosed dislocation alone.

E_{III} is the remaining energy in the strip; it is distributed over an area where the stress depends on the combined effects of all the dislocations. To evaluate E_{III}, we could sum the stress fields of the infinite array of dislocations and integrate the elastic energy density over the entire strip. However, the following simple physical argument gives formula (11.1) without the laborious mathematical calculation.

Suppose θ changes; consider the change in $E_\perp$:

$$dE_\perp = dE_I + dE_{II} + dE_{III}$$

For example, let θ decrease by $d\theta$, so that D increases by dD. $R = KD$ where K is constant, and $\theta = b/D$; therefore

$$-\frac{d\theta}{\theta} = \frac{dD}{D} = \frac{dR}{R} \tag{11.5}$$

The dashed lines in Fig. 11.3 show the new boundaries of the three regions. Consider in order the changes in the three energies:

E_I is the localized energy of atomic misfit at the dislocation core. It is independent of the other dislocations; hence it does not change.

The energy E_{II} increases: By definition of K, the stress in the E_{II} region depends only on the included dislocation; so the stress energy density does not change. The area of the E_{II} region increases as shown in Fig. 11.3. Thus dE_{II} equals the energy in the ring bounded by circles of radii $R = KD$ and $R + dR = K(D + dD)$; in this ring, the elastic stress field is the same as that around a single dislocation.

E_{III} does not change: The area of the E_{III} region increases, but the average energy per unit area decreases because the dislocations move farther apart. The following argument shows that these two effects exactly cancel: First divide the E_{III} region into small elements of area. Focus attention on one such element. When D increases, the area of this element increases as D^2. The following paragraphs will prove that the elastic energy density in the element varies *inversely* as D^2; therefore, (area) $\times$ (energy per unit area) = constant. Hence E_{III} remains constant as D varies.

The proof that energy density varies as $1/D^2$ has two steps. Step 1 shows, by a dimensional argument, that energy density remains constant if the ratio b/D is constant. Step 2 shows that, if everything else is constant, energy density varies as b^2. Conclusion: Energy density varies as b^2/D^2. (The reader may wish to prove these two steps as an exercise before going on.)

Step 1 follows directly from Fig. 11.1b. Imagine that the whole figure is photographically enlarged, so that b and D increase proportionally. The strain at any atom in the elastic region remains constant. Therefore elastic energy density (which varies as strain squared) remains constant.

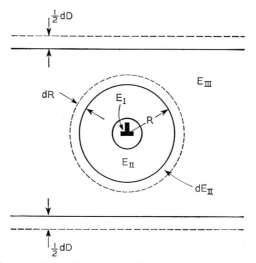

Fig. 11.3 As θ changes, D and R change. The solid lines show the boundaries of the three regions in Fig. 11.2; the dashed lines show the new positions of the boundaries after D has increased by dD.

Step 2 has already been proved in Sec. 8.4 for a single dislocation. The stress, strain, and displacement around a dislocation are proportional to the displacement b imposed on the cut (in forming the dislocation). The proportionality of everything to b follows from the linearity of elastic deformation and holds for any number of dislocations having equal Burgers vectors of magnitude b. Thus, if the dislocations remain fixed and b changes, then the energy density varies as b^2.

We have now shown that E_I and E_{II} remain constant as θ changes. Therefore the total change $dE_{\perp}$ is equal to dE_{II}. dE_{II} is easily calculated; it is the energy in the ring surrounding a single dislocation (Fig. 11.3). In that ring the stress, by definition, can be considered to be due entirely to the enclosed dislocation. Let us find the energy by imagining that the ring is cut and allowed to relax—so that the strain is completely relieved and the dislocation eliminated. For example, make a cut along the slip plane and apply forces to the two sides of the cut to maintain equilibrium. Gradually let the two sides of the cut have an offset b which relaxes the strain. Figure 11.4 shows the ring before and after the strain is relaxed. The energy in the ring is equal to the work done on the cut (against the forces applied to the cut to maintain equilibrium). In Sec. 8.4 we used this method of finding the energy in a ring around the dislocation; we also proved rigorously that all the work is done on the cut (the stresses on the inner and outer surfaces of the ring do no work).

The work done on the cut is one-half the force, which is τdR, times the displacement b; the factor of one-half comes from the linearity of elastic

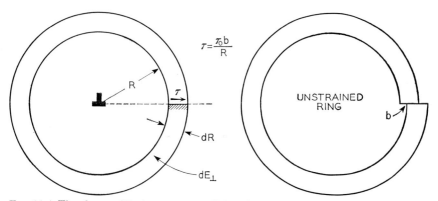

FIG. 11.4 The change $dE_\perp$ in energy per dislocation is the energy in the ring, which is the work done when the ring is cut and the strain allowed to relax, as shown.

stress and displacement. Since $R \gg b$, we use Eq. (11.4), $\tau = \tau_0(b/R)$. Thus

$$dE_\perp = \frac{1}{2}\tau b dR = \frac{b^2\tau_0}{2}\frac{dR}{R} \tag{11.6}$$

[Differentiating Eq. (8.20) with respect to R would give exactly the same result.] From (11.5), $dR/R = -d\theta/\theta$; so (11.6) becomes

$$dE_\perp = -\frac{b^2\tau_0}{2}\frac{d\theta}{\theta} \tag{11.7}$$

which is readily integrated to give

$$E_\perp = \frac{b^2\tau_0}{2}[A - \ln \theta] \tag{11.8}$$

The grain-boundary energy E per unit area is $E_\perp$ times the density of dislocations; $E = E_\perp/D = E\theta/b$. Thus

$$E = E_0\theta[A - \ln \theta] \tag{11.9}$$

where

$$E_0 = \frac{b\tau_0}{2} \tag{11.10}$$

and A is the constant of integration; A depends on the unknown energy of atomic misfit.

11.5 Physical Meaning of the E vs. θ Formula. This section discusses the physical meaning of the two terms in the expression for E vs. θ.

The term $E_0\theta A$ represents a constant energy per dislocation; it is proportional to the density $1/D = \theta/b$ of dislocations. The constant energy per dislocation is thus bE_0A; this includes not only the unknown energy of atomic misfit E_I, but also the constant term in the elastic energy; later in this section we shall discuss the several contributions to A in more detail.

The term $-E_0\theta \ln \theta$ comes entirely from the elastic energy; the variable term in the elastic energy *per dislocation* is $-bE_0 \ln \theta = bE_0 \ln (1/\theta)$. As θ decreases, the elastic energy per dislocation decreases; the reason is that the stress fields of the dislocations overlap and cancel. For example in Fig. 11.1 each dislocation produces a compression above it and a tension below. Between the dislocations these opposing stresses cancel and leave the material unstressed. As the dislocations come closer together, the opposing stress fields cancel over larger areas. The stress fields cancel not only between dislocations but especially in the areas to the right and left of the boundary. By calculating the stress field of all the dislocations (see Prob. 6), we find that, when the distance x from the boundary is of the order of D or larger, the elastic energy density varies approximately as $x^2 \exp (-4\pi x/D)$. Thus, as we move away from the boundary, the elastic energy decreases rapidly and becomes negligibly small when $x \gg D$.

When the spacing between dislocations increases without limit ($\theta \to 0$), the elastic energy per dislocation becomes infinite; this agrees with the fact (Sec. 8.4) that a single dislocation in an infinitely large crystal has infinite energy. However the elastic energy per unit area of grain boundary approaches zero as $\theta \to 0$, as it must for physical reasons. In mathematical terms: θ approaches zero faster than $-\ln \theta$ approaches infinity; so $-E_0\theta \ln \theta \to 0$ as $\theta \to 0$. The fact that energy per dislocation is sensitive to the spacing between dislocations explains why the energy of a dislocation array is determined by a macroscopic variable such as θ.[1]

We now consider in more detail the various contributions to A and the

---

[1] The author has shown that a two-parameter formula similar to (11.9) gives the energy per unit volume in a cold-worked metal as a function of the average density of dislocations for the hypothetical case where the distribution of dislocations remains similar as the average spacing changes. The derivation of this formula is given by Shockley (1952).

relation of A to the unknown energy of atomic misfit in the bad core of a dislocation. A involves the following three energies, each of which is a constant energy per dislocation (at least at small θ):

1. E_I, the unknown energy of atomic misfit in the bad material, which lies within a radius r_l of the center of the dislocation; r_l is also unknown.

2. There is an energy associated with the higher order terms in the expression for elastic stress, Eq. (11.3). This energy is highly localized in the good material immediately around the dislocation. Since it is part of E_{II}, call it $E_{II'}$. At small θ, $E_{II'}$ is independent of θ. Section 11.8 (2) will show how the E vs. θ formula must be modified when the dislocations are close enough together that the higher order terms are important in the region where the stress fields overlap appreciably.

3. We have seen that E_{III} is a constant energy per dislocation; E_{III} can be calculated by summing the stress fields of all the dislocations and finding the work done on the slip plane of a dislocation in forming the boundary (see Read and Shockley, 1950). The division of elastic energy between E_{III} and E_{II} is to some extent arbitrary and depends on the parameter K (see Shockley, 1952).

Read and Shockley (1952b) have shown that A is given directly in terms of the unknown E_I, r_l, and $E_{II'}$ by

$$A = \frac{2}{b^2 \tau_0} (E_I + E_{II'}) + 1 + \ln \frac{b}{2\pi r_l} \tag{11.11}$$

An experimental measurement of A does not give the core energy E_I directly. However, if calculations are ever made on an atomic basis, so that E_I, $E_{II'}$, and r_l can be evaluated, then (11.11) can be used to check the calculations with experimental measurements of grain-boundary energy.

K simply divided the energy between E_{II} and E_{III} for purposes of the derivation. Since this division is to some extent arbitrary, K does not appear in the final formula.

As used in this book E is understood to be *energy, not free energy;* except at the absolute zero of temperature, the two are not equal. At elevated temperatures, where grain boundaries come to equilibrium in the experiments, there is an appreciable contribution to free energy from the effect of the dislocations on the frequency of the normal modes of thermal vibration. However this effect is confined to the bad regions at the dislocation cores; hence, the change in free energy contributes additively to E_I and affects only the unknown parameter A. Shockley (1952) and Read and Shockley (1952b) have discussed this point in more detail.

11.6 Predictions from the Theory. This section shows how experimental measurements of E vs. θ could check the theory. Specifically it could check (1) the *form* of the formula and (2) the value of E_0. Both of these are derived from the elastic strain alone and are independent of the interatomic forces in the region of severe atomic distortion. Both are uniquely determined by the (anisotropic) elastic constants of the crystal and the dislocation model.

Figure 11.1 applies not just to the hypothetical simple cubic structure, but to any crystal where the atoms in a plane form a square array with each atom surrounded by four nearest neighbors. For example, it would apply to the {001} planes in face-centered cubic.

The ideal experimental procedure to check the theory would be as follows: Grow a number of controlled grain boundaries between face-centered cubic grains that have a common $<001>$ axis. Define the misfit by a rotation of each grain through an angle of $\theta/2$ away from the boundary, where the boundary is a plane of symmetry as in Fig. 11.1. Let the angular misfit θ be different in each bicrystal. Now measure the grain-boundary energies. (Chapter 13 discusses the techniques of preparing specimens and measuring energies.)

To compare the theoretical and experimental curves, plot E/θ vs. $\ln \theta$. When plotted in this way, the theoretical formula

$$\frac{E}{\theta} = E_0 \left[A - \ln \theta\right] \tag{11.12}$$

is a straight line; see Fig. 11.5a. The slope of the line is $-E_0$, and the zero-energy intercept is A. The theory predicts that

1. The experimental points at small θ should all lie on a straight line. This checks the *form* of the theoretical curve.
2. The slope of the straight line should be $-E_0 = (-\tau_0 b)/2$, where Eq. (8.16) with $\alpha = \pi/2$ gives τ_0 in terms of elastic constants. This would be a quantitative check of the theory.

The experimental plot would provide two additional pieces of information: One is the unknown parameter A, which is the logarithm of the angle at which the straight line, extrapolated to large angles, gives zero energy. The other is the value of θ above which the theory breaks down, and the points no longer fall on the straight line. It was assumed in the derivation that θ must be small; this would tell how small. Section 11.8 discusses, in detail, the small-θ limitation.

Figure 11.5b is a plot of $E = E_0\theta[A - \ln \theta]$ in the conventional way: E vs. θ. The curve goes through the origin; the density of dislocations (proportional to θ) approaches zero faster than the energy per dislocation (proportional to $- \ln \theta$) goes to infinity; so $\theta \ln \theta \to 0$ as $\theta \to 0$. The slope is infinite at the origin and decreases steadily; the curve reaches a maximum at an angle $\theta_m = e^{A-1}$ which depends on the unknown energy of atomic misfit.   The magnitude of the maximum is

$$E_m = E_0\theta_m \tag{11.13}$$

Typical values of E_m and θ_m are 600 ergs/cm² and 0.5 radian, respectively; or $E_0 \approx$ 1,200 ergs/cm² and $A \approx$ 0.3.

The unknown parameter $A = 1 + \ln \theta_m$ has almost no effect on the curve of Fig. 11.5b at small θ, where the energy is almost entirely elastic, $- \ln \theta \gg A$.

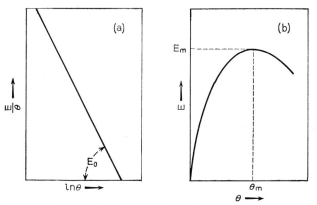

FIG. 11.5 Two ways of plotting the energy of a grain boundary vs. angle of misfit. (a) Plot of E/θ vs. $\ln \theta$.   (b) Plot of E vs. θ.   The parameters E_0, E_m, and θ_m are related by $E_m = E_0\theta_m$.   The straight line in a goes through zero energy at $\ln \theta = 1 + \ln \theta_m$, or $\theta = e\theta_m$.

The energy formula contains four quantities E, E_m, θ, θ_m; E_m and θ_m are constant when only θ varies.   The formula can also be written in terms of only two dimensionless quantities E/E_m and θ/θ_m:

$$\frac{E}{E_m} = \frac{\theta}{\theta_m}\left[1 - \ln \frac{\theta}{\theta_m}\right] \tag{11.14}$$

Now suppose we measure E vs. θ for a number of face-centered cubic metals, and plot E/E_m vs. θ/θ_m for each metal (each will have a different E_m and θ_m).   The theory predicts that all the experimental points will fall on the one theoretical curve (11.14).   The best available experimental data is plotted in this way in Fig. 13.2; the solid line is the theoretical curve.   This data is discussed in detail in Chap. 13; here we merely mention it in passing to show that the E vs. θ formula ties in with actual experimental measurements.   In these measurements, only relative energies were measured; so E_m is not known; θ_m for each set of measurements is listed on the figure.   These boundaries did *not* have the simple form in Fig. 11.1; also, they were not so controlled that only θ varied. Chapters 12 and 13 will discuss these boundaries and show that the formula (11.14) still applies as the best fit average curve; the lack of control of other degrees of freedom simply adds to the scatter.

One of the surprising features of Fig. 13.2 is that the theoretical curve fits the data even at relatively large angles, where the dislocations are only a few atoms apart. This also is discussed in Chap. 13; the small-θ limitation in general is discussed in Sec. 11.8. First, however, we give a short alternative derivation of E vs. θ; this derivation will help in estimating the range of θ where the formula should be valid.

11.7 Alternative Derivation of E vs. θ. The derivation in Sec. 11.3 brings out the physical meaning of the E vs. θ relation. This section presents a shorter and slightly more mathematical derivation, and brings out the small-θ limitation more accurately.

Read and Shockley (1950), in their original derivation, summed the stress fields of all the dislocations to find the shear stress acting on the slip plane of one dislocation. They then used the procedure of Sec. 8.4 to find $E_\perp$ from the work done on the slip plane of that dislocation. This section follows the same derivation but by-passes most of the mathematics; for example, we obtain the simple differential expression (11.7) from the integrated sum of the stress fields without having to carry out either the summation or the integration. All the terms in the sum vanish individually but one; that one represents the stress field of the dislocation on whose slip plane the work is calculated.

Take the origin at one dislocation in Fig. 11.1b and let the xz plane be the slip plane, as in Sec. 8.4. Let $\tau_{xy}(x,y)$ be the shearing stress due to a single dislocation. Equation (8.9) gives $\tau_{xy}(x,y)$ except near the dislocation. The shear stress on the slip plane of the dislocation at the origin is $\sum_{n=-\infty}^{n=\infty} \tau_{xy}(x,nD)$. As Sec. 8.4 showed, the energy $E_\perp$ per dislocation is $b/2$ times the shear stress integrated over the slip plane: Thus

$$E_\perp(D) = \frac{b}{2} \int_0^{\lambda D} \sum_{n=-\infty}^{n=\infty} \tau_{xy}(x,nD)\ dx \qquad (11.15)$$

where $\lambda \to \infty$ for an infinitely large crystal. We shall find that $E_\perp$ is independent of λ for $\lambda \gg 1$; that is, the energy is confined within only a few interdislocation spacings of the boundary; this result is a consequence of the dislocation model, which is always chosen to give zero strain far from the boundary.

The shear stress $\tau_{xy}(x,0)$ is not known, and in fact has no meaning, in the bad material at the origin. However, we can arbitrarily define τ_{xy} in the bad region by requiring it to give the correct total energy of a dislocation when integrated to $x = 0$ (Sec. 11.8 will show how this definition limits the derivation to small θ). For small θ, the assumed form of τ_{xy}

in the bad material affects only the constant energy per dislocation, which does not appear in the simple differential expression for $E_\perp$; we now proceed to derive this expression by differentiating $E_\perp$ with respect to D.

The concluding paragraph of this section will show that, when D is large enough that the first term in the series expression for stress is a good approximation, then the $n = 0$ term in Eq. (11.15) is the only term in the sum that depends on D; therefore differentiating with respect to D gives

$$\frac{dE_\perp}{dD} = \frac{b}{2} \lambda \tau_{xy}(\lambda D, 0) \tag{11.16}$$

Thus, as in Sec. 11.3, the change in $E_\perp$ is found from the stress on the slip plane of a single dislocation. Observe that $dE_\perp/dD$ depends only on the stress at distances equal to or greater than D from a dislocation. From (11.4) we have $\tau_{xy}(\lambda D, 0) = \tau_0 b/\lambda D$. Putting this in (11.16) gives

$$\frac{dE_\perp}{dD} = \frac{b\tau_0}{2D} \tag{11.17}$$

which is the same as (11.7) with $D = b/\theta$. (As an exercise the reader may wish to prove that only the $n = 0$ term depends on D—before going on to the answer in the following paragraph.)

Divide the x axis up into short segments of length $dx = D\, dx'$ (where x' is a dimensionless variable independent of D). Consider the work done on one segment by the stress due to the dislocation at $y = nD$ $(n \neq 0)$. Since stress varies inversely as distance from the dislocation, the product of stress times $dx = D\, dx'$ is independent of D.

11.8 Limitation of the Derivation to Small θ. When θ is large enough that the bad regions overlap, the dislocation model has no unique significance and the derivation of the E vs. θ relation does not apply at all. However, at smaller θ, there are three principal sources of error that become increasingly important as θ increases. These are the following:

1. The elasticity theory used in the derivation assumes that the geometry of the elastic region is not appreciably altered if the strain is relaxed. Suppose the strain along a grain boundary is relaxed by a cut and offset on the slip plane of every dislocation; this eliminates the dislocations and also the misfit. In the process, one grain rotates through an angle θ with respect to the other; the slip planes rotate through $\theta/2$ with respect to the boundary. Thus, for large θ, the shape of the elastic region is appreciably altered; hence the elasticity theory employed is invalid. This source of error may well be as large as the nonelastic effects 2 and 3 below.

2. The higher order terms in the elastic stress field have been neglected. These are most important in the immediate vicinity of a dislocation and contribute principally a constant energy per dislocation E_{II}, which affects

only the unknown parameter A. As θ increases, the higher order terms become important in the area where the stress fields of several dislocations overlap appreciably. Now, to calculate the elastic energy, we have to sum the higher order terms; Brooks (1952) has done this and shown that the higher order terms add an infinite series in powers of θ to $A - \ln \theta$; the first additional term is θ^2. The coefficients of the additional terms are not known at present. However, we would expect the formula to be valid at least for $\theta^2 \ll - \ln \theta$.

3. The stress fields of the various dislocations are superposed. However, at the core of a dislocation, the stress-strain relation is not linear and therefore the superposition principle does not hold. For example, in Eq. (11.15) we defined τ_{xy} in the bad region to give the correct energy per dislocation. However superposing a high elastic stress on the nonelastic distortion at a dislocation may give a state of distortion that is not the sum of the two taken individually. Suppose the stress field of the neighboring dislocations changes the nature of the atomic arrangement at the core of a dislocation; then the variation in energy per dislocation is not due simply to overlapping and canceling of the superposed elastic stress fields, and our formula fails. In other words, how we should define τ_{xy} in the bad region may depend on the spacing between dislocations. This effect may not be so serious in grain boundaries as it appears at first sight: in grain boundaries, symmetry generally requires that dislocations lie at positions of low or vanishing stress. For example, consider the stress at each dislocation in Fig. 11.1; observe that the stress fields of the other dislocations cancel in pairs; so each dislocation is at a point of zero stress. However if the dislocations are very close together, then the bad core of one dislocation overlaps with the high stress of another dislocation, and the superposition principle no longer holds.

Van der Merwe (1950) has carried out a more refined and elaborate mathematical derivation which, to some extent, avoids the above limitations. At small angles, van der Merwe's formula reduces to $E = E_0\theta[A - \ln \theta]$; the constant A is determined by an assumed approximate law for the nonlinear forces between atoms. Van der Merwe's analysis shows how some of the difficulties of an exact analysis can be overcome, and how a better knowledge of the forces between atoms could lead to a more exact formula.[1]

PROBLEMS

1. Add another plane of atoms in different elevation to make Fig. 11.1 represent the (001) plane in f.c.c.

[1] Van der Merwe applies the Peierls-Nabarro method to grain boundaries. For example, in the boundary of Fig. 12.2, van der Merwe treats each crystal grain as an

2. Draw a grain boundary made up of identical edge dislocations in the two-dimensional bubble model (see Lomer and Nye, 1952).

3. Consider a grain boundary in f.c.c. where the plane of the boundary is (110) and the two grains have a small relative rotation θ about the $[1\bar{1}2]$ axis, which is common to the two grains. Show that the grain boundary is a vertical row of *extended* edge dislocations. Consider how the separation of the partials (= width of the faults) varies with θ. Show that at large θ the separation increases as θ decreases; finally, at very small θ, the separation approaches a constant independent of θ. Show that $E = E_0\theta[A - \ln \theta]$ holds only in the range of very small θ and constant separation of the partials. Sketch roughly the form of the E/θ vs. $\ln \theta$ curve.

4. For a given θ, which has the lower energy—a grain boundary having many dislocations with small Burgers vectors or one having fewer dislocations with larger Burgers vectors?

5. Consider two parallel grain boundaries similar to Fig. 11.1; one has $\theta = \theta_1$, the other has $\theta = \theta_2$. Show that the two boundaries can reduce their energy by combining to form a single boundary with $\theta = \theta_1 + \theta_2$.

6. Consider the shear stress τ_{xy} for a vertical row of edge dislocations forming a simple grain boundary, as in Fig. 11.1. Using Prob. 4 of Chap. 8 and the relation

$$\sum_{n=-\infty}^{\infty} \frac{x}{x^2 + n^2} = \pi \coth \pi x$$

show that τ_{xy} is the real part of

$$\tau_0 b \frac{\pi^2 x}{D^2} \operatorname{csch}^2 \frac{\pi}{D} (x + iy)$$

What simple form does τ_{xy} take at distances from the boundary which are comparable to or greater than the spacing D between dislocations?

7. Use the results of Prob. 6 and the procedure of Sec. 8.4 to derive

$$E = E_0\theta[A - \ln \theta]$$

with

$$A = 1 - \ln \frac{2\pi R_0}{b}$$

where R_0 has the same meaning as in Sec. 8.4.

---

elastic continuum. He then uses the sine law (Sec. 2.7—Peierls-Nabarro) for stress vs. relative displacement across the grain boundary. His approach does not require an appreciable change in geometry of the elastic region—see 1 above—since the maximum displacement of a point on the boundary is $b/2$. Also, there is no mathematical infinity in the stress distribution and, consequently, no point where the solution cannot apply; all the parameters in the final formula are known.

In van der Merwe's treatment, the dislocation model of the boundary emerges from the mathematics; the transition from one grain to the other is relatively smooth over most of the boundary, with the severe misfit confined to discrete lines. At small angles, the solution reduces to a superposition of Peierls-Nabarro solutions (which, in turn, are equal to the conventional elasticity solution for a single dislocation except near the dislocation core). Thus, at small angles, van der Merwe's formula reduces to $E = E_0\theta[A - \ln \theta]$. However, his E increases monatomically with θ and therefore gives a poorer fit to the experimental data than our less rigorous formula, which has a maximum. Van der Merwe's analysis also rests on certain approximations which break down for large θ. The sine law of stress and strain is also subject to some question—see Sec. 2.7 and Lomer (1949).

8. Take account of the nonelastic effects discussed in Sec. 2.7 and show that the grain boundaries in Probs. 1 to 3 are under an average compressive stress that acts in the plane of the boundary and at right angles to the slip planes of the dislocations. Show that the magnitude of this stress is $c\theta$ + (higher order terms in θ) where c is independent of θ and less than unity. What is the physical meaning of c and how does it depend on atomic structure? Assuming relatively hard atoms (compression negligibly small compared to radius), find c for the boundaries in Probs. 1 to 3.

9. In Prob. 2, suppose the bubbles are relatively hard so that individual isolated dislocations are wide (in the sense defined in Sec. 2.7). Show that the dislocations in the grain boundary are wide and independent of θ at very small θ and that, at somewhat larger θ, the dislocations begin to get narrower as θ increases. (HINT: Use Prob. 7 of Chap. 2.) This effect was observed by Lomer and Nye (1952).

10. A deformation band may be visualized as a plane through which slip does not penetrate, or does not penetrate completely. Edge dislocations of opposite sign collect on opposite sides of the plane, which is normal to the slip vector. J. F. Nye (private communication) has observed (photoelastically) that deformation bands in silver chloride are under a compressive stress acting in the plane of the band and normal to the slip plane. Explain this using the general ideas of Prob. 8.

11. Suppose a grain boundary does not extend all the way through the crystal but ends abruptly on a line parallel to the dislocations. Find the stress distribution at distances from the end of the boundary which are large compared to D. [For the answer see Nabarro (1952).] Suppose τ_c is the critical stress for slip in a perfect crystal; at what value of D will the semi-infinite boundary become unstable and propagate catastrophically through the crystal? (This is a possible mechanism of kink formation; once a kink has started, the stress concentration at the ends of the kink can form new dislocations and permit the kink to grow.)

12. Consider a grain boundary in a structure made up of rigid atoms held together by long-range forces that can be represented by a hydrostatic pressure P. Show that the E vs. θ curve is a step function: $E = 0$ at $\theta = 0$; $E = \frac{1}{2}Pb$ at $\theta > \theta$. How is the curve modified if the atoms are slightly soft? Show that θ_m is determined by the hardness of the atoms (as defined in Sec. 2.7) and decreases as the hardness increases.

CHAPTER 12

GENERAL GRAIN BOUNDARIES

12.1 The Five Degrees of Freedom of a General Grain Boundary. The boundary in Fig. 11.1 is especially simple: the axis of relative rotation of the grains is a cube axis and the boundary lies in the symmetry, or mirror, plane of the bicrystal. In an arbitrary grain boundary, both the boundary plane and the axis of relative rotation of the grains may have any orientation. Thus the general grain boundary has five degrees of freedom: one grain can rotate with respect to the other; thus the difference in orientation of the grains has three degrees of freedom; the plane of the boundary can rotate in respect to the two grains—hence the orientation of the boundary has two degrees of freedom (rotation of a plane around its normal has no significance).

This chapter deals with the crystallography and energy of general grain boundaries. Section 12.2 introduces one more degree of freedom ϕ into the boundary of Fig. 11.1b by letting the grain boundary rotate about the common cube axis of the grains. Figure 11.1b corresponds to $\phi = 0$. The dislocation model and the energy are found as functions of ϕ and θ. The energy is again given by $E = E_0\theta[A - \ln\theta]$ where now E_0 and A are functions of ϕ.

Section 12.3 discusses so-called cusps, which arise because the spacing between dislocations cannot vary continuously but must always be an integral number of atomic planes.

Section 12.4 discusses what are called tilt and twist boundaries: to produce a tilt boundary, we rotate the grains about an axis in the plane of the boundary; in a twist boundary, the grains are rotated about the normal to the boundary. In certain special cases, tilt boundaries contain only edge dislocations, and twist boundaries, only screws.

Section 12.5 presents Frank's geometrical analysis of a general grain boundary. Frank has a simple procedure for finding the dislocation model for any arbitrary boundary. The boundary can always be made up of three sets of dislocations having different and noncoplanar Burgers vectors. Section 12.6 extends Frank's analysis to obtain an explicit formula for the directions and densities of the three sets of dislocations. Section 12.7 proves that $E = E_0\theta[A - \ln\theta]$ holds for the general boundary; θ is the magnitude of the relative rotation; E_0 and A depend on (1)

173

the orientation of the axis of relative rotation of the grains and (2) the orientation of the boundary. Note that 1 and 2 each have two degrees of freedom.

12.2 Two-degree-of-freedom Boundary. In Fig. 11.1 take one grain as fixed and let the other grain rotate about the cube axis normal to the drawing; this gives the one degree of freedom θ. To introduce another degree of freedom, let the grain boundary itself also rotate about the common cube axis of the grains; now we have two degrees of freedom. Figure 12.1 shows the two-degree-of-freedom boundary; ϕ is the angle between the boundary plane and the mean [100] direction of the two grains. The boundary makes an angle of $\phi + \theta/2$ with the [100] direction in one grain and an angle of $\phi - \theta/2$ with the [100] direction in the other grain; Fig. 11.1 is the special case of $\phi = 0$ or $90°$.

In Figure 11.1b the mismatch on the boundary is taken up by elastic deformation except where a plane of atoms ends on the boundary. The same is true of Fig. 12.1; now, however, two sets of planes end on the boundary; the number of each type is found from the figure as follows: The number of approximately vertical (100) planes coming into the boundary from above is equal to the distance EC divided by the spacing b between planes. The number coming up from below is AB/b. Hence $(EC - AD)/b$ planes end on the boundary. Take the trace AC of the boundary as unit length; then $EC = \cos(\phi - \theta/2)$, and

$$AB = \cos(\phi + \theta/2)$$

Thus

$$\frac{1}{b}\left[\cos\left(\phi - \frac{\theta}{2}\right) - \cos\left(\phi + \frac{\theta}{2}\right)\right] = \frac{2}{b}\sin\frac{\theta}{2}\sin\phi \doteq \frac{\theta}{b}\sin\phi$$

vertical planes end on unit length of the boundary. The edge of each plane is an edge-type dislocation, shown by the symbol $\perp$ in the figure. The same reasoning shows that

$$\frac{(CB - AE)}{b} = \frac{1}{b}\left[\sin\left(\phi + \frac{\theta}{2}\right) - \sin\left(\phi - \frac{\theta}{2}\right)\right] \doteq \frac{\theta}{b}\cos\phi$$

approximately horizontal planes end on the boundary in another set of edge dislocations; here the extra plane comes in from the right (slip plane vertical); these dislocations are denoted by the symbol $\vdash$. Thus the boundary consists of two sets of uniformly spaced dislocations. The spacings for the two sets are, respectively,

$$D_\perp = \frac{b}{\theta \sin\phi}$$

$$D_\vdash = \frac{b}{\theta \cos\phi} \tag{12.1}$$

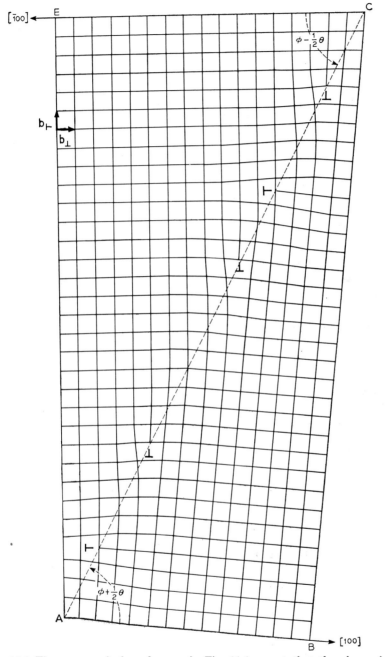

FIG. 12.1 The same grain boundary as in Fig. 11.1 except that the plane of the boundary makes an (arbitrary) angle ϕ with the mean of the (010) planes in the two grains (in Fig. 11.1 $\phi = 0$ or $90°$). Note that two sets of atomic planes end on the boundary in two sets of edge dislocations.

The geometrical conventions in Fig. 12.1 require that $0 \leqq \phi \leqq \pi/2$. When $\phi = 0$ or $\pi/2$, only one set is present, and we have the boundary of Fig. 11.1b.

Now consider the energy of the two sets of dislocations. This is the sum of three terms: (1) $E_\perp$ is the energy per dislocation of the $\perp$ set alone. (2) $E_\vdash$ is the energy per dislocation of the $\vdash$ alone. (3) Let $E_{\vdash\perp}$ be the energy of interaction per dislocation, which is equal to (strain associated with $\perp$) $\times$ (stress associated with $\vdash$), or vice versa.

The following argument shows that $E_{\perp\vdash}$ is independent of θ: $E_{\perp\vdash}$, by definition, comes from regions where the stress is due to the superposed stress fields of several dislocations; it is part of the energy E_{III} discussed in Sec. 11.4. Recall that the energy E_{III} remained constant when θ changed; the energy per unit area decreased and the area of the region increased in the same ratio. The same argument holds in Fig. 12.1, and the derivation of Sec. 11.3 applies to each set of dislocations individually; $E_{\perp\vdash}$ per dislocation enters only in the constant of integration. Thus Eq. (11.8) again gives $E_\perp$; a similar equation, with different A, gives $E_\vdash$. Observe that τ_0 is the same for the two sets of dislocations, which are crystallographically identical. The total energy E per unit area is $E_\perp/D_\perp + E_\vdash/D_\vdash$. Using Eqs. (12.1) for $D_\perp$ and $D_\vdash$, we have $E = E_0\theta[A - \ln \theta]$ as before; now however both E_0 and A depend on ϕ. E_0 is given by

$$E_0 = \frac{\tau_0 b}{2}(\cos \phi + \sin \phi) \tag{12.2}$$

E_0 varies in proportion to the total density $(1/b)(\cos \phi + \sin \phi)$ of dislocations—as is always true when the dislocations have equal τ_0's and b's. Since $0 \leqq \phi \leqq \pi/2$, E_0 varies by a factor of $\sqrt{2}$ as the boundary rotates about the normal to Fig. 12.1.

The dependence of A on ϕ is harder to calculate; it requires summing the stress fields of the doubly infinite array of dislocations. Read and Shockley (1950), who have done this for the isotropic case, find

$$A = A_0 - \frac{\sin 2\phi}{2} - \frac{\sin \phi \ln \sin \phi + \cos \phi \ln \cos \phi}{\sin \phi + \cos \phi} \tag{12.3}$$

where A_0 is the (at present) unknown value of A at $\phi = 0$ or $\pi/2$ (Fig. 11.1).

To summarize this section: adding another degree of freedom ϕ gives the same E vs. θ formula, where both E_0 and $A(\phi) - A(0)$ are known and depend on ϕ.

12.3 Energy Cusps. We have mentioned that the E vs. θ curve (Fig. 11.5b) has an infinite slope at $\theta = 0$. If the curve were extended to negative values of θ, it would be symmetrical about $\theta = 0$. Thus $\theta = 0$ is a cusp in the E vs. θ curve; the energy increases at an infinite rate as θ

deviates from $\theta = 0$. There are also cusps in E vs. the other degrees of freedom; for example, if a twin boundary deviates slightly from the twinning (mirror) plane, the energy increases at an infinite rate. The point $\phi = 0$ in the preceding section is also an energy cusp; the following shows this—first from the equations, then from a physical argument.

As ϕ approaches zero in Eqs. (12.2) and (12.3), $E_0 \to \tau_0 b/2$, and $A \to A_0 - 1 - \phi \ln \phi$. Thus, for small ϕ,

$$E(\theta,\phi) = E(\theta,0) - E_0 \, \theta\phi \ln \phi \qquad (12.4)$$

A plot of E vs. ϕ for constant θ has the same form at the origin as the E vs. θ curve, Fig. 11.5b.

The physical meaning of the energy cusp at $\phi = 0$ is this: At $\phi = 0$, there is only one set of dislocations spaced at $D_\vdash = b/\theta$. Let ϕ increase very slightly from $\phi = 0$. Now $D_\vdash = b/(\theta \cos \phi) \doteq b/\theta$; so the $\vdash$ remain unchanged. However, a second set—the $\perp$—are added; they are spaced at $D_\perp = b/(\theta \sin \phi) \doteq b/\theta\phi$ and, therefore, have an energy $E_0\theta\phi \ln \theta\phi$, which increases at an infinite rate with ϕ at $\phi = 0$.

Read and Shockley (1950) have shown that there are energy cusps at values of both θ and ϕ besides $\theta = 0$ and $\phi = 0$. The following shows why there are cusps at values of θ besides $\theta = 0$. The same argument applies to the other four degrees of freedom.

Take again the simple boundary in Fig. 11.1, where the dislocations are uniformly spaced at intervals of seven atomic planes. The E vs. θ derivation assumes that the dislocations are always *uniformly* spaced; however, the spacing must always be an integral number of atomic planes; hence the spacing is uniform only when $D/b = 1/\theta$ is an integer, and the formula is valid only at such points (note that the density of these points becomes infinite as $\theta \to 0$). For example, increase θ slightly over the value shown in Fig. 11.1 so that $D/b = 6.9$. Now we have a six spacing every 10 dislocations, or every 70 atomic planes. For an arbitrary deviation $\delta\theta$ from $\theta = \frac{1}{7}$, these six spacings occur at intervals of $b/(7\delta\theta)$. The energy due to the added dislocations comes from regions far from the boundary and contributes a term of the order $-(E_0/7)\delta\theta \ln \delta\theta$. (The effective strength of the perturbation is $b/7$.)

Similar $\delta\theta \ln \delta\theta$ cusps occur whenever the dislocations are spaced at integral numbers of atomic planes. Also cusps will occur at spacings such as $6\frac{1}{2}$, which corresponds to a regular alternation of six and seven spacings—a small deviation from this would require two six spacings to be adjacent. This reasoning leads to the conclusion that the E vs. θ curve has cusps at all values of θ for which D/b is a rational fraction. The same argument applies to deviations in ϕ and the other degrees of freedom from values which correspond to rational spacings. Actually, however, this fine structure will be smoothed out by statistical fluctuations except for certain prominent cusps. Most of the important cusps (besides $\theta = 0$) occur at relatively large θ's; twin boundaries are a particularly important example. Read and Shockley (1950) discuss cusps in considerable detail, especially in relation to the experimental measurements of Dunn and coworkers on silicon iron (Chap. 13).

12.4 Tilt and Twist Boundaries. It is convenient to represent the five degrees of freedom of a grain boundary by (1) the magnitude of the relative rotation θ that would bring the grains into perfect registry, (2) the axis of relative rotation, and (3) the orientation of the boundary. We let **u** be a unit vector parallel to the axis of relative rotation. The rotation of one grain relative to the other is a vector $\omega = \mathbf{u}\theta$. The three components of ω along three crystal axes would also represent the three degrees of freedom of relative rotation. (Using a vector to represent a finite rotation is a valid approximation when the rotation is small—as it is here. A vector can even represent a *single* large rotation; but *several* large rotations do not add vectorially.)

Specify the orientation of the boundary by the unit vector **n** normal to the plane of the boundary. We assume in this and the following chapters that the grain boundary is plane; the analysis, however, also applies to curved boundaries if the radii of curvature are large compared with the spacing between dislocations.

This section discusses what are called tilt and twist boundaries. In a tilt boundary the axis of relative rotation lies in the plane of the boundary; **u** and **n** are at right angles. In a twist boundary the axis of relative rotation is normal to the plane of the boundary; so **u** = **n**; here the plane of the boundary is a common crystallographic plane of the two grains. Figures 11.1 and 12.1 show pure tilt boundaries. They are made up of pure edge dislocations. The following paragraph describes the structure and energy of a simple twist boundary that contains only screw dislocations. The rest of the section discusses more general tilt and twist boundaries and shows that, in general, both edge and screw components are required in either type of boundary.

Figure 12.2 shows a twist boundary between two simple or face-centered cubic grains. Here the grains have a common {001} plane, which is the plane of the boundary, and also the plane of the figure. The open circles are atoms in the atomic plane just above the boundary; the solid circles are atoms in the plane just below. The figure shows that the boundary is a crossed grid of screw dislocations (compare with Fig. 2.3). Show that the spacing between dislocations is $D = b/\theta$ for each set.

The argument of Sec. 12.2 for the energy of two sets of dislocations applies to the twist boundary of Fig. 12.2; so again we have

$$E = E_0\theta[A - \ln \theta].$$

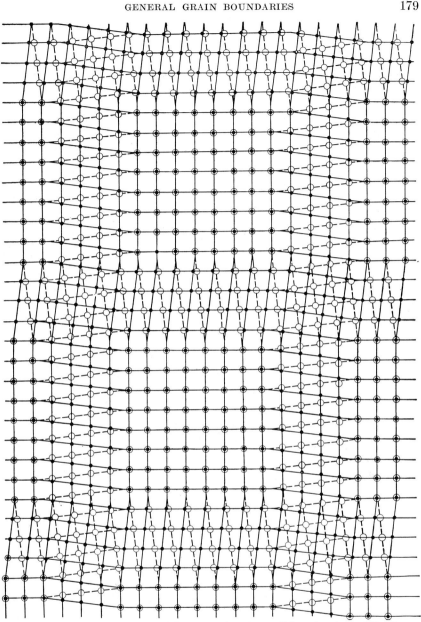

FIG. 12.2 A pure twist boundary. The boundary is parallel to the plane of the figure, and the two grains have a small relative rotation about their cube axis, which is normal to the boundary. The open circles represent the atoms just above the boundary, the solid circles, the atoms just below. The grains join together continuously except along the two sets of screw dislocations, which form a crossed grid.

As in Fig. 11.1, $D = b/\theta$; since the two sets of dislocations are crystallographically identical, the energy is just doubled—that is, $E_0 = b\tau_0$ where now τ_0 refers to the pure screw orientation. In the isotropic case $\tau_0 = G/2\pi$; in face-centered cubic, τ_0 is given by Eq. (8.17). A also is probably different for screw dislocations.

Any difference in orientation ω of the two grains can be resolved into orthogonal twist and tilt components; the twist component is $\mathbf{n} \cdot \boldsymbol{\omega} = \mathbf{n} \cdot \mathbf{u}\theta$. In general the dislocation model is *not* the superposition of the models for the twist and tilt components taken individually.

The following discusses the physical difference between twist and tilt boundaries and shows why Figs. 12.1 and 12.2 are special cases.

A pure twist boundary requires dislocations because corresponding atomic planes in the two grains do not intersect the boundary in parallel lines. The two sets of screw dislocations twist the adjoining atomic planes into register at the boundary; so the transition between grains is smooth everywhere except at the dislocations themselves.

In a pure tilt boundary, the atomic planes from the two grains meet the boundary along parallel lines; but the density of planes meeting the boundary is greater on one side; hence some planes end on the boundary in dislocations. As an exercise, prove that every plane ending on the boundary ends on a line parallel to $\mathbf{u}$. In Fig. 12.1, there are two $\mathbf{t}$ vectors at right angles to $\mathbf{u}$. Thus two sets of atomic planes can end on the boundary in edge dislocations whose Burgers vectors are $\mathbf{t}$ vector. This would not be true, for example, for the same boundary in body-centered cubic, where no $<111>$ $\mathbf{t}$ vectors are normal to $\mathbf{u} = [001]$; if dislocations with $\frac{1}{2}<111>$ Burgers vectors make up the boundary, the dislocations will be part edge and part screw. Such a pure tilt boundary is shown in Fig. 12.3. Observe that the screw components alternate in sign; the edge components are all the same. In a pure tilt boundary, the "unwanted" screw components always average out and contribute nothing to the misfit. They do however contribute to the boundary energy.

Incidentally, Fig. 12.3 shows how a disorientation of adjoining parts of a crystal could be produced by slip. Polygonized boundaries are actually formed in this way: the dislocations generated during deformation are rearranged into small-angle-of-misfit transition surfaces during annealing.

The boundary of Fig. 12.3 is symmetrical ($\phi = 0$). Suppose the boundary rotates about the axis of relative rotation of the adjoining grains (as in Fig. 12.1); now four sets of dislocations are required; the edge components are the same as in Fig. 12.1, and the screw components alternate in each set. Thus, in body-centered cubic with the axis of relative rotation along [001], the four Burgers vectors could be $\frac{1}{2}[111]$ alternating with $\frac{1}{2}[11\bar{1}]$ and $\frac{1}{2}[1\bar{1}1]$ alternating with $\frac{1}{2}[1\bar{1}\bar{1}]$.

The same reasoning shows that in general a pure twist boundary will contain dislocations with edge components; in general, the possible Burgers vectors will not lie in the plane of the boundary and therefore cannot be parallel to the dislocations. The edge components contribute to the energy without helping to accommodate the misfit. The fact that there are components that contribute to energy but not misfit explains why, for a given (arbitrary) misfit, the boundary energy varies with boundary orientation even in an elastically isotropic material.

Figures 11.1, 12.1, and 12.2 all show the atomic arrangement in planes where the atoms form a square array. However, the squares can be changed to parallelograms to represent a plane containing two primitive **t** vectors that are not at right angles, for example, the {110} planes of body-centered cubic or the {111} planes of face-centered cubic. This is the same transformation discussed in Sec. 2.6.

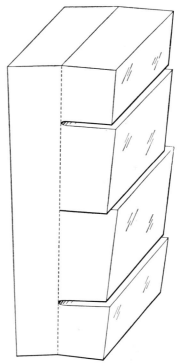

12.5 Frank's Formula for a General Grain Boundary. Suppose we are given a grain boundary; the crystal structure and θ, **u**, and **n**, are specified. What is the dislocation model? What is the orientation and spacing of dislocations having a given Burgers vector? Frank (1950) has a simple procedure for finding the dislocation model, or rather, the several possible models for a given boundary. This section presents Frank's formula from a pictorial viewpoint; the derivation is simplified by taking θ small.

The analysis applies to the general case of a grain boundary with five degrees of freedom, specified by a (small) angle of misfit θ and the two arbitrary

Fig. 12.3 A pure tilt boundary formed by dislocations with identical edge components and alternating screw components. The dislocations are represented by the slip that could have formed them. (Polygonized boundaries are actually made up of dislocations formed in slip.)

unit vectors: **u**, along the axis of relative rotation, and **n**, normal to the grain boundary. The following results, which have already been obtained for the special boundaries in the previous sections, will be shown to hold also for the general small-θ boundary:

1. The boundary is made up of sets of parallel straight dislocations uniformly spaced. Straight here means straight on a macroscopic scale:

on an atomic scale the dislocations may be curved or bent (Sec. 14.7).

2. The geometry of the boundary limits the dislocation model to only a few possibilities; the number of geometrically possible models is equal to the number of ways of resolving a given vector into **t** vectors. The correct model is the one having the lowest energy. In general, we can find the lowest energy model by calculating energies for only the one or two models having the lowest total dislocation density.

We continue to restrict the analysis to small θ boundaries, where the dislocations are many atomic spacings apart. It is always possible to produce a given disorientation of the adjoining grains by several different relative rotations $\omega = \mathbf{u}\theta$ each having a different θ. For example, to take an extreme case, θ is about $8°$ in Fig. 11.1; this corresponds to rotating each grain through $4°$ away from the boundary; however, we could have taken $\theta = 82°$ with each grain rotated $41°$ toward the boundary. The following applies only to boundaries where the relative orientation of the two grains can be produced by a small rotation; we take $\omega = \mathbf{u}\theta$ for that rotation. Read and Shockley (1950) have discussed dislocation models of large-θ boundaries.

Figure 12.4a shows a boundary of arbitrary orientation and arbitrary relative rotation $\omega = \mathbf{u}\theta$ about the axis **u**. This boundary is part tilt and part twist; that is, the axis of relative rotation has components both in and at right angles to the boundary.

Figure 12.4b shows the boundary of Fig. 12.4a with the upper grain removed. Frank's analysis shows that the boundary consists of sets of parallel straight dislocations. (For convenience, only one set is shown in the figure.) The orientation and density of each set is given by Frank's formula, which we now derive. The derivation is an extension of Burgers circuits and vectors to grain boundaries.

Choose any vector **V** lying in the boundary. One possible choice is shown in Fig. 12.4b. Then construct the vector **V'** by rotating **V** through the relative rotation $\omega = \mathbf{u}\theta$ of the two grains; the figure shows **V'** for the chosen **V**. **V'** has the same crystallographic indices in one grain that **V** has in the other. **V** and **V'** would be the same vector if there were no mis-fit—that is, if the specimen were a perfect single crystal instead of a bicrystal. Next construct the Burgers circuit shown in Fig. 12.4b. It begins at the end point of **V'** and goes along the solid line in the upper grain. It passes through the boundary at the common origin of **V** and **V'**. Continuing in the lower grain (dashed line), it ends at the end point of **V**; hence its closure failure is the vector $\mathbf{S} = \mathbf{V'} - \mathbf{V}$. This circuit is a Burgers circuit because it would close in a perfect crystal, where **V** and **V'** coincide. Since it does not close in the bicrystal, it must encircle dislocations. The sum of the Burgers vectors of the encircled dislocations is equal to the closure failure **S** of the circuit. The dislocations encircled by the circuit are also cut by **V**. **S** is therefore the sum of the Burgers vectors of the dislocations cut by **V**.

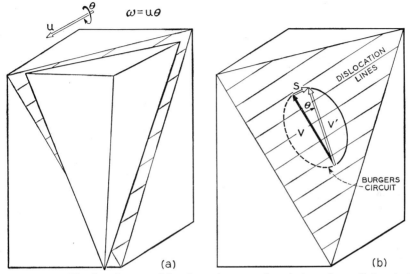

FIG. 12.4 (*a*) The five degrees of freedom of a general grain boundary: Cut a single crystal along two arbitrary planes, take out the wedge-shaped material between the two cuts, and bring the grains together again with a twist. The orientations of the two cuts and the magnitude of the twist define the five degrees of freedom. The definition in the text uses the magnitude of the relative rotation θ, the direction of the axis of relative rotation (parallel to the unit vector **u**), and the grain boundary normal **n**. The vector ω represents the (small) rotation of the top grain relative to the bottom one. (*b*) The top grain is not shown; the grain boundary consists of several sets of parallel dislocations (only one set is shown). The vector **V** is an arbitrary vector in the plane of the boundary. **S** = ω **X V** is the sum of the Burgers vectors cut by **V**.

For small θ, **S** is the vector, or cross, product of ω and **V**.

$$\mathbf{S} = \omega \times \mathbf{V} = (\mathbf{u} \times \mathbf{V})\theta \qquad (12.5)$$

The vector, or cross, product **u X V** is a vector normal to both **u** and **V**; its magnitude is equal to the area of the parallelogram whose sides are **u** and **V**; when **u** and **V** are parallel **u X V** = 0. Equation (12.5) is Frank's formula for the dislocation content of an arbitrary small-θ boundary. For the formula and its derivation without the small-θ approximation, see Frank (1950).

As an exercise, illustrate the above argument for the boundaries in Figs. 11.1, 12.1, and 12.2. Take two **V**'s in each case, construct the corresponding two Burgers circuits, and verify that Eq. (12.5) gives the correct **S** in each case.

We now show how Frank's formula gives the dislocation model when all we know are θ, **u**, **n**, and the crystal structure. As a simple example, take **u** = [001], **n** = [100] in a simple cubic bicrystal. (This is actually the boundary in Fig. 11.1.) The following argument derives the dislocation model from the given **u**, **n**, and θ using Frank's formula. The procedure is to choose one **V**, find the corresponding **S**, and then repeat for a second **V**. The only restriction on **V** is that it lie in the boundary.

First take **V** as unit vector in the [001] direction: **V** = **u** = [001]. Then, from (12.5), **S** = 0. This implies that **V** cuts *no* dislocations; so, the dislocations are all parallel to [001].

For the second **V**, take the unit vector in the [010] direction (up in Fig. 11.1). Now Eq. (12.5) gives **S** = θ[100]b = θ**b**/b where **b** = [100]. Thus the sum of the Burgers vectors cut by this **V** is θ**b**/b. The simplest model is therefore a row of identical dislocations with Burgers vector **b** and spacing $D = b/\theta$, which is the model shown in Fig. 11.1b.

As an exercise, carry through similar analyses for Figs. 12.1 and 12.2; verify that Frank's formula gives the correct dislocation model for the given θ, **n**, and **u**. For Fig. 12.1, express **n** in terms of ϕ and obtain Eqs. (12.1). Prove that, in any pure tilt boundary, all the dislocations are parallel to **u**. What is the necessary and sufficient condition that a boundary be made up of dislocations that are all alike?

Next consider the general case, where the **t** vectors are **b**$_1$, **b**$_2$, **b**$_3$, **b**$_4$, ... Suppose a given **V** cuts n_i dislocations having Burgers vector **b**$_i$ ($i = 1,2,3, . . .$). By definition

$$\mathbf{S} = n_1\mathbf{b}_1 + n_2\mathbf{b}_2 + n_3\mathbf{b}_3 + n_4\mathbf{b}_4 + \ . \ . \ .$$

Since both **S** and the n_i depend on **V**, we can write this equation as

$$\mathbf{S}(\mathbf{V}) = \sum_i n_i(\mathbf{V})\mathbf{b}_i \qquad (12.6)$$

From here it is a short step to prove rigorously that the dislocations are straight and that all the dislocations having the same Burgers vector are parallel. The proof follows directly from the fact that the magnitude of **S** is directly proportional to the length (magnitude) of the corresponding **V** for any choice of **V**. Since the **b**$_i$ in Eq. (12.6) are fixed, the number of dislocations of each type cut by **V** must increase in direct proportion to the length of **V**. Hence, the dislocations for each **b** are uniformly spaced as measured along any direction in the boundary; they are, therefore, parallel straight lines.

Observe that the values of n_i for two different directions of **V** uniquely determine the direction and spacing of the ith set of dislocations (dislocations whose Burgers vector is **b**$_i$). Thus two choices of **V** give the dislocation model.

If there are more than three t vectors, S can be resolved into components $n_i b_i$ in several different ways; each way represents a different model and a different arrangement of atoms. We then have to calculate energies to find which model has the lowest energy; that model should represent a well-annealed sample. The total number of dislocations in each model gives at least a rough idea of the relative energy and is much easier to calculate. The following section gives an explicit formula for the dislocation model for any choice of three Burgers vectors.

12.6 Densities and Directions of the Dislocations. Equations (12.5) and (12.6) show that the density of each set of dislocations is proportional to θ. Read and Shockley (1952b) define a quantity N_i where $N_i\theta$ is the density of the ith dislocation type; the dislocations are uniformly spaced at intervals of $D_i = 1/(N_i\theta)$. Observe that, when **V** is a unit vector normal to the dislocations, $n_i(\mathbf{V}) = N_i\theta$. This suggests defining a vector $\mathbf{N}_i$ which has the magnitude N_i, lies in the grain boundary, and is normal to the ith set of dislocations. Then n_i equals the dot, or scalar, product of $\theta\mathbf{N}_i$ and **V**; so

$$\mathbf{u} \times \mathbf{V} = \sum_i b_i \mathbf{N}_i \cdot \mathbf{V} \tag{12.7}$$

The $\theta\mathbf{N}_i$ completely specify the dislocation model. Now suppose we wish to make up a given boundary (given **u**, **n**, and θ) from three sets of dislocations having noncoplanar Burgers vectors $\mathbf{b}_i$ ($i = 1,2,3$). As an exercise show that

$$\mathbf{N}_i = \mathbf{b}_i^* \times \mathbf{u} - \mathbf{n}(\mathbf{n} \cdot \mathbf{b}_i^* \times \mathbf{u}) \tag{12.8}$$

where the $\mathbf{b}_i^*$ are the reciprocal vectors, defined by

$$\mathbf{b}_1^* = \frac{\mathbf{b}_2 \times \mathbf{b}_3}{\mathbf{b}_1 \cdot \mathbf{b}_2 \times \mathbf{b}_3}$$

with similar relations for $\mathbf{b}_2^*$ and $\mathbf{b}_3^*$ obtained by rotating subscripts. Equation (12.8) says that $\mathbf{N}_i$ is the projection of $\mathbf{b}_i^* \times \mathbf{u}$ in the plane of the grain boundary.

The above argument shows that any grain boundary can be made up of any three sets of dislocations having noncoplanar Burgers vectors. When there are more than three noncoplanar **t** vectors, then there are several ways of choosing the three Burgers vectors; each way gives a different model. To find the best model, first find the total dislocation density

$$\theta \sum_{i=1}^{3} N_i$$ for each model; in general this will be at least a rough indication of grain-boundary energy. Then calculate the energy for the model, or several models, for which the total dislocation density is least.

Next consider the question whether a three-dislocation model is better than, say, a four-dislocation model. Suppose we have found the lowest energy three-dislocation model; is it possible to lower the energy by adding a fourth set of dislocations? Show that, if $\delta \mathbf{N}_4$ represents the added fourth set, the directions and densities of the other three sets must be varied so that the change $\delta \mathbf{N}_i$ in $\mathbf{N}_i$ is

$$\delta \mathbf{N}_i = -(\mathbf{b}_4 \cdot \mathbf{b}_i^*) \delta \mathbf{N}_4 \qquad (12.9)$$

$\delta \mathbf{N}_4$ is arbitrary and can be chosen to minimize the energy. The condition that there be a $\delta \mathbf{N}_4$ which will lower the total dislocation density forms Prob. 5.

The following section extends the energy formula to the general grain boundary with arbitrary $\mathbf{u}$ and $\mathbf{n}$ and any number of sets of dislocations.

12.7 Energy of a General Grain Boundary. This section proves that $E = E_0 \theta [A - \ln \theta]$ gives the variation of energy with angle of misfit for any fixed orientation of the grain boundary and axis of relative rotation. The parameters E_0 and A vary with $\mathbf{u}$ and $\mathbf{n}$.

The proof is simply a generalization of the E vs. θ derivation in Sec. (12.2), where there were two sets of dislocations: The energy per dislocation of each set was found by ignoring the other set. The energy of interaction of the two sets contributed only a certain constant per dislocation. Exactly the same argument applies when there are three or more sets of dislocations. The energy per dislocation of the ith set is

$$E_i = \frac{\tau_{0i} b_i^2}{2} [A_i - \ln \theta] \qquad (12.10)$$

The A term includes the energy of interaction of the ith set with the other sets.

The total energy per unit area is $E = \theta \Sigma N_i E_i$. From Eq. (12.10),

$$E = E_0 \theta [A - \ln \theta] \qquad (12.11)$$

where

$$E_0 = \tfrac{1}{2} \sum_i \tau_{0i} N_i b_i^2 \qquad (12.12)$$

As an exercise obtain Eq. (12.2) from (12.12); use the method of Sec. 12.6 to find N_i for the two sets of dislocations (Fig. 12.1).

Read and Shockley (1952b) have used Eq. (12.12) to find the values of E_0 for various grain boundaries in face-centered cubic crystals; they used Eq. (8.16) and the anisotropic elastic constants to find the τ_0's.

PROBLEMS

1. Take $\mathbf{V}$ as a unit vector in the grain boundary. Show that the corresponding $\mathbf{S}$ is given by the following graphical construction: Let $\mathbf{S}$ and $\mathbf{V}$ have a common origin in the grain boundary. The end point of $\mathbf{S}$ is at the intersection of the following three surfaces:

a. A circular cylinder of radius $\mathbf{n} \cdot \mathbf{u}\theta$ where the axis of the cylinder goes through the origin and is normal to the boundary.

b. A plane through the origin and normal to $\mathbf{u}$.

c. A plane through the origin and normal to $\mathbf{V}$.

Thus show that, as $\mathbf{V}$ rotates and traces out a circle in the boundary, $\mathbf{S}$ traces out an ellipse. Find the orientation of the ellipse and its major and minor axes in terms of $\mathbf{n}$ and $\mathbf{u}\theta$.

2. A simple cubic crystal contains a cube-shaped volume of material that has a small difference in orientation from the surrounding crystal. The disoriented cube has faces parallel to $\{100\}$ planes and is rotated (relative to the rest of the crystal) about the [001] axis. Draw the distribution of dislocations on the faces of the cube.

3. Consider a bicrystal containing a pure tilt boundary. A torque is applied to the bicrystal about the normal to the grain boundary. Show that the boundary tends to rotate about an axis in the boundary and normal to the dislocations.

4. Plot $E_m(\phi) = E_0(\phi)\theta_m(\phi)$ vs. ϕ for the boundary of Fig. 12.1.

5. Consider a model consisting of three sets of dislocations. Introduce a fourth set corresponding to $\delta\mathbf{N}_4$ (Sec. 12.6). Show that the change in total dislocation density for small δN_4 is equal in magnitude to $(1 - \mathbf{a} \cdot \mathbf{n}_4)\theta\delta N_4$ where $\mathbf{n}_4$ is unit vector in the direction of $\delta\mathbf{N}_4$ and $\mathbf{a} = \displaystyle\sum_{i=1}^{3} (\mathbf{b}_4 \cdot \mathbf{b}_i^*)\mathbf{n}_i$ where $\mathbf{n}_i$ is unit vector parallel to $\mathbf{N}_i$.

In what direction should $\delta\mathbf{N}_4$ be taken for maximum reduction in total dislocation density?

Give some examples in both face-centered cubic and body-centered cubic where a fourth set of dislocations can decrease the total dislocation density.

6. Consider an arbitrary grain boundary with three sets of dislocations whose Burgers vectors have magnitude b and are mutually orthogonal. Resolve the vectors $\mathbf{n}$, $\mathbf{u}$, and $\mathbf{c} = \mathbf{u} \times \mathbf{n}$ into components n_i, u_i, c_i ($i = 1,2,3$) along three rectangular coordinate axes that are, respectively, parallel to the three Burgers vectors. Show that

$$E_0 = \frac{Gb}{4\pi(1 - \nu)} \sum_{i=1}^{3} \left[\sqrt{1 - u_i{}^2 - c_i{}^2} - \frac{\nu(\mathbf{n} \cdot \mathbf{u} - n_i u_i)}{\sqrt{1 - u_i{}^2 - c_i{}^2}} \right]$$

where G is the shear modulus and ν, Poisson's ratio (use isotropic elasticity).

CHAPTER 13

MEASUREMENTS OF GRAIN-BOUNDARY ENERGY

13.1 Introduction. Throughout the grain-boundary studies, there has been a continuous cross-stimulation between theory based on dislocation models and experiment. Dunn and coworkers' measurements of relative E vs. θ in silicon iron stimulated much of the theory in Chaps. 11 and 12. Aust and Chalmers made similar measurements on tin and lead. This chapter discusses briefly the experimental techniques and compares the results with the theory.

Section 13.2 discusses Dunn's technique of preparing tricrystals and determining energies. Section 13.3 deals with the formula used to calculate energies from the equilibrium configuration of the three boundaries in a tricrystal. Herring's exact formula is given together with the approximation used in practice; the latter neglects the dependence of energy on orientation of the boundary. Section 13.4 presents the experimental measurements of relative E vs. θ. This includes two sets of measurements by Dunn *et al.* and two by Aust and Chalmers. All four sets of data are well fitted by the theoretical formula, even at relatively large angles where the derivation would not be expected to hold.

Section 13.5 discusses measurements of absolute grain-boundary energy in silver, iron, and copper.

13.2 Dunn's Tricrystals. The measurements on silicon iron (about 3.5 weight per cent silicon, body-centered cubic) were made by Dunn and Lionetti (1949) and Dunn, Daniels, and Bolton (1950). These two series of measurements were especially well suited for comparison with the theory: the boundaries were all pure tilt; the axis of relative rotation was constant in each series—[110] in the first series, [100] in the second. Thus all the boundaries had two degrees of freedom θ and ϕ, as in Fig. 12.1. In the [110] series, the atoms have the same arrangement as in Fig. 12.1 except that the squares are replaced by parallelograms (Fig. 2.10 shows one dislocation).

The experimental procedure that Dunn *et al.* used was as follows: They prepared flat three-grain specimens by controlled grain growth; the growth nucleus of each grain was twisted into the desired orientation. Then the specimen was fed into a furnace so that growth proceeded from the oriented nuclei. The common axis of the three grains, [100] or [110], was always at right angles to the plane of the (flat) specimen.   They then annealed the tricrystals until the boundaries reached a constant configuration.   Three notches anchored the ends of the boundaries at the surface.

Figure 13.1 shows the three boundaries looking along the common axis of the grains.   The ϕ for each boundary is defined as in Fig. 12.1; it represents the orientation of the boundary in respect to the adjoining grains.   The energy of each boundary is a function of both ϕ and θ: $E_i = E(\theta_i, \phi_i)$.   The θ's are fixed by the fixed orientations of the grains; the ϕ's vary as the boundaries rotate and move toward the constant

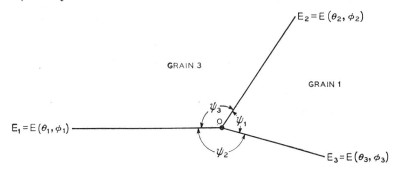

FIG. 13.1 Three grain boundaries that meet along a line (normal to the figure). Each boundary is defined by the angular misfit θ of the adjoining grains and the orientation ϕ of the boundary.

equilibrium state.   Each boundary tries to reduce its energy by (1) shrinking, to decrease its area, and (2) rotating toward an orientation of less energy.   Hence each boundary has an effective surface tension equal to its energy and is subject to a torque which is proportional to the derivative of energy with respect to boundary orientation.   C. Herring (1951) has derived the exact conditions for the equilibrium configuration; these are discussed in the next section.   Except in special cases, such as twin boundaries, a formula based on 1 alone seems to be a good approximation.   This is equivalent to treating each boundary as a two-dimensional soap film with surface tension equal to boundary energy per unit area.   In this approximation the equilibrium conditions reduce to the triangle of forces for the equilibrium of three forces acting at a point:

$$\frac{E_1}{\sin \psi_1} = \frac{E_2}{\sin \psi_2} = \frac{E_3}{\sin \psi_3} \tag{13.1}$$

The angles ψ_1, ψ_2, ψ_3 are shown in Fig. 13.1.   Dunn and coworkers measured the angles and calculated the ratios of the energies.   They made one boundary the same in each tricrystal and took its energy as the (unknown) unit of energy. Thus they got a curve of E vs. θ, where θ varied from a few degrees up to the twin orientation. Aust and Chalmers (1950) used the same procedure to get E vs. θ for tin and lead; their method of specimen preparation was somewhat different, and the grains did not all have a common axis throughout each set of measurements. Figure 13.2 shows the four sets of data plotted in terms of the dimensionless variables E/E_m vs. θ/θ_m. Section 13.4 discusses the data and its relation to theory; first, however, we shall give an exact treatment of the equilibrium conditions at the intersection of the three grains.

13.3 Herring's Exact Formula. Herring (1951) derived the equilibrium conditions taking account of the dependence of energy on boundary orientation. For calculating relative energies, it is convenient to express Herring's equations in the form

$$\frac{E_1}{(1 + \epsilon_2\epsilon_3)\sin\psi_1 + (\epsilon_3 - \epsilon_2)\cos\psi_1} = \frac{E_2}{(1 + \epsilon_1\epsilon_3)\sin\psi_2 + (\epsilon_1 - \epsilon_3)\cos\psi_2}$$
$$= \frac{E_3}{(1 + \epsilon_1\epsilon_2)\sin\psi_3 + (\epsilon_2 - \epsilon_1)\cos\psi_3}$$

$$(13.2)$$

where

$$\epsilon_i = \frac{\partial}{\partial\phi_i}\ln E_i = \frac{1}{E_i}\frac{\partial E_i}{\partial\phi_i} \tag{13.3}$$

The derivation of these equations forms Prob. 1.

If the ϵ's vanish, (13.2) reduces to (13.1). Consider the effect of neglecting the ϵ's in (13.2). No systematic measurements of E vs. ϕ have been made. However, we can calculate E from the theory, at least for small values of θ, where the theory may be expected to hold. At large θ, Eq. (12.3) probably does not give the correct variation of the unknown parameter A. However, there is some indication that, for large θ, the variations in A and E_0 with ϕ tend to compensate and leave E relatively independent of ϕ (see Prob. 4, Chap. 12); so possibly the neglect of the ϵ's is justified for large angles of misfit.

To estimate ϵ for a small-θ boundary, differentiate $E = E_0\theta[A - \ln\theta]$ with respect to ϕ:

$$\epsilon = \frac{1}{E}\frac{\partial E}{\partial\phi} = \frac{1}{E_0}\frac{\partial E_0}{\partial\phi} + \frac{1}{A - \ln\theta}\frac{\partial A}{\partial\phi} \tag{13.4}$$

Since $E_0 = \tau_0 b(\cos\phi + \sin\phi)/2$, the first term on the right in (13.4) is

$$\frac{1}{E_0}\frac{\partial E_0}{\partial\phi} = \frac{1 - \tan\phi}{1 + \tan\phi} \tag{13.5}$$

this term varies between $+1$ and -1. For small values of θ, where $A \ll -\ln\theta \gg 1$, the second term is small unless $\partial A/\partial\phi$ is quite large. In certain cases however, $\partial A/\partial\phi$ will be quite large; that is, the boundary will have a very high resistance to changing its orientation. Section 12.3 showed that, at small ϕ, A varies as $\phi \ln \phi$ so that E has an infinite derivative at $\phi = 0$.

It is not known whether or not the $\phi = 0$ cusp is large enough to prevent the boundary from rotating; however, when two grains are in a twin orientation, experiment has shown that the twinning plane is definitely a cusp in the energy vs. boundary orientation curve. Here, only one equation relates the three energies; we can equilibrate tensions only parallel to the strongly orientation-dependent boundary. If the energies of the other two boundaries are known independently, we can calculate the energy of a twin, or other orientation-dependent, boundary from the ψ's.

Cusp orientations can be detected by annealing a bicrystal with a boundary that runs obliquely across the crystal between two parallel faces. As long as the boundary does not encounter a cusp orientation, it rotates toward the minimum area orientation, at right angles to the two faces.

The consistency of experimental results based on the approximate formula (13.1) seems to indicate that, except for twin boundaries, the approximate formula is fairly accurate. At large angles of misfit, this may be due to the tendency of variations in A and E_0 with ϕ to cancel. At small angles, the apparent accuracy of the approximate formula may be explained as follows, without neglecting the orientation dependence of the small θ boundary: In general, a small-θ boundary occurs in a tricrystal containing two large-θ boundaries. (It is impossible to have only two small-θ boundaries, and three small-θ boundaries require too long to come to equilibrium.) If E_1 is the energy of the small-θ boundary, and if the other two boundaries are not strongly orientation dependent, we can take $\epsilon_2 = \epsilon_3 = 0$, and have

$$\frac{E_1}{\sin \psi_1} = \frac{E_2}{\sin \psi_2 (1 + \epsilon_1 \cot \psi_2)} = \frac{E_3}{\sin \psi_3 (1 - \epsilon_1 \cot \psi_3)} \quad (13.6)$$

In actual samples, where one energy E_1 is small, the opposite angle ψ_1 is near 180° and ψ_2 and ψ_3 are both near 90°. Away from cusp orientations, the second term in Eq. (13.4) can be neglected at small θ; thus $|\epsilon_1|$ is less than unity, (13.4) and (13.5); consequently $\epsilon_1 \cot \psi_2$ and $\epsilon_1 \cot \psi_3$ are negligibly small, and (13.6) reduces to the approximate formula (13.1).

13.4 Comparison between Theory and Experimental Measurements of Relative E vs. θ. This section compares the theoretical formula with measurements of relative grain-boundary energy vs. θ. In the experiments, the orientation of the boundary, as well as θ, varied; hence, a curve of E vs. θ would be expected to show some scatter for two reasons: (1) There is the scatter caused by using the approximate formula (13.1), which neglects the effect of boundary orientation.   We have seen that, if care is taken not to equilibrate tensions normal to certain prominent energy cusps, this may not lead to severe errors.   (2) Even if the energies are accurately measured, there will be some scatter because E is plotted vs. θ while actually E is also a function of the variable boundary orientation.   Section 12.2 showed that, in the [001] tilt boundary of Fig. 12.1, E_0 varies by a factor of $\sqrt{2}$ with boundary orientation; hence at small θ the energy also varies by a factor of $\sqrt{2}$.   There is some evidence that

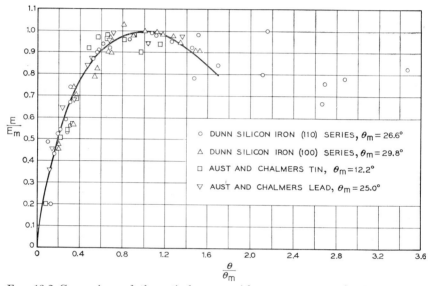

Fig. 13.2 Comparison of theoretical curve with measurements of relative grain-boundary energy.   The theoretical curve is given by $E/E_m = \theta/\theta_m[1 - \ln \theta/\theta_m]$; θ_m for each of the four sets of measurements is listed; the corresponding values of E_m are not known, since only relative energies are measured.

the variation in E is reduced at larger angles by a compensating variation in A.

Figure 11.5 illustrated two convenient methods of comparing the theoretical formula with measurements of energy vs. θ.   Both methods can be applied to the measurements of relative energy vs. θ to obtain a check of the form of the formula.   A quantitative check of the calculable parameter E_0 is, of course, not possible unless energies are measured on an absolute scale.

Figure 13.2 shows four sets of measurements: the two by Dunn and coworkers on silicon iron with axis of relative rotation [100] and [110], respectively, and two by Aust and Chalmers on tin and lead, respectively. As predicted by the theory, all four sets of data were well fitted with straight lines when plotted in the form E/θ vs. $\ln \theta$; see for example Read and Shockley (1953). In Fig. 13.2, the data are plotted in the form E/E_m vs. θ/θ_m. E_m is the maximum of the E vs. θ curve; the absolute value of E_m is unknown. θ_m is the angle at which the curve reaches its maximum; θ_m is listed for each set of data on the figure. Each θ_m was found from the zero intercept of the E/θ vs. ln θ curve. Section 11.6 showed that, when plotted as E/E_m vs. θ/θ_m, the theoretical curve is the same for all crystals. Hence all four sets of measurements can be represented on a single plot.

Figure 13.2 shows that the theoretical curve fits the data surprisingly well even at large angles. For example, the maximum of the curve occurs at 25 to 30° for the lead and silicon-iron series; this corresponds to about one dislocation every other atomic plane, in contrast to the assumption $D \gg b$ made in the derivation. The agreement at large angles is probably due in part to a fortunate cancellation of errors, which causes the formula to be valid beyond the range of validity of the derivation; also θ_m, which is chosen to fit the data, has almost no effect on the curve at small angles; hence θ_m is chosen to *make* the curve fit at large angles.

The two salient features of the theoretical curve are the rapid rise of E with θ at small θ and the relatively broad flat maximum; both features are clearly reproduced by the experimental data.

13.5 Comparison with Measurements of Absolute Energies. This section compares the quantitative predictions of the theory with measurements of absolute grain-boundary energy in silver, iron, and copper. There are, at present, no measurements of absolute energy vs. θ that have sufficient accuracy at small θ to give E_0 from the slope of E/θ vs. ln θ. To compare the quantitative predictions of the theory with absolute-energy measurements, we have to use the theory at large angles, well beyond the range of validity of the derivation. The fact that the proper choice of θ_m makes the form of the curve fit measurements of relative E vs. θ at large angles suggests, but does not require, that the energy in the relatively flat, large θ, part of the curve should be approximately given by $E_m = E_0\theta_m$, with E_0 calculated from the elastic constants, and θ_m determined from a plot of E vs. θ.

Silver. For comparison with the theory, the best measurements of absolute energy are those of Greenough and King (1951). They measured E/E_s vs. θ for silver, where E_s is the surface energy of silver. E_s has been measured independently. Greenough and King's grain boundaries were all pure tilt; however, the axis of relative rotation was not a simple crystallographic direction, and it varied from boundary to boundary. Figure 13.3 is a plot of the experimental data; each point is the average of values obtained with several different techniques for measuring the thermally etched groove angle where a grain boundary meets the surface. The ratio of grain-boundary energy to surface energy is obtained from the triangle of forces, Eq. (13.1), where now two of the energies are E_s. If the groove is symmetrical and the groove angle is ψ, then the grain-boundary energy is $E = 2E_s \cos(\psi/2)$.

The scatter in Fig. 13.3 is somewhat greater than in Fig. 13.2, especially at low angles. An E/θ vs. ln θ plot is not helpful here since it magnifies the scatter at low angles. However, the experimental points plotted as E/E_s vs. θ seem to be well fitted by the theoretical curve (solid line) with

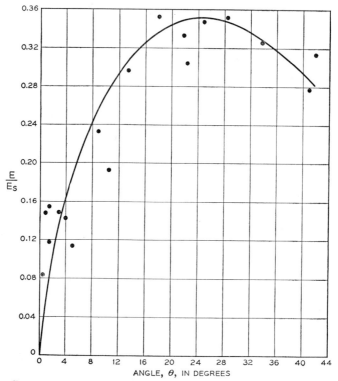

FIG. 13.3 Greenough and King's measurements of the ratio of grain-boundary energy E to surface energy E_s in silver. E_s is known independently and is about 1,300 ergs/cm².

$\theta_m = 25°$. It is interesting that θ_m was also 25° for the Aust and Chalmers data on lead, which is also face-centered cubic.

Fisher and Dunn (1952), in their review of experimental data on surface energies, conclude that the best value for the surface energy of silver in the temperature range 650 to 850°C is 1,140 ergs/cm². They obtain this value from Sawai and Nishida's measurements on silver foils under tension; the surface tension is simply related to the applied load for zero creep rate (for a lower load at these temperatures, the foils would shrink under their own surface tension).

Shuttleworth (discussion of Fisher and Dunn, 1952) has pointed out that taking account of transverse grain boundaries in the foils raises the value of surface energy by about 15 per cent; this makes $E_s = 1,310$ ergs/cm^2. Using this value for Greenough and King's data, where the boundaries came to equilibrium at 900°C, we find that the maximum energy $E_m = 0.35\ E_s$ in Fig. 13.3 is 460 ergs/cm^2. For $\theta_m = 25° = 0.436$ radian, $E_0 = E_m/\theta_m = 1,050$ ergs/cm^2. We now compare this with the theoretical value.

E_0 depends on the unknown orientation of the axis of relative rotation and grain-boundary normal. Since the boundaries were all pure tilt, they had three degrees of freedom (in addition to θ). As the best theoretical estimate of E_0 for this data, take the average of E_0 with respect to the one degree of freedom ϕ for the pure tilt boundary of Fig. 12.1. Using (12.2), we have

$$<E_0>_{\text{av}} = \frac{\tau_0 b}{2}\frac{2}{\pi}\int_0^{\pi/2}(\cos\phi + \sin\phi)d\phi$$

$$= \frac{4}{\pi}\left(\frac{\tau_0 b}{2}\right)$$

where τ_0 is given by Eq. (8.16) with $\alpha = \pi/2$; the elastic constants C_{11}, C_{12}, C_{44} refer to the temperature 900°C where the boundaries came to equilibrium. The elastic constants are not known at that temperature and are probably about 15 per cent lower than at room temperature. The room temperature values from Schmid and Boas (1935) give $E_0 = 1,185$. Reduced by 15 per cent to correct for temperature, $E_0 = 1,030$, as compared with the measured value of 1,050. Thus the theory and experiment agree well within the uncertainties.

C. Herring (private communication) has called attention to two additional sources of uncertainty in these experiments. (1) The surface energy is orientation dependent and therefore exerts a torque that may be appreciable, especially since the grain-boundary energy is smaller (by a factor of three or more) than the surface energy; consequently the simple triangle of forces may not be a good approximation. This might account for some of the scatter in Fig. 13.3. (2) H. Udin (unpublished) has shown that the surface energy is dependent on the oxygen content of the atmosphere. Thus, unless the atmosphere in Greenough and King's experiments was the same as in the silver-foil tests, the values of E_s might be different.

Iron. There are no other available measurements of absolute energy vs. θ. However, Van Vlack (1951) measured the intergranular energy for α iron with about 4 per cent of silicon by making a statistical analysis of dihedral angles in multiphase systems consisting of liquid copper, liquid copper sulfide, and iron. The liquid copper–liquid copper sulfide interfacial energy was measured (independently) from the differential depression of their interface in two capillary tubes of unequal radii. Van Vlack obtained 760 ergs/cm² for the average intergranular energy at the temperature, 1105°C, of the experiment. His boundaries were not controlled; all five degrees of freedom, including θ, varied.

To compare Van Vlack's value with the theory, we make several assumptions: First, if the boundaries were randomly distributed over all possible values of θ, then the statistical analysis gives the average of E over θ. In Dunn's data on silicon iron (Fig. 13.2), the average E is about $0.85 E_m$. If we further assume that the average E in the controlled experiments of Dunn is equal to the average energy of the uncontrolled boundaries in Van Vlack's experiment, then we can determine the E_0 for silicon iron from $E_0 = E_m/\theta_m$. Taking $E_m = 760/0.85 = 895$ ergs/cm² and using the values of θ_m from Fig. 13.2 gives $E_0 = 1,920$ for the (110) series and $E_0 = 1,720$ for the (100) series. Brooks (1952) has calculated the theoretical E_0's from the elastic constants of α iron reduced 15 per cent for temperature. Averaging over ϕ, Brooks finds $E_0 = 2,910$ for the (110) series and 2,620 for the (100) series; in both cases the theoretical value is high by 52 per cent. In view of the assumptions and uncertainties involved in the comparison, this discrepancy, although disappointing, is not crucial.

Copper. Fisher and Dunn (1952) list four independent determinations of the intergranular energy of copper, again measured by a statistical study of dihedral angles in multiphase systems where one interfacial energy was known independently. The average of the four independent values is 550 ergs/cm². Again assuming that this average is 0.85 of the maximum for an E vs. θ curve, we have $E_0 = E_m/\theta_m = 650/\theta_m$. Calculating the average E_0 for the simple boundary of Fig. 12.1 (as was done for silver) gives $E_0 = 1,390$, which agrees with the measured value if θ_m for copper is $650/1,390 = 0.465$ radian $= 26.5°$. This is reasonable in view of the measured value of $\theta_m = 25°$ for the other two face-centered cubic metals, silver and lead.

These quantitative comparisons indicate that the theory gives values of the right order of magnitude (probably within a factor of less than 2) for the energies of large-angle grain boundaries. However, a crucial quantitative check of the theory would be to measure absolute energy vs. θ for small values of θ with sufficient accuracy to give the slope E_0 of an E/θ vs. ln θ plot, and rigidly to control the orientations of the adjoining grains and grain boundary as was done, for example, in the experiments of Dunn. *Agreement between theory and experiment here would be very strong evidence for the validity of the theory.*

PROBLEM

Derive Herring's relations for Fig. 13.1; verify that they reduce to Eq. (13.3).

CHAPTER 14

THE MOTION OF A GRAIN BOUNDARY

14.1 Pressure on a Grain Boundary. Chapter 4 showed how the motion of a dislocation is associated with a macroscopic deformation of the crystal in which externally applied stresses can do work; this work is conveniently represented by a force on the dislocation. The same is true of a small-angle-of-misfit grain boundary, which is an array of dislocations. The force per unit area, or pressure, on a grain boundary is defined as the work done per unit area of boundary per unit distance moved, in other words, the work done per unit volume swept out by the boundary in its motion. We shall see that the pressure depends on the way in which the dislocations on the boundary move; for example, there is one pressure tending to produce pure glide and another tending to produce a combination of glide and climb. This chapter discusses types of boundary motion and the driving forces and resistances to each type. In all cases the pressure on the boundary can be found either from the macroscopic deformation of the bicrystal or from the sum of the forces on the dislocations.

An important distinction will be drawn between glissile and sessile grain boundaries: A *glissile* boundary can move freely by pure slip. A *sessile* boundary can move only by diffusion or by forcing dislocations through one another's stress fields against strong forces of interaction. Glissile boundaries are a very special case. The motion of a glissile boundary was predicted by Shockley (1949) and subsequently observed by Parker and Washburn (1952) in one of the most important verifications of dislocation theory.

The discussion in this chapter applies only to small-angle-of-misfit boundaries; here the dislocation model has a unique significance. The motion of a large-angle-of-misfit boundary can probably be described more conveniently in terms of a local rearrangement of the disordered atoms on the boundary.

Section 14.2 discusses the simplest case of boundary motion: namely, pure glide of the boundary in Fig. 11.1. The more general tilt boundary in Fig. 12.1 can move in three different ways (Sec. 14.3); each way is associated with a different pressure (Sec. 14.4). Sections 14.5 and 14.6 discuss the pressures, motions, and resistances to motion for a pure tilt boundary composed of equal numbers of two kinds of dislocations on non-orthogonal slip planes. The resistance to motion in the general case is discussed (Sec. 14.7) and glissile and sessile boundaries are distinguished (Sec. 14.8). Section 14.9 describes the Parker-Washburn experiment and shows how it provides a powerful tool for studying dislocation dynamics.

14.2 Glide of a Simple Boundary under Stress. Take the simple boundary of Fig. 11.1, where the dislocation model is a vertical row of identical dislocations. Apply a shearing stress τ as shown in Fig. 14.1a. This section determines the pressure on the boundary, first from the forces on the dislocations and then from the macroscopic deformation.

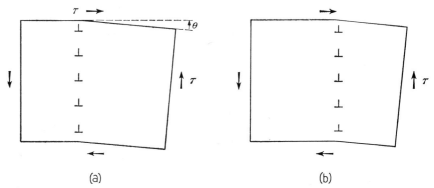

(a)   (b)

F<small>IG.</small> 14.1 Showing how the simple boundary of Fig. 11.1 moves under an applied stress; the motion produces a macroscopic deformation in which the crystal yields to the applied stress τ.

Since τ acts on the slip planes and in the slip direction of the dislocations, there is a force τb per unit length on every dislocation. The direction of the force is normal to the boundary. Thus there is a pressure P on the boundary equal to the force per unit length per dislocation times the density of dislocations. For this simple case, the pressure is

$$P = \tau\theta \qquad\qquad (14.1)$$

tending to move the boundary to the right by pure glide.

Next derive Eq. (14.1) from the work done on the external surface of the crystal when the boundary moves. Figure 14.1b shows how motion of the boundary is associated with a macroscopic shear in which the crystal yields to the applied stress τ. Observe that the work done by τ is $\tau\theta$ per unit volume swept out by the boundary.

The boundary in Fig. 14.1 is a particularly simple one: it consists of an array of identical dislocations with their slip planes at right angles to the boundary; hence the boundary can move by a uniform glide of all the dislocations. The motion of the boundary in Fig. 14.1 can be predicted from the slipping motion of a single dislocation. Here is an ideal example of a macroscopic phenomenon uniquely determined by dislocation theory without special assumptions; here experimental observations can check theoretical predictions and throw considerable light on the atomic mechanism of slip. Section 14.9 shows how this was actually done in the Parker-Washburn experiment.

The motion of an arbitrary boundary is, however, much less simple, as the following examples illustrate.

14.3 Motion of the Boundary in Fig. 12.1. This case is slightly more general; the grain boundary is made up of two sets of dislocations on orthogonal slip planes. Begin with the case of $\phi = 45°$, where the boundary is symmetrical and has equal numbers of the two sets of dislocations. This section discusses successively three different types of boundary motion.

Glide. Suppose the boundary moves to the right by pure glide: the $\perp$ glide to the right and the $\vdash$ glide down. Since the slip planes are orthogonal, the shearing stress is the same on each set of planes; there are equal numbers of each set, and each set moves the same distance; hence the work done by the applied stress is the same in magnitude for each set of dislocations. However, work is done *by* the applied stress on one set of slip planes and *against* the applied stress on the other; hence the total work is zero and the pressure tending to produce a sidewise motion of the boundary by pure slip vanishes. As an exercise derive the same result by finding the macroscopic deformation associated with the glide of each set of dislocations (see Shockley, 1952).

Splitting. What effect *is* produced by an applied stress if only glide is permitted? Suppose the applied stress on the slip planes tends to move the $\perp$ to the right; then the $\vdash$ tend to move up; thus the stress tries to split the boundary into two boundaries and move the two sets of dislocations apart. The forces between dislocations, however, try to hold the boundary together. The resistance to splitting may be simply visualized as follows: If the boundary splits, the material between the two sets of dislocations is severely strained. Thus energy is needed to split the boundary. Section 14.6 calculates the resistance to splitting from the forces between dislocations.

As an exercise, extend the above argument to the more general case of arbitrary ϕ, where there are unequal numbers of the two sets of dislocations. Show that there is still no pressure tending to make the boundary glide; if only glide is permitted, any applied stress will try to split the boundary.

Uniform Motion of All the Dislocations. Suppose all the dislocations move uniformly along the boundary normal; such motion requires climb as well as glide except when the slip planes of all the dislocations are parallel, $\phi = 0$ or $90°$. In general, uniform motion of all the dislocations requires some of the dislocations to climb out of their slip planes; hence the motion requires mass transport. For example, suppose all the dislocations in Fig. 12.1 move at right angles to the boundary (so that the boundary moves to the right and down). Atoms must be added onto the edges of the vertical (100) planes that end on the boundary in edge dislocations, and the (010) planes that end on the boundary must lose atoms. Since an edge dislocation can be either a source or sink for vacancies, atoms can move from the edges of the shrinking (010) planes to the growing (100) planes by diffusion of vacancies in the opposite direction. The following argument determines (1) the macroscopic deformation and (2) the driving force for diffusion of vacancies from one set of dislocations to the other.

The macroscopic deformation is exactly the same as in Fig. 14.1, where the dislocations also move normal to the boundary. Moving all the dislocations uniformly normal to the boundary is the same as putting the boundary in a different place in the crystal. It does not matter whether the dislocations move by pure glide or combined glide and climb. This is *not* so if the dislocations cut across one another in their motion—even though the *plane* of the boundary moves sidewise, the boundary as a *configuration* is not simply moving sidewise. The deformation in Fig. 14.1 is the same if we replace the simple boundary by any pure tilt boundary where the dislocations move at right angles to the boundary. The pressure favoring such motion is therefore $\tau\theta$, where τ is the shear stress acting on the plane of the boundary and in the direction at right angles to the axis of tilt. The following paragraph shows how the pressure $\tau\theta$ provides a driving force for diffusion.

Figure 14.2 shows the boundary of Fig. 12.1 for the case $\phi = 45°$; here there are equal numbers of the two types of dislocations; the figure shows three dislocations. A shear stress τ is applied as shown. Figure 14.3 shows the same stress referred to the crystal axes. It consists of a tensile stress on the (010) planes and a compressive stress on the (100) planes. Since there is no shear on the slip planes, there is no force trying to make the dislocations glide. However, there is a force on each set at right angles to its slip plane; the dislocations on which (100) planes end want to climb in the positive direction (up and to the right); the other set of dislocations wants to climb down and to the right. Figure 14.2 shows the force on each set. The sum of the forces (per unit area) defines a pressure tending to move the boundary to the right. The magnitude of the pressure is $\tau\theta$—as can be verified from the forces on the dislocations and the density of dislocations.

To sum up the above argument: the applied stress τ is equivalent to tensile and compressive components σ_{010} and σ_{100} on the crystal planes; the compressive component tries to squeeze out the (100) atomic

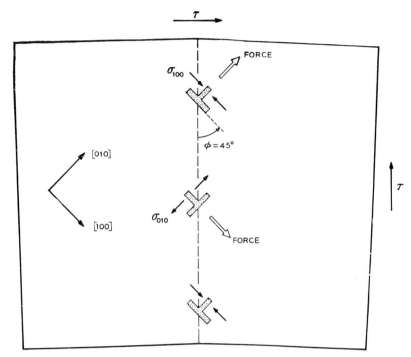

FIG. 14.2 The boundary of Fig. 12.1 with $\phi = 45°$. The boundary consists of equal numbers of the two sets of dislocations uniformly spaced. The applied stress τ produces a force on each dislocation at right angles to its slip plane.

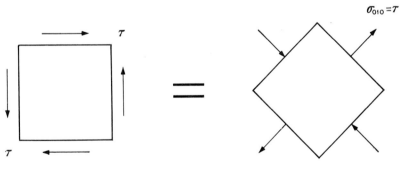

FIG. 14.3 The applied shear stress τ is equivalent to tension and compression on the 45° planes; thus, in Fig. 14.2, the applied shear stress produces a force normal to the slip planes.

planes ending on the boundary and the tensile component encourages the growth of the (010) planes.   Thus the stress provides a driving force for the diffusion of vacancies from one set of dislocations to the other.

As an exercise extend the above argument to the case of arbitrary ϕ in Fig. 12.1; show that the work done when the dislocations all move at right angles to the boundary is $\tau\theta$, independently of ϕ.

Read and Shockley (1950, 1952b) and Shockley (1952) have discussed the role of diffusion in grain-boundary motion in more detail.   They suggest that such diffusive motion might explain the "viscous-grain-boundary" behavior studied by Zener (1948) and Kê (1949), which is characterized by an activation energy equal to the activation energy for self-diffusion.

14.4 Three Types of Boundary Motion and the Corresponding Pressures.   The preceding section shows that there are different driving forces, or pressures, for different types of motion.   This section reviews briefly the three types of motion illustrated in Sec. 14.3 and defines the pressure in each case.

1. The boundary moves by pure glide; all the dislocations glide in their slip planes and remain in the plane of the boundary.   Call the work done per unit volume swept out P_g.   In general this type of motion has a high resistance since the relative displacement of the different sets of dislocations is opposed by forces between dislocations.

2. There are two sets of dislocations and they both move by pure slip, but one set moves to the right of the boundary and the other to the left; so the boundary is split.   The work done per unit volume between the two boundaries defines a pressure P_s that tries to split the boundary. Again the two sets of dislocations have to move through one another's stress fields.   When there are three or more sets of dislocations, the boundary can split in several different ways; there is a pressure for separating any two sets.

3. All the dislocations move along the boundary normal, so that the boundary moves as a whole.   The work done per unit volume swept out defines a pressure P_n.   This type of motion, in general, involves a combination of glide and climb and therefore requires mass transport by diffusion.   For an arbitrary boundary, defined by unit normal **n** and relative rotation **u**θ,

$$P_n = \tau\theta_{\text{tilt}} \tag{14.2}$$

where θ_{tilt} is the tilt component (component in the plane of the boundary) of **u**θ, and τ is the applied shear stress acting on the plane of the boundary and in the direction normal to the axis of tilt, which is parallel to the projection of **u** in the plane of the boundary.

For the simple boundary of Figs. 11.1 and 14.1, $P_g = P_n = \tau\theta$ and $P_s = 0$.

For the boundary of Fig. 12.1, $P_g = 0$ except for $\phi = 0$. For any ϕ, $P_s = \tau_{sp}\theta$ where τ_{sp} is the shear stress on the slip planes of the dislocations.

P_g and P_s tend to produce pure slipping motions which in general require dislocations to move through one another's stress fields. Such motion is opposed by the forces between dislocations, which try to hold the dislocations in a minimum energy configuration. P_n tends to produce a uniform motion of the dislocations, where the rate of motion is limited by diffusion.

14.5 Pressure on a Pure Tilt Boundary When Slip Planes Are Not Orthogonal. This section discusses the motion of a boundary similar to the one in Fig. 12.1 except that the two sets of slip planes are not orthogonal. Again let the boundary be symmetrical, so that there are equal numbers of the two types of dislocations; call them A and B dislocations. Figure 14.4 shows three dislocations of the array. This figure could represent, for example, a {110} plane in body-centered cubic, where $\psi = \cos^{-1}\left(\frac{1}{3}\right)$. We shall, however, carry through the analysis with ψ arbitrary.

The spacing D between similar dislocations is

$$D = \frac{2b}{\theta}\cos\frac{\psi}{2} \tag{14.3}$$

(Recall that, in a pure tilt boundary, the dislocations are all parallel and the sum of all the Burgers vectors is $n\theta$ per unit length of boundary.)

This section derives P_g and P_s for a uniform distribution of applied stress having components σ_x, σ_y, τ as shown in Fig. 14.4.

First take P_g: let each dislocation move by pure slip, so that the boundary is displaced unit distance to the right; each dislocation moves a distance $\sec(\psi/2)$ on its slip plane. Let τ_A and τ_B be the shearing stress components on the two sets of slip planes, respectively. Then P_g is equal to $b(\tau_A + \tau_B) \sec(\psi/2)$ divided by D. Express τ_A and τ_B in terms of σ_x, σ_y, and τ, and show that only τ contributes to P_g and that

$$P_g = \frac{2\tau\theta}{1 + \sec\psi} \tag{14.4a}$$

For $\psi = 90°$, $P_g = 0$ as in Fig. 12.1. For $\psi = 0$, the two sets of dislocations are the same and $P_g = \tau\theta$, as in Fig. 14.1.

Now let the boundary split. From the work done in separating the two sets of dislocations, show that

$$P_s = \left(\frac{\sigma_x - \sigma_y}{2}\right)\theta\tan\frac{\psi}{2} \tag{14.4b}$$

The stress $\frac{1}{2}(\sigma_x - \sigma_y)$ is the shear stress acting on the planes at 45° to the boundary (Fig. 14.4, lower right). The stress σ_x, σ_y, τ is equal to the sum of a pure shear τ on the plane of the boundary, a pure shear

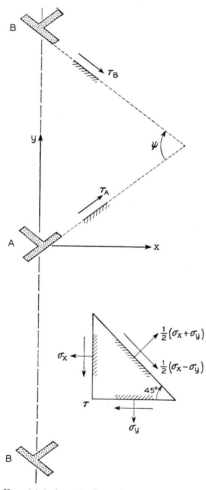

$$\tau_{45} = \tfrac{1}{2}(\sigma_x - \sigma_y) \qquad (14.5)$$

on the 45° planes, and a hydrostatic pressure $\frac{1}{2}(\sigma_x + \sigma_y)$. τ tends to produce glide of the boundary, τ_{45} tends to split the boundary, and the hydrostatic pressure has no effect.

The maximum value of ψ in Fig. 14.4 is 90°, at least for an elastically isotropic medium. If ψ were greater than 90°, the two sets of dislocations would attract and combine to form a single set of dislocations. Thus the maximum P_s is θ times the shear stress on the slip planes, and the maximum P_g is $\tau\theta$.

The derivation of P_g and P_s for the more general case where the grain boundary in Fig. 14.4 makes an arbitrary angle ϕ with the symmetry plane forms Prob. 1.

14.6 Resistance to Motion Due to Forces between Dislocations. If the boundary in Fig. 14.4 moves or splits by pure glide, then the A and B dislocations move relative to one another, and work is done against the forces of interaction, which try to hold the dislocations in a minimum energy configuration. This section discusses the variation of boundary energy with relative

Fig. 14.4 A grain boundary made up of equal numbers of two parallel sets of dislocations A and B. The angle ψ between the two slip planes is arbitrary. The stress components on the x and y axes and the 45° plane are shown in the lower right.

position of the two sets of dislocations. It is concluded that an applied stress of the order of θ times the shear modulus is needed to make the boundary glide or split.

Figure 14.4 shows the minimum energy configuration: alternate A and

B dislocations equally spaced at intervals of $\frac{1}{2}D$. Take an xy coordinate system fixed with respect to the B set, and let x and y be the coordinates of an A dislocation; let the origin be the minimum energy position, as shown in the figure. For fixed θ and ψ, the grain-boundary energy E varies with x and y.

Consider how this variation enters the E vs. θ relation: Section 12.7 showed that the energy of interaction of several sets of dislocations contributes to the $E_0A\theta$ term; that is, the interaction energy per dislocation is independent of θ. Any relative displacement of the various sets of dislocations can affect only the interaction energy. The variation of E with relative position of the sets must therefore come from the $E_0\theta A$ term. Thus A must be a function of x and y. Actually A is a function of the dimensionless variables $x' = x/D$ and $y' = y/D$ where Eq. (14.3) gives D.

The calculation of $A(x',y') - A(0,0)$ is straightforward; the final result and various steps in the calculation form problems at the end of this chapter.

The physical meaning of the variation of E with relative position and the effect of this variation on boundary motion can be appreciated as follows: In general, an A and a B dislocation repel one another (if they attracted, the two sets could combine and form a single set with a reduction in energy). First suppose the boundary moves to the right by pure slip, $x = 0$, $y \to D/2$; the A and B sets come together and there is a net repulsive force in the y direction acting between approaching pairs and opposing the motion.

The splitting of the boundary is a little less simple to visualize. Once the two sets of dislocations have been separated by a distance $x \approx D$, the repulsive forces tend to move them farther apart. However, we first have to overcome the stabilizing forces that keep all the dislocations in a vertical row. These forces can be understood as follows: Consider the simple case $\psi = 0$, where there is only one set of dislocations; however, continue to call alternate dislocations A and B, respectively. Figure 9.1 shows that the x component of force between like edge dislocations is attractive for $y^2 > x^2$. The same is true of an array of like dislocations, such as the simple grain boundary of Fig. 11.1. If one dislocation moves off the boundary, the attractive x components of force pull it back; so the boundary is stable. Essentially the same argument applies to the boundary in Fig. 14.4; the x component of force is attractive when $y = 0$ and x is less than a critical value of the order of D.

Now consider the equilibrium of the boundary under externally applied pressures P_s and P_g. First suppose the two sets of dislocations move apart a distance dx with $dy = 0$. P_s does an amount of work $P_s dx$, which must go into the A term in E. Thus the equilibrium condition in the x

direction is

$$P_s = \frac{\partial E}{\partial x} = E_0\theta \frac{\partial}{\partial x} A(x',y')$$

$$= \frac{E_0\theta^2}{2b} \sec \frac{\psi}{2} \frac{\partial A}{\partial x'} (x',y') \tag{14.6}$$

By the same reasoning

$$P_g = -2 \tan \frac{\psi}{2} \frac{\partial E}{\partial y}$$

$$= -\frac{E_0\theta^2}{b} \sec \frac{\psi}{2} \tan \frac{\psi}{2} \frac{\partial A}{\partial y'} (x',y') \tag{14.7}$$

These equations and Eqs. (14.4) show that τ and $\tau_{45} = \frac{1}{2}(\sigma_x - \sigma_y)$ uniquely determine the equilibrium values of x and y. The plot of τ and τ_{45} vs. x' and y' for $\psi = \cos^{-1} \frac{1}{3}$ forms a problem at the end of the chapter.

The equilibrium equations can also be obtained from the vanishing of the net force on each dislocation; the net force is the sum of the forces due to (1) the externally applied stress, τ and τ_{45}, and (2) the stress fields of other dislocations.

The critical values of applied pressure required to move or split the boundary are proportional to $E_0\theta^2/b$; hence the critical stress is proportional to $\tau_0\theta \approx G\theta$ where G is the shear modulus. The factor of proportionality depends on ψ and is of the order of unity for typical cases. Thus it appears that a distinguishable boundary ($\theta > 10^{-4}$ radian) would probably neither move nor split by pure slip at values of applied stress lower than the critical stress for appreciable plastic flow.

14.7 Resistance to Slipping Motion in the General Case. Figure 14.4 is a special case: there are equal numbers of two sets of parallel dislocations; so the same force acts on all the dislocations of one set; the dislocation distribution is specified by only two coordinates x and y. This section discusses (1) the general case of parallel dislocations (pure tilt boundary), where the densities of the two or more sets are not rationally related; and (2) the general boundary, where the several sets are not parallel.

1. In general, if there are a total of N parallel dislocations on the boundary, $2N$ coordinates are needed to specify the detailed arrangement of dislocations. In equilibrium, the two components of force on each dislocation must vanish; this gives $2N$ equations to determine the $2N$ coordinates. The same general conclusions apply as in the simpler case of Fig. 14.4. Glide of the boundary means moving dislocations past one another against forces of interaction, which are of the same magnitude as in Sec. 14.6. Hence a stress of the order of $G\theta$ is required to move the boundary by pure slip.

2. Thus far we have considered the interference between dislocations

in pure tilt boundaries, where the dislocations are all parallel. If the boundary has any twist component, $\mathbf{n} \cdot \mathbf{u} \neq 0$, then the different sets of dislocations are not parallel. A boundary made up of nonparallel sets of straight dislocations remains unchanged (in structure and energy) as it glides, even though each set of dislocations glides on a different set of slip planes; hence the forces between dislocations do not resist the motion.

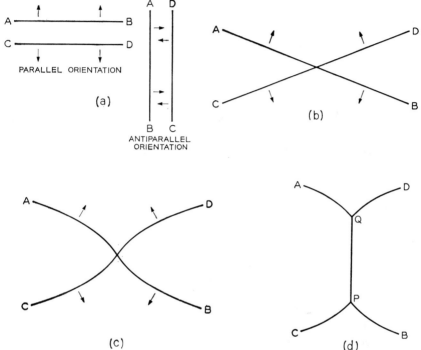

FIG. 14.5 (a) Two dislocations AB and CD repel in the parallel orientation and attract in the antiparallel orientation. (b) If the dislocations cross, they exert torques on one another. (c) The torques tend to twist the dislocations toward the antiparallel orientation. (d) The antiparallel sections attract and combine to form nodes P and Q.

However, intersecting sets of dislocations are straight only in a macroscopic, statistical, sense. Where the dislocations cross, they exert high local forces on one another. In general, the local forces produce a torque which twists the dislocations into a curved configuration. The following paragraph illustrates a simple case where intersecting dislocations become curved.

Figure 14.5 shows two dislocations AB and CD which exert a uniform repulsion on one another when they are parallel. If one were rotated through 180° in the plane of the figure, they would attract; call this the *antiparallel* orientation. Figure 14.5a shows both the parallel and antiparallel orientations. To make the argument quite concrete suppose the dislocations are both pure edge dislocations having the same Burgers vector; let it be normal to the figure. The incomplete atomic planes are therefore in the plane of the drawing

Now suppose the dislocations cross, Fig. 14.5b, so that the two incomplete atomic planes partially overlap. Where they overlap, the compressive stress tries to squeeze out each plane. Likewise each incomplete plane wants to grow into the area where the two regions of tensile stress overlap. The resulting forces are shown by the arrows in the figure. Observe that each dislocation exerts a torque on the other; the torques try to twist the dislocations locally into the antiparallel orientation. The same argument can be stated in terms of the force on each dislocation due to the stress field of the other; the important component of stress is σ_x, where the x axis is normal to the figure.

The torques try to make the dislocations climb, that is, move in the plane of the figure. Suppose the specimen is annealed at a temperature where appreciable diffusion can occur. Then the dislocations move, by climb, toward the configuration shown in Fig. 14.5c. Now the dislocations are curved; associated with the curvature of each dislocation is a restoring force that opposes the force of the other dislocation.

The above argument holds for any two dislocations that repel one another when they are parallel. When they cross, they try to turn themselves locally into the antiparallel orientation, in which they attract. The final configuration may be that shown in Fig. 14.5d, where the section PQ is a single dislocation formed by combination of the two sections that have rotated into the antiparallel orientation.

Nodes, like P and Q in Fig. 14.5d, or curved dislocations, prevent the dislocations from gliding freely. In general, each set of dislocations glides on a different slip surface; hence the antiparallel or curved sections of dislocation must move apart if the boundary is to glide. However, the forces between dislocations resist such motion. Conclusion: Again the boundary has a high resistance to motion by pure glide, that is, the boundary is sessile.

14.8 Glissile and Sessile Grain Boundaries. These were mentioned briefly in Sec. 14.1. A glissile grain boundary is one that can glide freely without interference from the forces between dislocations. A sessile boundary can move only by diffusion or by somehow overcoming the forces between dislocations. We have already seen two examples of glissile boundaries: One is the simple boundary of Fig. 11.1 where there is only one set of dislocation. The other was the $\phi = 45°$ boundary in Fig. 12.1 for an elastically isotropic material. (Recall that there is no force between orthogonal edge dislocations lined up on the 45° lines, Fig. 8.2.) However there is also no driving force for the motion of the

$\phi = 45°$ boundary; Sec. 14.3 showed that the applied stress on the slip planes simply tries to split the boundary. The glissile boundary in Fig. 14.1 is one example of a slightly more general type: even when there are two or more sets of dislocations, the boundary is glissile if all the slip planes are parallel.

A glissile boundary in an otherwise perfect crystal would move at the applied stress necessary to overcome whatever frictional resistance there may be to pure slip of a single dislocation. In actual crystals, however, the boundary would have to move through internal stress fields associated with other dislocations or other types of imperfections, and the dislocations on the boundary would have to cut through other dislocations (Sec. 6.9).

14.9 The Parker-Washburn Glissile Boundary. Consider what is the most fundamental experiment in dislocation dynamics that could be done. It would be to observe the motion of a single dislocation; this would be the dislocation equivalent of the oil drop experiment in electron physics. The next most fundamental experiment would be to study the identical motion of a number of identical dislocations; Parker and Washburn (1952) have done such an experiment. They used the simplest example of an array of identical dislocations, namely, a simple grain boundary like the one shown in Fig. 14.1. This section describes their experiment and shows how it verifies predictions from dislocation theory. As early as 1948, Shockley predicted that the boundary in Figs. 11.1 and 14.1 would move under an applied stress.

Parker and Washburn's boundaries are symmetrical pure tilt boundaries in zinc bicrystals. The axis of relative rotation lies in the basal plane and normal to a close-packed row of atoms. The plane of the boundary is normal to the basal plane, or rather to the mean basal plane of the two grains. Thus the boundary is a vertical row of identical pure edge dislocations, as in Figs. 11.1 and 14.1. The angle of misfit θ is about $2°$; so the dislocations are about 30 atomic planes apart; thus the dislocation model has a unique significance. The Parker-Washburn boundary is the simplest example of a glissile boundary.

To observe the boundary, Parker and Washburn cleaved the bicrystal on the basal plane and looked at the cleavage surface through a microscope with oblique illumination. (This is the same as looking at the crystal in Fig. 14.1 from above.) Figure 14.6 shows three micrographs of the cleavage surface. In Fig. 14.6 the axis of relative rotation is a vertical line in the plane of the figure. The location of the boundary is revealed by the difference in brightness of the two grains (due to the difference in orientation under oblique illumination). The irregular horizontal line in Fig. 14.6 is a step in the cleavage surface and serves as a reference.

Parker and Washburn loaded the bicrystal so that an applied stress acted on the basal plane and in the slip direction (as in Fig. 14.1). As predicted, the boundary moved under the applied stress. The three micrographs show successive positions of the boundary: Fig. 14.6a shows

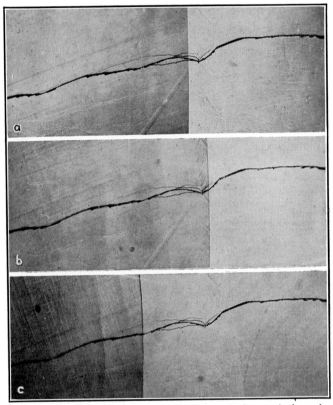

FIG. 14.6 Parker and Washburn's micrographs of a moving grain boundary in zinc. The boundary is normal to the plane of the figure, and the two grains have a relative rotation about an axis that is parallel to both the grain boundary and the plane of the figure. The brightness of the two grains is different because of the orientation difference under oblique illumination. This is the grain boundary of Fig. 14.1 viewed looking down from above. (a) The initial position of the boundary. Under an applied shear the boundary moves to the right to the position shown in b. In c a reverse stress has moved the boundary back beyond the initial position. The irregular horizontal line is a step in the surface, which is a cleavage surface parallel to the basal plane.

the initial position. Under the applied stress, the boundary moved to the position shown in Fig. 14.6b. A reverse stress moved the boundary back to the left beyond the original position—see Fig. 14.6c. The total motion in Fig. 14.6 is about 0.3 mm to the right followed by about 1 mm to the left.

The dislocations in the Parker-Washburn boundary are probably extended dislocations (since they lie in the basal plane). The force on the dislocations and their predicted motion, however, are independent of whether or not they have split. The boundary will be glissile provided only that the slip planes of the dislocations are parallel; thus a pure tilt boundary with the axis of relative rotation lying in any direction in the basal plane would also be glissile.

To conclude: Parker and Washburn have performed a macroscopic experiment in plastic deformation where the result follows directly from dislocation theory. This was possible because, although many dislocations were involved, they were all alike; hence the result follows directly from the behavior of a single dislocation. *The Parker-Washburn boundary is a powerful research tool for studying the basic atomic mechanism of slip.*

PROBLEMS

1. Show that, when the boundary in Fig. 14.4 makes an angle ϕ with the symmetry plane of the two grains,

$$P_g = \frac{2\tau\theta \cos \psi}{\cos \psi + \cos \phi}$$

$$P_s = -\frac{\theta}{\sin \phi}\left[(\cos \psi - \cos \phi)\tau_{45} + \frac{\tau \sin 2 \phi}{2(\cos \psi + \cos \phi)} \right]$$

2. Suppose that there is only one dislocation of each set in Fig. 14.4; show that in the case of isotropic elasticity the total energy of the pair is

$$b^2\tau_0 \left(- \cos \psi \ln r + \frac{x^2}{r^2} \right) + \text{const.}$$

where one dislocation is at the origin, the other at x, y. The constant includes the self-energies of the two dislocations.

Show that, in the notation of Probs. 2 and 3 of Chap. 8, the energy can be written as

$$b^2\tau_0 \, \text{Re} \left(- \cos \psi \ln Z + \frac{x}{Z} \right) + \text{const.}$$

3. Use the result of the last problem to show that the energy of one B dislocation in the stress field of all the A dislocations is

$$\text{Re } b^2 \, \tau_0 \left(- \cos \psi \ln \sinh \frac{\pi Z}{D} + \frac{x\pi}{D} \coth \frac{\pi z}{D} \right) + \text{const.}$$

HINT: Use the summation formula of Prob. 6, Chap. 11.

4. From the result of the last problem show that $E = E_0\theta[A - \ln \theta]$. Find E_0 and show that

$$A - A_0 = \text{Re} \, \frac{\pi x}{D} \left(\frac{\pi x}{D} \tanh \frac{\pi Z}{D} - \cos \psi \ln \cosh \frac{\pi Z}{D} \right)$$

where now the origin is taken at the minimum energy position, where $A = A_0$.

5. Take $\cos \psi = \frac{1}{3}$ in the preceding problem and calculate τ and τ_{45} vs. x and y for static equilibrium; plot τ and τ_{45} vs. x for various values of y.

APPENDIX

This appendix derives the stress distribution around a screw disloca-tion in an isotropic crystal. The same general analysis applies to an edge or any other straight dislocation. However, in the anisotropic case, the equations are rather cumbersome.

Use cylindrical coordinates r, θ, z, and let the dislocation lie along the z axis. The region of elastic strain is bounded by a small cylinder of radius $r = r_l$ along the z axis; inside this cylinder, the following analysis does not apply. Let the elastic region extend to infinity, and the stress vanishes there. Assume that, in the elastic region, the stress and strain are analytic, that is, continuous and continuously differentiable. This appendix finds the most general analytic distribution of stress and shows that it includes a screw dislocation.

For convenience, use the notation and basic elasticity equations of Timoshenko (1934). Page 200 of Timoshenko shows that, when nothing varies with z, the component of displacement w in the z direction can be treated independently of the components u and v at right angles to z. Likewise the stress components τ_{rz} and $\tau_{\theta z}$ (Timoshenko, 1934, p. 277) can be treated independently of the other stress components; they must satisfy the equation of equilibrium in the z direction

$$\frac{\partial}{\partial r} r\tau_{rz} + \frac{\partial}{\partial \theta} \tau_{\theta z} = 0 \tag{A.1}$$

As an exercise derive (A.1) from the static equilibrium of an element of volume. The strains (Timoshenko, p. 277) are given by

$$\frac{\tau_{rz}}{G} = \gamma_{rz} = \frac{\partial w}{\partial r}$$
$$\frac{\tau_{\theta z}}{G} = \gamma_{\theta z} = \frac{1}{r} \frac{\partial w}{\partial \theta} \tag{A.2}$$

Observe that the two strain components depend on a single component of displacement; we can therefore get another equation by eliminating w from the two equations (A.2); this is called the compatibility equation. In terms of stress it is

$$\frac{\partial}{\partial \theta} \tau_{rz} = \frac{\partial}{\partial r} r\tau_{\theta z} \tag{A.3}$$

213

Verify (A.3) by differentiating Eqs. (A.2).   Eliminating $\tau_{\theta z}$ from (A.1) and (A.3) by differentiation gives

$$\frac{\partial}{\partial r} r \frac{\partial}{\partial r} r \tau_{rz} + \frac{\partial^2 \tau_{rz}}{\partial \theta^2} = 0 \tag{A.4}$$

for τ_{rz}.   The same procedure gives an identical equation for $\tau_{\theta z}$.

Since the stress is continuous, the distribution of stress on any circle $r = $ constant is given by a Fourier series; the coefficients of $\sin n\theta$ and $\cos n\theta$ vary from one circle to another, that is, they are functions of r. Thus

$$\tau_{rz} = R_0(r) + R_1(r) \cos \theta + R_2(r) \cos 2\theta \cdots$$
$$R_n(r) \cos n\theta \cdots S_n(r) \sin n\theta \cdots \tag{A.5}$$

with a similar expression for $\tau_{\theta z}$.

Substituting (A.5) into (A.4) gives

$$\frac{\partial}{\partial r} r \frac{\partial}{\partial r} r R_n = n^2 R_n \tag{A.6}$$

with an identical equation for $S_n(r)$.   Verify that the solution of (A.6) is a linear combination of r^{n-1} and r^{-n-1}.   Since the stress vanishes at $r = \infty$, only negative powers of r are allowed.   Thus the general solution for τ_{rz} is

$$\tau_{rz} = \frac{A_0}{r} + \sum_{n=1}^{\infty} \left(\frac{A_n \cos n\theta + B_n \sin n\theta}{r^{n+1}} \right) \tag{A.7}$$

where the A's and B's are constants.

To find $\tau_{r\theta}$, substitute (A.7) into (A.3) and integrate; this gives

$$\tau_{r\theta} = \frac{C_0}{r} + \sum_{n=1}^{\infty} \left(\frac{-B_n \cos n\theta + A_n \sin n\theta}{r^{n+1}} \right) \tag{A.8}$$

where C_0 is an additional constant of integration.

Now consider the physical meaning of the constant coefficients C_0, B_n, A_n.   The stress acting on the boundary $r = r_l$ between the good and bad regions is unknown; it depends on the interaction of the bad material with the surrounding good material.   This interaction specifies $\tau_{rz} = \tau_{rz}(r_l, \theta)$ on the cylindrical surface $r = r_l$ ($\tau_{\theta z}$ does not act on the cylindrical surface).   If the stress distribution $\tau_{rz}(r_l, \theta)$ were known, and were expanded in a Fourier series in terms of $\sin n\theta$ and $\cos n\theta$, the coefficients would uniquely specify the constants A_0, A_n, B_n ($n = 1,2,3, \ldots$) in Eq. (A.7). Thus all the constants in the general solution except C_0 are determined by the unknown interaction with the bad material.   In other words we know the general solution but not the boundary conditions on the inner boundary $(r = r_l)$ of the elastic region. Consequently, the coefficients of the higher order terms in Eq. (A.8) are unknown. The first term, however, is independent of the boundary conditions on $r = r_l$. In the following we show that the C_0/r term represents a dislocation and is uniquely determined by the discontinuity in w (z component of the Burgers vector).

Begin by expressing w as a differential

$$dw = \frac{\partial w}{\partial r} dr + \frac{\partial w}{\partial \theta} d\theta \qquad (A.9)$$

Equations (A.2) give the partial derivatives of w in terms of stress; substituting them into (A.9) gives

$$dw = \frac{1}{G} (\tau_{rz} dr + r\tau_{\theta z} d\theta) \qquad (A.10)$$

Substituting Eqs. (A.7) and (A.8) for τ_{rz} and $\tau_{\theta z}$ into (A.10) gives

$$G\, dw = A_0 \frac{dr}{r} + C_0\, d\theta + \sum_{n=1}^{\infty} A_n \left(\cos n\theta \frac{dr}{r^{n+1}} + \frac{\sin n\theta}{r^n} d\theta \right)$$
$$+ \sum_{n=1}^{\infty} B_n \left(\sin n\theta \frac{dr}{r^{n+1}} - \frac{\cos n\theta}{r^n} d\theta \right)$$

The right-hand side is a perfect differential; integration gives

$$w = \frac{1}{G} \left[A_0 \ln r + C_0 \theta - \sum_{n=1}^{\infty} \frac{1}{n} \left(\frac{A_n \cos n\theta}{r^n} + \frac{B_n \sin n\theta}{r^n} \right) \right] \qquad (A.11)$$

Notice that the term $(C_0\theta)/G$ is multivalued and gives a discontinuity in displacement $\Delta w = (C_0 2\pi)/G$. It does not matter at what value of θ the discontinuity occurs; hence the surface of discontinuity, or cut, may be any surface terminating on the z axis. The discontinuity in displacement $(C_0 2\pi)/G$ is constant; in other words, the two sides of the cut are displaced (relative to one another) by a rigid body translation. In good crystalline material, the discontinuity in displacement must be a lattice translation vector; $(2\pi C_0)/G$ must therefore be the z component of a lattice translation vector. Thus if $C_0 \neq 0$ the solution represents a screw dislocation, or dislocation with screw component. A similar analysis of the u and v components of displacement leads to an edge dislocation as part of the general analytic solution for stress. When the dislocation is pure screw,

$$\Delta w = b; \qquad \text{so } C_0 = Gb/2\pi$$

It is now a simple step to derive the stress distribution on the slip plane; the slip plane is defined as the plane containing both the dislocation and its Burgers vector. For a screw dislocation, the dislocation and Burgers vector are parallel; hence the slip plane may be any plane containing the dislocation. Taking the plane $\theta = 0$ as the slip plane, the shearing stress τ on the slip plane and in the slip direction is $\tau = \tau_{\theta z}(r,0)$, which from (A.8) with $C_0 = \dfrac{Gb}{2\pi}$ is

$$\tau = \tau_0 \frac{b}{r} + \tau_1 \frac{b^2}{r^2} \cdots \tau_n \frac{b^{n+1}}{r^{n+1}} \tag{A.12}$$

where

$$\tau_0 = \frac{G}{2\pi}$$
$$\tau_n = -\frac{B_n}{b^{n+1}} \tag{A.13}$$

Thus the first term in (A.12) is uniquely determined by the elastic constants of the material. The coefficients of the other terms depend on the B's and therefore on the interaction of the good material with the bad.

The general solution represented by equations (A.7), (A.8), and (A.11) is not confined to the case where the excluded region along the z axis is a dislocation. The excluded region might, for example, be a hole in the crystal to which external stresses were applied. One particularly simple case is represented by the A_0 term: Suppose the excluded region is a rigid rod of radius $r = r_l$ cemented to the surrounding elastic material. Let an external force be applied to the rod; show that all the coefficients vanish except A_0 and that $2\pi A_0$ is the force per unit length on the rod.

The A_0 (net force) and C_0 (dislocation) terms in the general solution have the same dependence on r. Both give an elastic energy that depends logarithmatically on the size of the crystal.

For simplicity we have derived only the z component of the displacement (and the associated stress components $\tau_{\theta z}$ and τ_{rz}). The same approach gives the u and v components for a general analytic stress field around a singularity. In all cases, the general solution includes a discontinuity in displacement, which is always a rigid body displacement of the two sides of the cut (or surface of discontinuity). In a real crystal the relative displacement of the two sides of the cut must be a translation corresponding to a t vector (or the sum of several t vectors). In general continuum theory the rigid body motion may include a relative rotation of the two sides of the cut about the z axis, which would involve cutting out or inserting a wedge; this is called a wedge dislocation. The wedge dislocation involves no z component of displacement; hence, it did not appear in (A.11).

REFERENCES

Aust, K. T., and B. Chalmers (1950): *Proc. Roy. Soc. (London)*, A**201**:210–215; A**204**: 359–366.

Bardeen, J., and C. Herring (1952): "Imperfections in Nearly Perfect Crystals" (W. Shockley, editor), Chap. 10, Wiley, New York.

Barrett, C. S. (1952a): "Structure of Metals," McGraw-Hill, New York.

Barrett, C. S. (1952b): "Imperfections in Nearly Perfect Crystals" (W. Shockley, editor), Chap. 3, Wiley, New York.

Barrett, C. S. (1953): *Acta Metallurgica*, **1**:2–7.

Bilby, B. A. (1950): *J. Inst. Metals*, **76**:613–627.

Bragg, W. L. (1940): *Proc. Phys. Soc. (London)*, **52**:54–55.

Bragg, W. L., and J. F. Nye (1947): *Proc. Roy. Soc. (London)*, A**190**:474–481.

Bragg, W. L., and W. M. Lomer (1949): *Proc. Roy. Soc. (London)*, A**196**:171–181.

Brooks, H. (1952): Theory of Internal Boundaries, Paper 2 in "Metal Interfaces," ASM, Cleveland, Ohio.

Brown, A. F. (1952): *Advances in Physics*, **1**:427–479.

Burgers, J. M. (1939): *Proc. Koninkl. Ned. Akad. Wetenschap.*, **42**:293–325; **42**:378–399.

Burgers, J. M. (1940): *Proc. Phys. Soc. (London)*, **52**:23–33.

Burton, W. K., and N. Cabrera (1949): *Disc. Faraday Soc.*, **5**:33–39, 40–48.

Burton, W. K., N. Cabrera, and F. C. Frank (1949): *Nature*, **163**:398–399.

Burton, W. K., N. Cabrera, and F. C. Frank (1951): *Phil. Trans. Roy. Soc.*, A24C 299–358.

Chen, N. K., and R. B. Pond (1952): *Trans. AIME*, **194**:1085–1092.

Cottrell, A. H., and B. A. Bilby (1949): *Proc. Phys. Soc. (London)*, A**62**:49–62.

Cottrell, A. H., and B. A. Bilby (1951): *Phil. Mag.*, **42**:573–581.

Cottrell, A. H. (1952): *Phil. Mag.*, **43**:645–647.

Cottrell, A. H. (1953): "Dislocations and Plastic Flow in Crystals," Oxford, New York.

Dawson, I. M., and V. Vand (1951): *Nature*, **167**:476; *Proc. Roy. Soc. (London)*, A**206**:555–562.

Dunn, C. G., and F. Lionetti (1949): *Trans. AIME*, **185**:125–132.

Dunn, C. G., F. W. Daniels, and M. J. Bolton (1950): *Trans. AIME*, **188**:1245–124.

Eshelby, J. D. (1949a): *Proc. Phys. Soc. (London)*, A**62**:307–314.

Eshelby, J. D. (1949b): *Phil. Mag.*, **40**:903–912.

Eshelby, J. D., W. T. Read, and W. Shockley (1953): *Acta Metallurgica*, **1**:251–359.

Fisher, J. C. (1952): *Trans. AIME*, **194**:531–532.

Fisher, J. C., and C. G. Dunn (1952): "Imperfections in Nearly Perfect Crystals" (W. Shockley, editor), Chap. 12, Wiley, New York.

Fisher, J. C., E. W. Hart, and R. H. Pry (1952): *Phys. Rev.*, **87**:958–961.

Foreman, A. J., M. A. Jaswon, and J. K. Wood (1951): *Proc. Phys. Soc. (London)*, A**64**:156–163.

Forty, A. J. (1952): *Phil. Mag.*, **43**:949–957.

Forty, A. J. (1953): *Phil. Mag.* (in press).

Frank, F. C. (1949): *Proc. Phys. Soc.*, A**62**:131–134.

Frank, F. C., and J. H. van der Merwe (1949): *Proc. Roy. Soc. (London)*, A**198**:205–216.

Frank, F. C., and W. T. Read (1950): *Phys. Rev.*, **79**:722–723.

Frank, F. C. (1950): Carnegie Institute of Technology Symposium on the Plastic Deformation of Crystalline Solids (Pittsburgh Report), pp. 150–151, Office of Naval Research (NAVEXOS-P-834).

Frank, F. C. (1951): *Phil. Mag.*, **42**:809–819.

Frank, F. C. (1952): *Advances in Physics*, **1**:91–109; see also *Phil. Mag.*, **42**:1014–1021 (1951).

Fullman, R. L. (1951): *J. Applied Phys.*, **22**:448–455.

Galt, J. K., and C. Herring (1952): *Phys. Rev.*, **85**:1060–1061.

Greenough, A. P., and R. King (1951): *J. Inst. Metals*, **79**:415–427.

Griffin, L. J. (1950): *Phil. Mag.*, **41**:196–199.

Griffin, L. J. (1952): *Phil. Mag.*, **43**:827–846.

Gyulai, Z., and D. Hartly (1928); *Z. Physik*, **51**:378–387.

Harper, S. (1951): *Phys. Rev.*, **83**:709–712.

Heidenreich, R. D., and W. Shockley (1948): Report of a Conference on the Strength of Solids, pp. 57–75, University of Bristol, England, Physical Society, London.

Herring, C. (1951): "The Physics of Powder Metallurgy" (W. F. Kingston, editor), Chap. 8, McGraw-Hill, New York.

Kê, T. S. (1949): *J. Applied Phys.*, **20**:274–280.

Lacombe, P., and N. Yannaquis (1947): *Métaux & corrosion*, **22**:35–37.

Lacombe, P. (1948): Report of a Conference on the Strength of Solids, pp. 91–94, University of Bristol, England, Physical Society, London.

Lomer, W. M. (1949): *Proc. Roy. Soc. (London)*, A**196**:182–194.

Lomer, W. M. (1951): *Phil. Mag.*, **42**:1327–1331.

Lomer, W. M., and J. F. Nye (1952): *Proc. Roy. Soc.*, A**212**:576–584.

Mathewson, C. H. (1951): *Trans. Conn. Acad. Arts Sci.*, **38**:213–246.

Mott, N. F. (1952): *Phil. Mag.*, **43**:1151–1178.

Nabarro, F. R. N. (1947): *Proc. Phys. Soc. (London)*, **59**:256–272.

Nabarro, F. R. N. (1952): *Advances in Physics*, **1**:269–394.

Nye, J. F. (1953): *Acta Metallurgica*, **1**:153–163.

Orowan, E. (1953): "Dislocations in Metals" (M. Cohen, editor), Chap. 3, AIME, New York (in preparation).

Parker, E. R., and J. Washburn (1952): *Trans. AIME*, **194**:1076–1078.

Peach, M., and J. S. Koehler (1950): *Phys. Rev.*, **80**:436–439.

Peierls, R. E. (1940): *Proc. Phys. Soc. (London)*, **52**:34–37.

Read, W. T., and W. Shockley (1950): *Phys. Rev.*, **78**:275–289. See also a preliminary report, *Phys. Rev.*, **75**:692(1949).

Read, W. T., and W. Shockley (1952a): "Imperfections in Nearly Perfect Crystals" (W. Shockley, editor), Chap. 2, Wiley, New York.

Read, W. T., and W. Shockley (1952b): "Imperfections in Nearly Perfect Crystals" (W. Shockley, editor), Chap. 13, Wiley, New York.

Read, W. T., and W. Shockley (1953): "Dislocations in Metals" (M. Cohen, editor), Chap. 2, AIME, New York (in preparation).

Schmid, E., and W. Boas (1935): "Plasticity of Crystals" (English translation), F. A. Hughes and Co. Ltd., London, 1950.

Seitz, F. (1950): Carnegie Institute of Technology Symposium on the Plastic Deformation of Crystalline Solids (Pittsburgh Report), pp. 1–36, Office of Naval Research (NAVEXOS-P-834).

Seitz, F. (1952): "Imperfections in Nearly Perfect Crystals" (W. Shockley, editor), Chap. 1, Wiley, New York.

Shockley, W. (1949): Dislocation Theory, in "Cold Working of Metals," pp. 131–147, ASM, Cleveland, Ohio.

Shockley, W. (1952): Dislocation Models of Grain Boundaries, pp. 431–484, in "L'État solide." (Report of the 9th International Solvay Conference, Brussels, Belgium, 1951), Stoops, publisher.

Timoshenko, S. (1934): "Theory of Elasticity," 1st ed., McGraw-Hill, New York.

van der Merwe, J. H. (1950): *Proc. Phys. Soc. (London)*, A**63**:616–637.

Van Vlack, L. H. (1951): *Trans. AIME*, **191**:251–259.

Verma, A. R. (1951): *Phil. Mag.*, **42**:1005–1013. *Nature*, **167**:939; **168**:430–431; **168**:783–784.

Vogel, F. L., W. G. Pfann, H. E. Corey, and E. E. Thomas (1953): *Phys. Rev.* **90**: 489–490.

Volmer, M., and W. Schultze (1931): *Z. physik. Chem.*, A**156**:1–22.

Zener, C. (1948): "Elasticity and Anelasticity of Metals," University of Chicago Press, Chicago.

NAME INDEX

SUBJECT INDEX